C000264916

GOVERNANCE
AND
THE SCLEROSIS THAT HAS SET IN

Governance

and
the sclerosis that has set in

ARUN SHOURIE

ASA

Rupa . Co

First Published 2004
Fourth Impression 2005
Fifth Impression 2005

Published by

ASA Publications
A-31, West End,
New Delhi 110 021

Rupa . Co
7/16, Ansari Road, Daryaganj,
New Delhi 110 002

Sales Centres:

Allahabad Bangalore Chandigarh Chennai
Hyderabad Jaipur Kathmandu
Kolkata Mumbai Pune

ISBN 81-291-0524-1

Typeset by
Pradeep Kumar Goel, 2/18, Ansari Road, New Delhi 110 002

Printed in India by
Gopsons Papers Ltd., A-14 Sector-60, Noida 201 301

For our parents
For our Adit
For Anita

Taat maat guru sakha tu....

Contents

Introduction
   1. Thought @ the speed of Government   3

Enterprises?
   2. Discoveries: or the real condition of public sector enterprises   25
   3. Disentangling the Government   43

A coral reef
   4. Regulators, licenses, technologies   69

An institution
   5. "A parking lot"   95

A sector
   6. Environment: the vital lesson   147
   7. Demand, and file   161
   8. Converting a great problem into a greater opportunity   181

A matter of life and death
   9. Acting on the facts   207

The real lesson
   10. Towards an enabling State   233

Index   257

Introduction

Thought @ the speed of Government

Some time in early 1999 – I was unable to fix the precise date – two officers in the Ministry of Steel made some notings on the files that passed through their desks. What caught the eye of their colleagues and superiors was not any thing they had written, but the fact that they had used red and green ink.

Accordingly, on 13 April 1999, the Ministry of Steel wrote a "D.O. letter" to the Department of Administrative Reforms and Public Grievances. Can officers use inks other than blue or black?, the Ministry wanted to know. Are there Guidelines on the question? If so, could these please be forwarded to the undersigned....

The letter arrived at the Department of Administrative Reforms six days later though the buildings of the two organizations are less than a kilometer away.

Research began. Consultations commenced. Ultimately it was decided that, as the matter concerned ink and as the Directorate of Printing had the requisite expertise on ink-related matters, the opinion of that Directorate had to be obtained.

Accordingly, an "O.M." – an Office Memorandum – was sent on 3 May 1999 to the Directorate of Printing. Will the Directorate kindly clarify whether any officer is authorized to use any ink other than blue or black for noting, drafting and correspondence in the Secretariat.

Deliberations, consultations, cogitation now began in the Directorate of Printing. After three weeks of thought, on 21 May 1999, the Directorate wrote to the Department of Administrative Reforms. There are no orders/instructions/guidelines in respect of use of different colours of ink, they noted. They had a view, nevertheless, based, it turned out, not on their perceived area of expertise, namely the properties of ink, but on hierarchy. Heads of Department may be permitted to use any colour of ink, they opined. However, as far as other officials/Government servants are concerned, only blue or black ink may be used in noting, drafting and correspondence. The

Department of Personnel and Training, Ministry of Home Affairs, may, however, be consulted, they concluded.

The letter reached the Department four days later.

After deliberating on the suggestion of the Directorate of Printing for three weeks, on 15 June 1999, the Department of Administrative Reforms issued an "O.M." to the Department of Personnel and Training "seeking clarification in the matter with request to provide copy of instructions/guidelines, if any, on the same." The DoPT was also requested to furnish their views/comments on the question so that necessary guidelines may be evolved in case there are no such guidelines/instructions.

It was now the turn of the Department of Personnel and Training to think, deliberate, hold meetings on.... Three weeks passed in these. On 6 July 1999, the Department of Personnel and Training wrote to the Department of Administrative Reforms. The question as to which ink may be used in notings/draftings/correspondence pertains essentially to the Manual of Office Procedure, the Department of Personnel noted, and, under the Allocation of Business Rules, the Manual of Office Procedure is regulated by the Department of Administrative Reforms. Hence, the Department of Administrative Reforms and Public Grievances may take a view in the matter.

A perfect answer, as you can see. Throw the ball back....

On 28 July 1999 the officer concerned in the Department of Administrative Reforms recorded that as the decision on the use of different colours of ink has to be taken by the Department itself, the criterion for adjudging the issue should first be settled. He proposed that the matter be judged in terms of the longevity of the notings in inks of different colours. When a file is closed, he noted, it is recorded as "A", "B" or "C" category. In case it has been designated as an "A" or "B" category file, it has to be kept permanently. Hence, the colour of the ink that is used for noting and correspondence in the file should be long lasting, and it should not fade with the passage of time. The matter, went the concluding recommendation, may be taken up for discussion at the Senior Officers Meeting.

The next level of officer to whom the file went reasoned that the matter was not as simple as that. Accordingly, he recorded that longevity would also be affected by the quality of the ink that had been used, as well as on whether ball-point pens or ink-pens had been used. So, these factors too needed to be decided along with the question of the colour of the ink.

In view of the criterion that had been agreed upon – the durability of the noting – and the multiplicity of factors that were likely to affect it – the colour of the ink, the quality of the ink as well as the type of writing instrument that had been used, it was felt that views of the National Archives of India had to be ascertained. After all, they are the ultimate custodians of Government records; and they are the ones who would know the legibility or otherwise of notings made in different colours, etc. in files in years past. The suggestion was taken up for consideration in the Senior Officers Meeting. It was approved.

And so, a letter was sent to the Director General, National Archives of India on 12 August 1999. It sought comments of the National Archives on the longevity of notings made in different colours of ink.

The Deputy Director of the National Archives replied on 27 August 1999. Every record creating agency, he wrote, in creating records of permanent nature should use fountain pen inks and ball point inks of permanent nature prescribed by the Bureau of Indian Standards as IS:221-1962, IS:220-1988, and IS:1581-1975 in respect of fountain pen inks of blue/black colour; and IS:8505-1993 in respect of ball point pen ink. So far as fountain pen ink of permanent nature is concerned, the National Archives declared, the prescribed colour is blue-black, while for ballpoint inks, the colours are blue, black, red and green.

But this of course left the matter precariously ambiguous. On this reading of options, if an officer was using a fountain pen, he would be obliged to use blue-black ink; but if he was using a ball point pen, he could without further thought use blue, black, red or green. Longevity clearly was not a sufficient criterion to clinch the question.

The letter from the National Archives was accordingly placed before the Senior Officers Meeting on 22 September 1999. It was decided in accordance of the view of the Chairman that the Department of Administrative Reforms obtain the instructions that are contained in the relevant manual for the armed forces, in particular the Army, and the existing instructions on the matter. Joint Secretary (Establishment) was charged with the twin tasks.

Consequent on the decision taken, as the phrase goes, in the Senior Officers Meeting, a D.O. was addressed on 4 October 1999 to the Joint Secretary (O&M) in the Ministry of Defence seeking a copy of the instructions contained in the relevant manual of the armed forces/ Army so as to finalise the implementation of a Uniform Ink Colour Code in the Central Secretariat.

The same day another communication was sent to the Department of Personnel and Training seeking existing instructions on the subject. Incidentally, such instructions as exist are available in printed form.

The Ministry of Defence replied on 22 December 1999. It stated that red coloured ink is used by the Chief of Army Staff/Chief of Naval Staff/Chief of Air Staff; green coloured ink is used by Principal Staff Officers; and blue or black colour ink is used by all other officers.

As nothing had been heard from the Department of Personnel and Training, the Department of Administrative Reforms sent a reminder on 4 January 2000. Could the DoPT forward the existing instructions on the matter of colour of ink that may be used in notings/drafting/ correspondence...?

In response to the reminder, on 9 February 2000 the Department of Personnel and Training reiterated that the matter is essentially a part of office procedure, and would accordingly be the concern of the Department of Administrative Reforms and Public Grievances. Hence, they have no information to furnish on the matter. They stated further that there is no reference to using red ink in para 38 of the Manual of Office Procedure.

The rest of February and almost the whole of March were taken up in thought within the Department of Administrative Reforms. At last, on 28 March 2000, a proposal was put up for an amendment and an addition to be incorporated in the relevant paras of the Manual of Office Procedure "in regard to use of different coloured inks in the activity of noting/drafting/correspondence."

A reply was finalized on 5 April 2000 for the Ministry of Steel, the original querist, so to say.

It was sent on 27 April 2000 – after having received the approval of officers at various levels within the Department of Administrative Reforms.

But there was a much more consequential outcome. Two additions were made in the Manual of Office Procedure – a singular achieve- ment. The bureaucratic equivalent of getting a new word into the Oxford Dictionary. Chapter 6 of the Manual deals with "Action on Receipts". It was enlarged to include para 32, sub-para 9 which now reads,

> "Notes and orders will normally be recorded on note sheets in the Notes Portion of the file and will be serially numbered. Black or blue ink will be used by all category of staff and officers. Only an officer of the level of Joint Secretary to the Government of India and above may use green or red ink in rare cases."

A good bureaucratic solution, as you would have noticed: discretion allowed, but circumscribed!

And Para 68, sub-para 5 of the Manual of Office Procedure now reads,

> "Initial drafting will be done in black or blue ink. Modifications in the draft at the subsequent levels may be made in green or red ink by the offices so as to distinguish the corrections made."

Another good solution, as you would have noticed: neither option ruled out; a proper function for each option.... Some ambiguity, of course. Para 32(9) says that only officers of Joint Secretary level and above may use red or green ink, and that too only in rare cases. Para 68(5), on the other hand, does not limit the use of these colours to any particular rank; and it does not say that the corrections and amendments for which these colours are used have to be of an especially rare kind.

Solution? The two sub-paras are to be, as the courts remind us, "read harmoniously"!

Even then, not all problems have been solved, I am constrained to record! After all, in view of what the Deputy Director of the National Archives had pointed out, may it not be that the ink that is being used by officers does not bear that ISI mark?....

A model way to finalize a model document

Projects worth hundreds of crore have to be executed. Disputes arise, allegations fly because some words are inserted in, some words are left out of clauses in Tender Documents. International aid agencies have their own manuals. The documents we put out have to be harmonized with them. Each project is delayed by the time that is taken in drafting these documents. Once begun, the process is stalled by disputes, litigation.... By the mid-1980s everyone concerned agrees that the only way out is to put together a Model Tender Document.

At last, on 3 February 1987, a committee is formed by the Department of Economic Affairs, Ministry of Finance, to draft the Model Tender Document for civil works in the case of projects in which international competitive bids are to be invited. A former Secretary of the Ministry of Water Resources, M.G. Padhye, is made its Chairman.

The Committee labours intensively, and submits its report in December of the same year, 1987.

In a parallel exercise, at its first meeting – on 29 June 1987 – a Group of Ministers decides to appoint another committee to draw up the Model Tender Document for its consideration. This gets to be known as the Vir Amar Prakash Committee after its Chairman, a former member of the Central Water Commission. This Committee takes cognizance of the Model Tender Documents finalized by the Central Public Works Department, as well as the ones finalized by the Padhye Committee for International Competitive Bidding.

February 1988: the Vir Amar Prakash Committee submits its report to the Cabinet Secretariat. It suggests that the Model Documents finalized by the Padhye Committee for International Competitive Bidding can, with a few modifications, be used for Local Competitive Bidding also.

The report is put up to the Group of Ministers. The Group meets on 28 April 1988 and decides to authorize the Ministry of Urban Development to coordinate all aspects of the matter relating to the finalization of tender documents. It also decides to have the report of the Vir Amar Prakash Committee circulated to all Ministries for their views.

Seven months pass as the Ministry of Urban Development strives to secure the comments of other Ministries. At last, on 9 December 1988, the Ministry of Urban Development submits its report containing the comments of other Ministries on the report of the Vir Amar Prakash Committee which, as we just saw, had commended the Model Documents prepared by the Padhye Committee.

The Group of Ministers decides that the matter may be further examined by the Ministry of Law.

Eight months pass. The matter is again before the same Group of Ministers. The Ministers decide that Vir Amar Prakash will go through all the documents and develop a single formulation of the Model Draft Contract – and that he will do so in consultation with the Ministry of Law, and after obtaining the views of other Ministries.

On 20 June 1990 the World Bank draws attention to some differences between its practices and the Model Document developed by the Padhye Committee. Accordingly, the Ministry of Water Resources sets up a third Committee under the Chairmanship of V.B. Patel, a former Chairman of the Central Water Commission. He is tasked to review the matter and finalize a Document that would be acceptable to both the Government of India and the World Bank.

On 25 October 1990, the Committee of Secretaries decides that a self-contained paper on the Model Tender Document be prepared for consideration of the Cabinet Committee on Economic Affairs. It decides further that this paper should be prepared by the Ministry of Urban Affairs – after obtaining the comments of the Ministry of Power, the Ministry of Finance, and the Ministry of Water Resources.

18 January 1991: the Patel Committee – not to be confused with the Vir Amar Prakash Committee which in turn is not to be confused with the Padhye Committee – submits its report. It has modified some clauses so as to bridge differences. But admittedly a few differences remain.

A year passes.

January 1992: the report of the Patel Committee is forwarded to the Department of Economic Affairs and, through it, to the World Bank to sort out the aforesaid differences.

6 May 1992: the Committee of Secretaries decides that the Ministry of Urban Development shall set up a Standing Inter-Ministerial Technical Committee to review the system for, the procedures of, the methods used in, as well as the technology relating to contract management in regard to the construction industry. The Committee shall function under the Chairmanship of the Secretary, Planning Commission.

24 September 1992: the Standing Inter-Ministerial Technical Committee *is* set up – but under the Ministry of Urban Development. It holds its first meeting that day.

1 May 1993: in response to the report of the Patel Committee which has been sent to it, the World Bank points out that its Board has made it mandatory for borrowers to use its Standard Bidding Documents for International Competitive Bidding in projects aided by it. However, it agrees to some modifications to take account of local requirements.

In response, a Task Force is formed by the Department of Economic Affairs, Ministry of Finance, on 25 May 1993 under an Additional Secretary, with members from various Ministries and Departments to suggest modifications, "if any" as is invariably provided, to the World Bank documents. The Task Force observes that the "Standard Bidding Documents for International Competitive Bidding" are in fact already being used in all World Bank assisted projects negotiated after 1 May 1993.

26 September 1994: almost exactly two years after its first meeting, the Standing Inter-Ministerial Technical Committee holds its second meeting.

June 1995: the sub-group that had been set up under the Chairmanship of the Director General, CPWD, reports to the Standing Inter-Ministerial Technical Committee that the CPWD has adopted the revised contract form for its works since 1 June 1995. This revised form is being circulated to the Standing Inter-Ministerial.Technical Committee for its consideration.

20 May 1996: the Department of Economic Affairs states that the Task Force – recall, it had been formed on 20 May 1993 – is presently revising the already indigenised Standard Bidding Documents of World Bank aided projects – in view of the latest 1995 Guidelines issued by the World Bank, and that the subject is still under process.

31 October 1996: by now the task of preparing a "Model Contract/ Bidding Document for Project Implementation" has been assigned to the Department of Programme Implementation. The Committee of Secretaries meets to deliberate upon the paper that this Department has finalized on the matter. At the meeting, the Department gives a resume of the work that has been done over the years by the Expert Groups and Committees. It indicates that the Standard Bidding Documents that have been issued by the Ministry of Finance and are applicable at present to World Bank aided projects may be used as standard reference. The Department also points out that it may be advantageous to study successful projects and draw lessons from them. One factor that causes delays in the execution of several projects is the application of risk and cost clauses. A mechanism must accordingly be put in place "which ensures flexibility and yet prevents misuse by defaulting contractors."

Decisions along these lines are taken. The Committee of Secretaries also sets up a two-member group consisting of Secretary, Department of Programme Implementation, and Additional Secretary, Expenditure, to scrutinize the Guidelines that will be prepared in accordance with the decisions that have been taken.

That is on 31 October 1996.

2 September 1998: that is, almost two years later, the Department of Programme Implementation points out: "The Ministries have either not felt the need or have not reported progress made. There is no information about action taken by the DEA to issue SBDs [the Standard Bidding Documents] for the bilaterally funded projects."

I am taken into Government. Among my charges are the very same Department of Programme Implementation, and Department of Administrative Reforms. I am also the MOS for Planning. One of the hosts of bodies that function under the loose umbrella of the Planning Commission is the Construction Industry Development Council. A participant at a seminar organised by the Council says that one of the factors that is holding back the industry, is that huge amounts are locked up in disputes. Actually, it turns out that huge amounts are locked up because the Government, having lost arbitration cases, has not paid up. A quick survey by the Construction Industry Development Council reveals that this figure is in the range of *Rs. fifty three thousand crore.* And one of the factors, he narrates, that breeds both delays and corruption is that there is no standard form for tenders, etc.

I then discover the foregoing history. The Secretary of the Council, a thorough professional, volunteers to put together yet another Standard Document that would meet everyone's concerns. He labours hard, and swiftly.

A voluminous document is ready by June 1999.

We study it within the Department. It seems very thorough to us.

A letter is accordingly sent on 2 July 1999 to the Cabinet Secretariat, Ministry of Surface Transport and the Department of Expenditure about this work having been completed, and urging that the exercise that has been going on for *twelve years* be brought to a conclusion, and the standard document, updated for the umpteenth time, be adopted.

The Department of Expenditure suggests that the Department of Programme Implementation obtain the comments of public sector undertakings like NTPC, GAIL, HPCL, BIL....

The document is circulated.

The Department tries and tries to extract comments from the undertakings and departments.

The last set of comments that we have been asked to elicit are received only by 27 January 2000.

We are told to prepare a draft note for the Cabinet Committee on Economic Affairs.

As part of this note we are to incorporate the comments of other Ministries. Hence a new hunt begins.

By June even this is done.

I lose track as I am assigned other portfolios....

An idea that takes off

Among these is a dream portfolio – Development of the Northeast. Many influential persons from the region press proposals for airports – for entirely new ones, for enlarging the buildings that stand at the existing airports, for lengthening the landing tarmacs. But the existing airports are so little used, I find. Why is everyone so keen on new ones?, I inquire. Why do they want runways to be extended when the existing ones can take all the aircraft that are going to land here in the foreseeable future? I am swiftly awakened to the lure of contracts for constructing buildings, for getting land beyond the two ends of the runway assigned to oneself and then getting compensation for the land when the runway has to be extended....

I insist that we will not spend further money on airports. A paper by Professor Rodham Narasimha about low-budget airlines in Europe has planted an alternative in my mind: instead of squandering money on the little-used airports, we will deploy it to commence an air-taxi service. Let Indian Airlines take a few planes on lease and fly them from one airport in the Northeast to the next throughout the day. The Northeast will be linked. Gradually a market will emerge. A person having to go from Silchar to Guwahati, will not have to go first to

Kolkata, spend the night there in a hotel, and take the flight next day to Guwahati....

Tenders are floated. Two technical committees are set up to evaluate offers. Searches for the best take so long that the principal potential supplier informs IAC that the aircraft have already been leased to another airline. The process begins again. Again, it takes so long that the supplier informs IAC that the remaining aircraft too have been committed to another country. The process begins a third time.... But at least the aircraft are plying today – all the advantages that Professor Narasimha had anticipated are manifest. And IAC can claim that they were able to bring the lease rent down from the initial offer....

A slip

In the mid-1990s, there was an IDA credit for a forestry project in Madhya Pradesh. In June 1996, Additional Central Assistance of Rs.143.42 lakhs was to be credited to the account of the Government of Madhya Pradesh. The release was to be made notionally in the books of the Central Accounts Section at the RBI offices in Nagpur, credited in the account of Controller Aid Accounts and Audit, and the amount was to be recovered from the state in full – all the entries were to have been just book entries. By some inadvertence, the communication from the Controller Aid Accounts and Audit to the Project Monitoring Unit, Department of Economic Affairs specified the amount as Rs.1,394.51 lakhs. This caused an excess release to, and an excess recovery from, the Government of Madhya Pradesh of Rs.1,251.09 lakhs – Rs.1,394.51 lakhs *minus* Rs.143.42 lakhs.

All the entries were mere book entries. No one was any poorer or richer. But a year later, on 11 June 1997, the accountants noticed that an excess Rs.1,251.09 lakhs had been released and recovered. This was brought to the attention of the Plan Finance Division for rectification.

Since both the release and the recovery had been notional, the Plan Finance Division had to make the adjustments also only notionally. As luck would have it, on 16 September 1997 the Division actually deducted the amount from the actual Additional Central Assistance that was due to Madhya Pradesh.

This one error entailed not one but two discrepancies in the books. In one set of books – the one for notional entries, the Madhya Pradesh Government had been "given" an amount which it should not have been "given". In the other set of books – the one which records "real" money being transferred, the Madhya Pradesh Government had been deprived of an amount which should not have been taken from it.

On 20 April 1998, the eye of the Accountant General of Madhya Pradesh fell on the error by which the amount had been deducted in fact instead of being deducted notionally. He therefore requested that the amount be released/refunded in cash.

On 10 June 1998, the Director, Project Monitoring Unit requested that the excess ACA amount which had been notionally released and which was outstanding under the Deposit Head in the books of the Controller Aid Accounts and Audit, be notionally recovered and the entries brought in line. He requested that the appropriate entries be made in the books of the Central Accounts Section, RBI, Nagpur – by entering a notional credit in the accounts of the Government of Madhya Pradesh and a notional debit in the books of the Controller Aid Accounts and Audit.

By now the Comptroller and Auditor General of India had stepped in. His eye had fallen on the amount that had been deducted in fact. He took strong exception to the appearance of a minus balance in the 1996/97 Finance Account of the Government of Madhya Pradesh. Accordingly, the Accountant General of Madhya Pradesh sent another communication on 19 June 1998: please credit the account of the Government of Madhya Pradesh, and debit the account of the Controller Aid Accounts and Audit, under the Major Civil Head 8,443- Civil Deposit....

2 July 1998: the Plan Finance Division requests the Controller Aid Accounts and Audit to refund Rs.1,251.09 lakhs to the state Government.

10 July 1998: the Controller Aid Accounts and Audit requests the Plan Finance Division to supply a copy of the sanction number.... dated 13 August 1996 "as the same is not available in this office for taking further necessary action."

13 August 1998: Controller Aid Accounts and Audit advises the Reserve Bank of India, Central Accounts Section, Nagpur to refund the amount to the Government of Madhya Pradesh by crediting the account of the state Government and by contra-debiting the account of the Controller Aid Accounts and Audit with the RBI, New Delhi.

1 September 1998: the Reserve Bank asks the Controller Aid Accounts and Audit to furnish regular Inter-Government Advice for the normal IGA transfer and also furnish specimen signatures.

7 October 1998: the Controller Aid Accounts and Audit requests the Plan Finance Division to take "necessary action" to issue the Inter Government Advice for this Inter-Governmental Adjustment Transaction.

10 November 1998: the Accountant General, Madhya Pradesh asks the Controller Aid Accounts and Audit to endorse to his office for necessary action a copy of the advice sent to the RBI, Nagpur.

4 December 1998: the Controller Aid Accounts and Audit again requests Plan Finance-I Division to release the payment to the Madhya Pradesh Government. He records that the state Government is pressing for an early settlement of this long-pending case.

11 December 1998: the Accountant General, Madhya Pradesh again informs all concerned that the amount of Rs.1,251.09 lakhs has not yet been credited to the account of the state Government.

12 December 1998: the Reserve Bank of India, Central Accounts Section, Nagpur, requests Controller Aid Accounts and Audit to arrange Inter Government Advice in the prescribed format as well as the specimen signatures for contra-debiting the amount.

30 December 1998: the Central Accounts Section, RBI, Nagpur again requests Controller Aid Accounts and Audit to forward the Inter Government Advice along with the specimen signatures of the authorized officials.

We are into the New Year.

11 January 1999: the Accountant General, Madhya Pradesh, requests the Plan Finance Division to settle the issue early.

On the same day, the Government of Madhya Pradesh requests the Controller Aid Accounts and Audit to release the payment immediately as the state is facing financial hardships.

21 January 1999: the Accountant General, Madhya Pradesh, once again requests Controller Aid Accounts and Audit to release the amount – this has been outstanding now for two years, he emphasizes.

28 January 1999: the Plan Finance-I Division in turn asks another wing of the Finance Ministry to intimate the present position regarding the adjustment of excess Additional Central Assistance of Rs.1,251.09 lakhs.

The same day, the Project Monitoring Unit requests the Controller Aid Accounts and Audit to rectify the matter immediately.

As nothing has happened, the Madhya Pradesh Government again requests that the amount be refunded – plus an interest @ 13%.

16 February 1999: the Controller Aid Accounts and Audit requests the Pay and Accounts Office, Ministry of Finance to refund the amount of Rs.1,251.09 lakhs to the Government of Madhya Pradesh by issuing Inter Government Advice because of the excess recovery of ACA in August 1996.

The financial year is over. The amount has still not come.

8 April 1999: the Madhya Pradesh Government writes yet again – release the amount, please.

At last – on 9 April 1999 – the Pay and Accounts Office, Ministry of Finance issues the sanction for Rs.1,251.09 lakhs. It requests Central Accounts Section, Reserve Bank of India, Nagpur to credit the account of the state Government. He endorses a copy of the sanction to the Accountant General, Madhya Pradesh.

An error made in June 1996 is at last put to rest – just about three years later. But that is when the Central and state Governments were involved, and the Comptroller and Accountant General of India, and the Accountant General of the state, and the Reserve Bank of India, and the CAA&A, and the CAS, and the PF Division, and the PMU Division.... What if just you or I had been the victim of the original error?

Matters big and small

This way of doing things – a mindless, endless shuffling in slow motion – is not a device, it is more than a habit. It has become nature. You will find it in every aspect of governance – big or small.

❑ Even as the Government is making announcements after announcements that it will downsize, even as it is setting up one Committee of Secretaries after another to implement directives of successive Prime Ministers to this effect, routine requests of persons to proceed on study-leave take months and months and references upon references to higher authorities; requests of those who had gone on study-leave to the effect that, as they do not now want to continue in government, they should be allowed to retire, take just as long to get approved.

❏ An officer is caught taking a bribe. The processes to bring him to book take *eighteen years* – and in the end it is the Government that settles for a nominal show of censure.

❏ The Disinvestment Commission finds that, even as its competitors are racing ahead, the proposal of BALCO to set up a cold roll mill at Korba has been making the rounds for *eight years*. This clearance at least comes – though after eight years. But the clearance for setting up a plant for 100% captive power generation hasn't come at all, the Commission finds.

❏ Determined efforts of the Government to reduce the number of Joint Secretary level posts began in 1991. They continue.

❏ The National Textile Corporation hurtles from rack to ruin – of the 129 mills, only 25 are working to capacity; thirty-odd are physically shut – the Government continues to spend seven hundred crore every year on paying wages to workers in these and other mills whose factories are locked. The deliberations on what to do about the Corporation go on for twelve years and more. Every scheme hinges on selling the land of mills that are lying closed in Bombay. Discussions – as if these were negotiations over Kashmir – go on between the Government of Maharashtra and the Central Government for all these years. Chief Ministers come and go, Prime Ministers come and go, the discussions go on, one formula following another. They are still going on.

❏ In 1977 Government adopts a Retention Price Scheme for fertilizer plants. The price at which urea is to be sold to farmers is notified by Government. The Government determines what the cost of producing urea is for each plant in the country – separately. It determines what is the net worth of each plant. It fixes the rate of return on that net worth which is "reasonable". Each plant is permitted to "retain" only that part of the price which, given the cost of production as estimated by the Government, will fetch it that "reasonable" rate of return – on net worth as determined by the Government. The difference between the "retention price" and the price that the farmer pays comes out of the Exchequer as subsidy. The retention price for each plant is fixed for three years at a time. Over the decades, this scheme becomes one of the principal shackles on the industry, as well as one of the principal sources of corruption in the sector. Pulled in one direction and then the other, successive governments are not able to make up their minds on the constituents of the price. The "sixth pricing period" is to end on April 1994. As it is not able to choose, the Government announces that it will continue till 26 August 1996 the arrangement that had been prevailing – and which on all hands had become obsolete. August 1996 comes. Still no decision. The "sixth pricing period" is therefore extended yet again – till 30 June 1997. Still no decision. Four years later, alternatives are still being weighed – till finally, after meetings upon meetings, a new pricing policy is evolved in 2002.

The delays become the occasion for collecting octroi, so to say. They make for heartlessness: a person who has suffered injustice is condemned to trudge from office to office – till his spirit gives way. Opportunities are lost. Economic progress is arrested.

And the next round of administration is made even more tortuous. For at each stage of "processing", at each pass as the alternatives are weighed, yet another squiggle is added to the forms, yet another loop to the process. To continue with that last example, the price that a fertilizer plant was allowed to "retain" came to depend on

❑ Its capacity – for on that depended the amount it could be deemed to have invested, which, in turn, was a factor that went into determining its costs of production; but there were further distinctions – between "licensed capacity", "design capacity", and "installed capacity".
❑ The extent to which the capacity – licensed/design/installed – was·utilized. This depended not just on actual utilization, but on that as well as the "norm" for such utilization – this was to prevent a plant from using the installed capacity to excess, thereby bringing down its unit costs and thereby reaping an "unfair" margin!
❑ Feedstock – naphtha?, fuel oil?, natural gas?
❑ Whether the input has been imported or indigenously procured.

❑ Cost of inputs: not just the actual cost, but also with reference to "input norms" prescribed by the Government.

❑ The "costed year" – the year for which Government chose to calculate the costs of inputs. The effect of choosing one year instead of another spelt hundreds of crore – and this did not accrue proportionately to all plants; the manna would fall differentially.

❑ The catalyst that is used, and its "normal" life as determined by the Government.

❑ Net Fixed Assets – in some phases and for some purposes this meant "net fixed assets as of date 'X'"; in other phases and for some other purposes this meant "the average net fixed assets for the preceding 3 years".

❑ "Capital additions" – in some phases this included all capital expansions, in others it was restricted to outlays for installing specified energy saving devices.

❑ "Capital works in progress" – much arcane scholarship was required for estimating the precise figure.

❑ Selling expenses.

❑ Dealers' Margin.

❑ Secondary freight costs.

❑ The quantum of subsidy that the Government would give in any particular period.

❑ The Fertilizer Pool Equalization Charge.

❑ The Equated Freight.

❑ Vintage Allowance – a construct that required the most esoteric determination: as plants had been set up at different times, this differential was inserted so that the later, more efficient plants did not acquire an "unfair advantage" over the earlier, less efficient plants!

❑ There was much tussle over whether the magnitudes should be determined for each plant or for groups of plants: when a simplification was attempted, the minimum number of groups that could be thought of came to nine! "Pre-92 gas based (land-fall) units; pre-92 gas based (non-land-fall) units; post-92 gas based units; pre-92 naphtha based units with annual capacity less than 5 lakh metric tonnes; pre-92 naphtha based units with annual capacity more than 5 lakh metric tonnes; post-92 naphtha based units, Fuel Oil/Low Sulphur Heavy Stock units with annual capacity less than 5 lakh metric tonnes; Fuel Oil/Low Sulphur Heavy Stock units with annual capacity more than 5 lakh metric tonnes; mixed energy units...." This was the order of complexity in the formula designed to *simplify!*

The more complex the formula, the more the interstices in which scholarship can be honed, or, in the alternate, bargains struck.

In Chapter 3 I take up the telecom licensing system as I found it when I was given charge of the Communications Ministry to illustrate what happens as each effort to plug the loopholes that resulted from the previous effort at "improvement" propels governments to still more zealous efforts at improvement.

This book

In this book I give accounts and illustrations – of the state of affairs as well as of the consequences – from diverse fields. From government departments to public sector enterprises, to courts, to an institution like the Planning Commission. From the passing of laws to the enforcement of laws that are passed. From environment to National Security.

As will become evident, by now the malaise affects all institutions of State. It affects all aspects of governance.

It is not difficult to think up remedies that should be put in place. And I have retained several specific ones that spring up in the context of the example that I am writing about – whether it is the environment or an institution like the Planning Commission. But the essays illustrate what happens to such ideas. The malaise is well known to those in the system too. Accordingly, proposals for reforming that system are adopted from time to time, and decrees go out to implement the measures "in a time-bound manner". But in every case, the proposal is put through – some would say, it *has* to be put through – the same mill!

And it is ground to dust in the same mill. There are huge cost and time over-runs, reports of the Department for Programme Implementation show. *Decision:* these must be curbed. *Solution:* responsibility for the cost and time over-runs must be fixed in each case. *Device:* Standing Committees are set up in 23 ministries to affix responsibility in each case where there has been a time or cost over-run. But soon it is noticed that these Standing Committees are preparing reports, and these reports are just getting filed. No action follows. *Device:* each time a proposal comes to the Cabinet Committee on Economic Affairs for outlays, it must contain the report of the Standing Committee on that project and Ministry – about the over-runs and who was responsible, and the action that has been taken. I study 35-odd reports. Each of them concludes, *each of them* concludes that it has *not* been possible to affix responsibility – that the over-run has taken place because of "systemic" deficiencies.... I give up reading the reports.... The reader will get a glimpse of this feature as he steers through the coils through which we were put as we tried to implement the Government's decision to privatize its hotels.

Literally, the situation of which the seer speaks: "If the salt have lost its saltness, wherewith shall it be salted?"

Yet, *this* is the reform that has to be realized today. In the first phase, mere announcements amounted to reform. "We hereby abolish Industrial Licensing.... We hereby abolish the Directorate General of Technical Development.... We hereby open the insurance sector to foreign investment...." Each of these spelled a major advance. But now, *actual governance* has to be changed.

That is the theme of each essay. I have retained the essays as they were written – for each is a whole in itself and I did not have the heart to chop and stitch limbs. But also because each essay contains information that will alternately delight and infuriate the reader – and this detail would have been lost in the stitching.

Thus while the subjects and locale differ, a single theme runs through all the essays.

And the moral too is the same – the way to reform this system is not to tinker with this procedure or that institution; but to just jettison the function, to hack away the limb wherever this is possible.

A leaner machine, like a leaner body will then be easier to improve.

For we need to improve the State. As the penultimate chapter shows, there are several tasks that only the State can discharge.

Enterprises?

2

Discoveries: the real condition of PSUs

The Indian Tourism Development Corporation has operated thirty-two hotels. *Thirty-one* of them made a loss in 2001/2002. The solitary exception was the Lalitha Mahal Palace in Mysore. A heritage property, as a hotel the dream of a hotelier, of a guest, yet it made a princely profit of only Rs.86 lakhs. In the three years from 1999 to 2001, the Hotels Division of ITDC made a cumulative loss of over Rs.105 crore.

Of these hotels, eight are in Delhi: Ashok, Samrat, Janpath, Ranjit, Kanishka, Indraprastha, Qutab, and Lodhi.

Every single one of them has been running in loss: to earn Rs.42 crore, the Ashok Hotel spends Rs.51 crore. And this in spite of the fact that it is charged a ground rent of *Rs. twenty five thousand a year* only – as against the *Rs. fourteen crore a year* that the Land and Development Office insisted the hotelier who wins the competitive bid for running the property on lease must pay.

On commencing the process for privatizing these properties in Delhi we discovered that:

❑ Not one of them, *repeat not one of them* had the title deed or lease documents in order – the documents were either just not available, or the lease was in dispute, and that in spite of the fact that the hotels had been in operation for up to *forty-five years;*

❑ Not one of them, *repeat not one of them* had a Completion Certificate – and that in spite of the fact that the buildings had been constructed *twenty* to *forty-five years* earlier; indeed, even the Building Plans on the basis of which Completion Certificates could be given – "with retrospective effect" so to say – were not available;

❑ Not one of them, *repeat not one of them* had even the mandatory Certificate from the Fire authorities.

As a consequence these hotels owned by the Government have been encoiled in litigation for decades – often with limbs of the Government itself! A typical case is that of Lodhi Hotel.

It was in 1966 – that is, *thirty-five years ago* – that the ITDC purchased the buildings of this Hotel from the Department of Urban Development: the premise was that a "Corporation" of the Government would be able to run hotels better than a mere "Department" of the Government. The value of the buildings had to be determined for fixing the property tax that the Corporation would have to pay the Municipal Corporation of Delhi. The task was assigned to yet another arm of the Government – the Central Public Works Department. It valued the buildings on the basis of "depreciated replacement cost".

But there was another variable: the tax the ITDC would have to pay would depend not just on the value of the buildings, it would also depend on who owned the land on which the buildings stood. The Municipal Corporation fixed the tax on the premise that the land was owned by the ITDC. The Department of Tourism and the Land and Development Office disputed this assumption: they maintained that the land was owned by the Department of Urban Development and could only be deemed to be on lease to the ITDC. In its turn, ITDC asserted that the property tax must be computed on the premise that the asset to be taxed comprised the buildings alone, that the land did not come into the reckoning at all – as it was not on ownership basis but on leasehold basis. The dispute ended in the High Court of Delhi. Hearings followed hearings – for *ten years*. Ultimately, the High Court directed that the dispute be resolved by the Joint Assessor and Collector of the Municipal Corporation. That was *two years* before the matter came to the Disinvestment Ministry. All that happened was that the Municipal Corporation and the ITDC kept sending letters to each other.

But that very fact now came in handy for thwarting privatization. The bidders would not bid for the Hotel till the issue was resolved, and, on the other side, the various limbs of Government would not resolve the issue. Indeed, they would flag this dispute as one of the reasons why privatization had to be postponed! Naturally, indefinitely.

That is how matters stood in September 2001. I called all concerned to a meeting. There was no issue of principle that I could detect. There was not even an issue of law. The question was one of fact. It turned on who "owned" the land – the Department of Urban Development or the ITDC, both limbs of the same governmental structure. "But there must be *some* document – of lease or ownership," I said in exasperation. That was the problem, the officials explained: the original documents were not, as they had not been, available!

As long ago as 1981 the Chandigarh Administration gave the ITDC land on lease of 90 years to build a hotel. The land was given on the condition that the hotel would be built within three years. Nine years passed. No hotel. The Chandigarh Administration issued a notice to ITDC: show cause why the lease should not be cancelled. Letters to and fro for four years, but no hotel – just the shell of an incomplete structure. And so in 1994, the Chandigarh Administration cancelled the lease. ITDC filed an appeal with the Estate Office of that very Administration. The appeal was rejected. ITDC filed a review petition before the Advisor to the Governor. The plot was restored to ITDC. Now it was the turn of the Chandigarh Administration: *it* filed a writ in the Punjab and Haryana High Court against restoration of the plot to the ITDC by the Advisor – that is, the person discharging the functions of a Cabinet Minister – to the head of its own Government, the Governor. Two years later, the High Court decreed that the status quo after the Advisor's order continue – that is, the plot would be with ITDC. That was four years ago. But the shell remained as it was – *twenty years* after ITDC got the land on the undertaking that it would build a hotel within *three years,* there was still no hotel.

So, when the proposal to disinvest the property was commenced, a dispute arose: what proportion of the "unearned increase" in the value of the property will go to the Chandigarh Administration and what proportion to ITDC? Learned arguments from each side. Meetings. Correspondence. The *shastras* cited. The former maintained that ITDC was entitled to no more than the value of the *malba* – the debris – that would result from the demolition of the shell. ITDC maintained that it should get what it would be entitled to according to the formula that had been arrived at in regard to the properties in Delhi....

And remember, both the Chandigarh Administration and ITDC are limbs of the same Central Government!

Whole contingents

The dispute about the tax that one part of the Government must pay another part; the sort of issue on which it turned – as to which part of Government "owns" the land; the fact that the issue, instead of being resolved by discussion within the governmental structure, ended up in Court; that in that forum it took years; that the Court eventually directed a limb of the same governmental structure to resolve it; that what that limb did was to commence correspondence with other limbs; that the matter remained locked in correspondence – none of this is unique to ITDC and its hotels. Indeed, it is typical of what has become of governance today. Enterprise after enterprise, we discovered as we began the process of privatization, is bogged down in the same swamp.

Hindustan Teleprinters purchased about 15 acres in Hosur from the State Industries Promotion Corporation of Tamil Nadu, SIPCOT. The land was not put to use. SIPCOT issued a notice to HTL to show-cause why the land should not be taken back by the former. The notice became a matter of protracted meetings, consultations, correspondence.

Ten years later, in 1993, HTL purchased another 15.92 acres from another undertaking of the Tamil Nadu Government, the Tamil Nadu Small Industries Development Corporation. As HTL did not put this land to use either, SIDCO issued a show-cause notice: show-cause why the land should not be repossessed. SIDCO was even more emphatic because HTL had forgotten to pay maintenance charges regularly – the arrears by now amounted to Rs.18 lakhs. Meetings, consultations, and of course correspondence – "with reference to the above the undersigned is directed to state...."

Paradeep Phosphates, we found, had been engaged in a prolonged battle with the environmental authorities of the state about what it was inflicting on the environment, about the corrective equipment it had promised to install and had not. Eventually, a public interest case was filed in the Orissa High Court against this undertaking. Even that did not stir the company into action. The financial bids were to be received on 8 February 2002. Just two days before that final date, that is on 6 February, we received a fax from the plant's management informing us that *a month earlier* the Orissa High Court had issued an order that the entire plant would be shut down on the 15th of February unless such and thus had been done. Hadn't someone, we were compelled to wonder, held on to the information, and sent it at the penultimate moment to scare away the bidders?

IPCL, GAIL and ONGC – one and all owned by the same entity, the Government of India – had been engaged in a dispute about the way Natural Gas supplied by GAIL and the C2/C3 components of Natural Gas supplied by ONGC would be priced. The dispute had been going on for six years!

IPCL – owned by the Central Government – and the same Government's Central Excise Department had been encoiled in a hotly contested dispute about the excise liability of the former: the dispute turned on the way a product of IPCL, Pyrolysis Gasoline, was to be classified. The dispute had been going on for eight years. By now the Excise Department was claiming that IPCL owed it Rs.570 crore on this count alone. "How can bids be invited till the bidders can be told what the outcome of this dispute is going to be between two arms of the Government?," those who wanted to block privatization demanded.

VSNL – another undertaking of the Central Government – was involved in a similar dispute with another limb of the same Government, this time the Income Tax Department. VSNL had been paying Rs.101 crore since 1986; with the switch in the telecom regime, this amount had been increased to 12 per cent of the revenue as license fee. VSNL maintained that this fee was "revenue expenditure". The Income Tax Department maintained this was "capital expenditure". On this premise it declared that VSNL owed it Rs.600 crore. "Naturally, no bids can be invited till the issue is resolved, and the bidders can be told that they will have to or that they will not have to pay this huge amount to the Income Tax Department," proclaimed those who wanted to thwart prospective bidders.

National Fertilizers Ltd.: environmental clearance for the Nangal expansion yet to be received…. Title deeds for the Vijayapur II plant not yet settled….

And so on, with exasperating regularity. And you can guess at one reason why such disputes continue for decades. Entire contingents on either side are dedicated to advancing the case of that side. Preparing the papers for that dispute, keeping track of it, attending hearings in court on that matter, briefing superiors about what transpired, drafting correspondence about it, filing the communications about it that come and go – these are the be all and end all of the official life of so many. These "tasks" are what they specialize in. These are *all* they specialize in. Our equivalent of Keynes' prescription: put people to dig holes, and fill them.

More on the hotels

But to get back to the ITDC Hotels. My colleagues ran into encroachments galore: in some cases – elsewhere as much as in Delhi – the ITDC hotels had encroached on the land of others; in other instances, others had encroached on the land of ITDC! In Ashok Hotel in Delhi – not in distant Manipur, but right here in Delhi; not on the outskirts of Delhi, just three-four hundred yards from the Prime Minister's house – *three hundred and forty seven* quarters had been constructed illegally. The NDMC maintained that the Completion Certificate for the Ashok and Samrat Hotels could only be given after these unauthorised quarters were demolished. But it is easier to bring down Pakistani bunkers across the Line of Control than these! And so, no Completion Certificate. As no Completion Certificate, no privatization!

In instance after instance – for example, Kanishka, Indraprastha, right here in Delhi – the licenses and permits required for operating the hotels, and the bars and restaurants in them had expired; in some cases they just did not exist.

In instance after instance – for example, Kanishka, Ranjit, Janpath, Lodhi, Qutab, Ashok to confine ourselves to Delhi alone – agreements with those who were operating shops and commercial establishments in the hotels had either expired, or just did not exist.

The Lease Agreement for operating Hotel Airport Ashok at the Kolkata Airport – the Hotel came up *thirty years ago,* in 1971-72 – did not exist, and ITDC was engaged in a dispute with the Airports Authority about it.

The License Agreements for operating the restaurants at the Airports in Kolkata and Aurangabad did not exist either.

The Kovalam Beach Hotel is, on all counts, ideal property for a hotel. Yet its occupancy rate in 2001/02 was a miserable 24%. It too registered a loss: of Rs.3.5 crore. Its land area is 25.78 hectares. On the records of the state Government, however, of this area ITDC has a clear title to only 16.5 hectares. One of the most valuable parts of the complex, Halcyon Castle, is *not* among the areas to which ITDC has a clear title! Indeed, it turns out that the balance 9.2 hectares have been under the occupation of the Kerala Tourism Development Corporation and private parties! Not just that. While this large area has been under the occupation of other entities, ITDC is the one that has been paying taxes on it!

Hotel Ashok in Varanasi presented an even more delicious illustration of the way things are. ITDC purchased 9.42 acres for the Hotel from the Department of Tourism in 1976. But it turns out that there is no record of the Department of Tourism having acquired the land and owning it at all! Although ITDC had been paying taxes on it since 1976, the land revenue records showed that the land actually belonged to Major General S. Shamsher Jung Bahadur Rana of Nepal. Elaborate searches revealed no document that could establish that the Department of Tourism ever acquired the property. We had no option but to disclose this – how should I put it? – "ambiguity" to the bidders, and ask them to submit bids for the Hotel on an "as is where is" basis!

Hotel Ashok in Khajuraho presented a double-barreled "ambiguity". The records revealed, on the one hand, that it owned 0.254 acres of which it was not aware, and, on the other, that it had encroached on 0.583 acres of a private party's land – and built 16 rooms and the Chef's residence on them! To implement the decision of the Cabinet, my colleagues had to first ensure an out-of-court settlement with the private party. It cost Rs.11 lakhs.

Yet this condition – the opacity of accounts, the encroachments, the undisclosed liabilities – itself became the occasion for further calumny, "You have given away Government money to the private party – even *after* privatization"!

Yet another charge!

Every sale and purchase agreement of the kind that is entered into while privatizing a unit, every merger and acquisition agreement has a clause for what are known as "post-closure adjustments". A unit may be purchased on, say, 31 December 2001. At that time the audited accounts that will be available will be only those as of 31 March 2001 – and that too, if we are lucky. This clause, therefore, provides that if, when the audited accounts of the unit till 31 December become available, it is found that the firm owed someone Rs.X crore which it had not remembered or not disclosed, the Government would pay the new owners Rs.X crore. On the other hand, if it turns out that the firm had amount Rs.Y crore due to it, or some asset which it had forgotten to include in its statement of assets and liabilities, the new owners will pay the Government Rs.Y crore.

It turned out that Modern Foods had not been following prudent accounting methods. For instance, norms of prudence require that amounts which have remained due for over three years be provided for as doubtful recoveries. But Modern Foods had been showing amounts which others – chiefly the governments of Delhi, UP, Bihar – had not paid it for over five years as good and recoverable amounts. It had made no provision for them. Similarly, no provision had been made for unusable and "slow-moving" raw materials, unusable stores, amounts due towards gratuity. The result was inevitable. Provisions had to be made for all these, and many similar items. During 1999-2000, when the provisions were made, the net loss of the company rose from Rs.13 crore to Rs.48 crore. The increase of Rs.35 crore was directly attributable to provisions under these heads. As it did not know the imaginative accounting methods of the company, the Government had quite literally not disclosed these additional liabilities to the bidders at the time of bidding, and therefore had to pick up the bill. But you can guess what was alleged in the papers and elsewhere.

In Hindustan Teleprinters we discovered contingent liabilities regarding claims that others had made on the Company but which had not been included in the balance sheets as debts. These related to Sales Tax: Rs.11 crore; Income Tax: Rs.3 crore; Excise Duty: Rs.1 crore. These claims were pending against the Company. Each of them related not to what the successful bidder would do henceforth. They arose from what the company had or had not done under Government ownership.

That is one thing we learnt: it is only when you begin privatizing governmental units that you get to know their real condition.

But there was more – that was even more shocking. The hotels we learnt had not been depositing even the statutory dues – towards Provident Fund, Gratuity etc. In 13 hotels that were being privatised in the first batch, ITDC was in default on this count by *Rs.31.50 crore*. In the remaining Hotels of the Corporation, the estimates revealed to our horror, the Corporation had failed to deposit about *Rs.80 crore*.

Regard for the law

That last bit – about the hotels not having deposited even what the statutes mandated them to deposit on pain of punishment – led us to gather information about other Public Sector Units that we may be asked to handle. We were able to gather preliminary information about 68 of these crown jewels – excluding the hotels. They traversed several sectors, and were in the care of 16 ministries – in a word, a representative lot. It turned out that between these 68 jewels, they had not deposited statutory dues – to the extent of *Rs. one thousand five hundred and seventy eight crore*. In addition, they had not paid even the wages of their workers to the extent of *Rs. three hundred and fifty seven crore*.

The law says that senior personnel in units – Directors, managers, etc. – that do not deposit what is due towards gratuity etc. will be severely punished. The punishment is to extend up to a year in prison. How is it that these organizations – owned and operated by Government – had been violating the law in this blatant manner? How is it that no one had ever been punished on that count? What would Government have been doing, what would our champions of the Public Sector have been shouting if these figures related to private firms?

The only way to safeguard jobs is for the units to be competitive. That, as has been documented times without number, the Public Sector Units are not. But efficiency apart, do facts such as the preceding ones show that keeping property – for instance, public land – in the hands of Public Sector Units is the way to safeguard even those tangible public assets? Do facts about defaults on statutory dues show that keeping these units in the Public Sector – a sector in which no one is ever brought to book, in which no one *can* ever be brought to book – is any way to safeguard even money that the workers have been guaranteed by law, to say nothing of their jobs?

Indeed, I would wager a law: the more strident champions of the Public Sector are about a particular unit, the more unaccountable it is.

The "progressives"

You have to just think of reforming the work-culture of a unit in West Bengal or Bihar, for instance, to say nothing of privatising it, and a howl goes up. Writs are filed. Stay orders obtained. Legislatures are brought to a standstill. Committed journalists add to the din. What are the facts about Public Sector Units in these most progressive of states?

There are 13 units of the Central Government in (the old) Bihar. *Seven* of them have been declared sick for years – and are lying in that mortuary, the Bureau of Industrial and Financial Reconstruction. There are 37 Central Government undertakings in West Bengal. *Twenty* of them are in the BIFR.

Note three things about them.

A unit is not declared "sick" and referred to the BIFR just because it has incurred losses for a year or two. It is declared "sick" and sent to the BIFR only after it has incurred losses for *four years in a row*, and only after its net worth has been eroded by 50 per cent or more of its peak net worth in the immediately preceding four years. In Bihar, for instance, the net worth of two other central public sector units has become negative though they have not yet been referred to BIFR. In Bengal the number of such units is eight! The net worth of these eight has sunk to *minus Rs. eighteen hundred and forty three crore.*

Second, these units of Bihar and Bengal have been rotting in the BIFR for up to a decade: of the 20 units from Bengal that are with the BIFR, for instance, *twelve* were referred to it in *1992!*

Neither the BIFR, nor what is called the Operating Agency – an investment institution like the ICICI or IDBI, say; neither the Central nor the state Government has been able to find any way to revive them: in several cases attempts have been made to get private entrepreneurs to enter into joint ventures for reviving the units, in several other cases attempts have been made to induce private entrepreneurs to take them over. To little avail.

In several instances, having spent years and heaps of public money in these fruitless chases, the BIFR has had to recommend that the units be closed. Governments have not been able to act on the recommendation. Political pressure has been mounted to prevent closure. Stay orders have been secured from the courts. Pledges have been made that new revival schemes will be explored. And all the while, the public exchequer has continued to be bled – to keep the corpses around.

The condition of public enterprises of the states is of course much, much worse. And among enterprises of state governments, the condition of those that are owned and operated by the Governments of Bihar and Bengal is much, much worse than of those in other states.

In March 2000, the year for which a study done for the CAG's office was able to get data, Bihar had 54 public sector undertakings. *Thirty-two* of these were reported to be "non-working". A total of Rs.8,168 crore had been invested in the 54. In turn they had accumulated net losses of *Rs. five thousand and sixty crore*.

The report of the CAG on West Bengal for 1999 furnishes data about the state's public sector units. There are 77 of these – 65 of them are Government Companies, 12 are Corporations. Taking share capital and loans together, *Rs. ten thousand six hundred and thirty three crore* have been invested in them. Against this investment of Rs.10,633 crore, the state Government received *Rs. 71 lakhs* from two Government Companies and *Rs.2.4 crore* from one Corporation! Finances of the West Bengal Government have been under severe strain for years: even if the Central Government borrows, it has to pay around 10% as interest. As against this, the rate of return from the state's Companies is an abysmal *zero point zero four per cent!* The CAG's report on West Bengal for the year ended March 2001, [p.15, Volume I, Civil] gives an instructive table in this regard.

Year	Percent return on investments	Rate of interest on Government's borrowing
1995/96	0.02	14
1996/97	0.02	13.85 & 13.75
1997/98	0.05	13.05
1998/99	0.01	12.15 & 12.50
1999/2000	0.03	11.85 & 12.25
2000/01	0.08	10.52, 11.80, 12, 10.50

Through these years, capital expenditure as a percentage of the state's total expenditures kept dwindling: it was 12 per cent in 1996/97, and 5 per cent in each of the following years. In the meanwhile, the expenditure locked in "incomplete projects", the CAG found, had increased from Rs.766 crore in 1996/97 to Rs.1,083 crore! The ratio of "capital outlay" to "capital receipts" "has been less than even 0.50 during the last five years," the CAG noted, "and came down drastically from 0.43 in 1996-1997 to 0.14 in 2000-2001 indicating that almost the entire capital receipts were spent either on revenue expenditure or on repayment of debt." "As there is no return from such application of capital receipts, the sustainability of operations of government are [*sic.*] weakened considerably," warned the CAG.

But then how did the state manage to continue this state of affairs? "Government of India provided special treatment to the state government despite the poor performance," records the CAG – and that about a state whose rulers have always won by alleging neglect and discrimination by the Centre! "The special treatments were accorded through (i) special loan from HUDCO for infrastructure development and (ii) additional plan assistance for state plan schemes. Substantial amounts (Rs.2,912.87 crore) of these expenditures were transfers to deposits and shown as expenditure in the accounts. These reflect poorly on the quality of expenditure...." "Persistent lack of balance from current revenues, galloping deficits, mounting interest payments, declining tax compliance indicated continued poor financial condition of the government," the CAG concluded. ".... Due to its precarious ways and means position the state government had to resort to huge ways and means advances and overdrafts throughout the year."

But there was an even more ingenious device, it turns out, involving the state's enterprises. The corporations of the state were in such a condition that they could not raise funds on their own. The state itself was straining against the borrowing limits prescribed by the Reserve Bank. No problem! The state government provided a "guarantee" so that the corporations could borrow. And the corporations put the money at the disposal of the state government! The "guarantees" provided by the state government amount to Rs.5,606 crore in 1999/2000. They increased to Rs.9,677 crore in 2000/01. Giving details for one year, the CAG recorded, "The guarantees given during 2000-2001 included Rs.4,277 crore guaranteed against loans obtained by WBIDFC (Rs.2,812 crore), WBKV & IB (Rs.871 crore) and WBPDCL (Rs.594 crore)...." And later in its report we learn what happened to these amounts.

"WBIDFC [the West Bengal Infrastructure Development Finance Corporation] raised Rs.4,540.55 crore during 1999-2001 through bonds/bank loans for the purpose of infrastructure development of the state," the CAG noted, "but spent only Rs.291.54 crore while the remaining funds were kept in the Deposit Account raising serious doubts about the stated purpose of raising these funds. Six government companies and statutory corporations parked schemes of Rs.281.47 crore, meant for implementation of various development schemes, in their deposit accounts with the Government."

Examining the Rs.1,567.93 crore that had been raised in 1999/2000 by the West Bengal Infrastructure Development Finance Corporation through bonds and bank loans ostensibly for infrastructure development, the CAG found that Rs.1,117.93 crore of this had been placed by the Corporation "in the Deposit Accounts with Pay and Accounts Officer, Kolkata, for utilization by the state government for other purposes. During the year 1999-2000, an aggregate of Rs.1,215 crore was taken by the state government from WBIDFC as loan."

But that, it turned out, was not even one-third of the story! The CAG observed,

> "Scrutiny (September 2001) revealed that Rs.582.31 crore remained in the Deposit Account of WBDIFC as on 31 March 2000 awaiting conversion to loans. In addition, during the year 2000-2001, WBIDFC raised Rs.2,972.62 crore through bonds (Rs.1,689.85 crore), loans from Housing and Urban Development Corporation (Rs.590.77 crore) and term loans (short term: Rs.542 crore, and long term: Rs.150 crore) from commercial banks at interest rates varying from 11.75 to 14 per cent per annum for the purpose of infrastructure development of the state. Out of Rs.2,972.62 crore, Rs.2,549.07 crore were parked in the Deposit Account with PAO, Kolkata. The state government converted Rs.2,508.89 crore into loans repayable in 92 equated monthly installments along with interest at the rate of 18 per cent per annum. Thus, the total loans received by Government from WBIDFC amounted to Rs.3,723.89 crore, of which Government repaid principal amount of Rs.183.59 crore and paid interest of Rs.485.76 crore during 1999-2001."

How very convenient! You can't borrow. Therefore, you get a

corporation under you to borrow. Then, instead of using the amount for the purpose for which that entity borrowed it, the corporation puts it as a deposit with you. And you convert that deposit into a loan to yourself!

The CAG's account continues:

"Further, out of Rs.4,540.55 crore raised by WBIDFC during the years 1999-2001 through bonds and loans for the purpose of infrastructure development in the state, only Rs.291.54 crore (6.4 per cent) had been utilized for the specific purpose and the remaining fund was parked in the Deposit Account. Thus, the actual use of the funds did not match the stated purpose of raising these loans. The state government used the WBIDFC as a vehicle of borrowing to improve the ways and means position of the government."

And clearly this Infrastructure Development Corporation was just one of the instruments to be put to such use! Examining other companies of the state, the CAG records,

"Mention was made [in the previous report of the CAG for 1999-2000] about parking of funds aggregating Rs.1,304.72 crore as on 31 March 2000 in the deposit accounts of 36 Government Companies and 2 Statutory Corporations. Further, test check revealed that during 2000-2001 various departments of the state government drew Rs.479.79 crore on the ostensible purpose of loans and advances to 4 Government Companies and 2 Statutory Corporations but deposited the amount in the deposit accounts of these institutions...."

And all this was facilitated by another feature – one which, if it had occurred in the case of private companies, would have raised a shout, it would have invited prosecution. It turns out that of the 65 Government Companies of West Bengal, *only fifteen* had finalised the accounts for 1998/99. Accounts of the remaining 50 Companies were in arrears for periods ranging *from one year to fifteen years*. Out of the 12 Corporations, *only one* Corporation had finalised its accounts for 1998/99 within the stipulated period. The accounts of 9 Corporations – for which information could be obtained – were in arrears *from one to nineteen years*.

A test check of the accounts revealed that of forty state under-takings *twenty-five* had understated their losses, and *eight* had overstated their profits!

"But why is the Government not rehabilitating the units first?," progressives demand at the Centre. In fact during the last decade, successive central governments have implemented a large number of "revival packages". These have cost the taxpayer around *Rs. forty thousand crore*. Each time the package was put up for approval, all sorts of forecasts were made – how in two years sales would increase by X per cent, how net profits would become positive in the third year.... I leave it as an exercise for the reader to find out how many units were turned around as a consequence, how many lived up to the forecasts that were made while extracting the "revival package".

"But that is because you fellows do not really want to help public sector units, the packages have been just for show," progressives retort.

So, why not consider the fate of units in West Bengal? After all, the Government of *that* state at least cannot be accused by its own votaries to not have wanted to revive its units.

The CAG reports that the West Bengal Government set up an Industrial Reconstruction Department in 1973. Till March 1999, the state Government had taken over 20 sick units for revival. *Eighteen of these twenty* units continued to remain sick. Their paid up capital was *Rs.65 crore*. As against this, after what we must assume were strenuous and dedicated efforts at reviving them, the accumulated losses of the units were *Rs. seven hundred and four crore!*

The units must remain in the public sector so as to ensure accountability, the progressives argue. If government holding is allowed to fall below 51 per cent, the managements will escape from the purview of CAG etc., they allege. In point of fact, accountability will *increase* were government ownership to be diluted. The lament of the CAG in the West Bengal case explains the state of accountability in these units, and bears testimony to his own helplessness:

"The Comptroller and Auditor General of India has repeatedly commented in the Audit Reports of the state [West Bengal] on the failure of the Heads of Departments and the Management of the undertakings in timely preparation of the *pro forma* accounts. Accountant General (Audit) reminded Principal Secretary (Finance) and the Secretaries of the concerned departments periodically in this matter. But there was little improvement in the situation and most of these undertakings have not finalized their accounts for periods up to 10 years or more.... The Principal Secretary/Secretary of the department concerned neither initiated action against the defaulting Heads of Departments for their failure to prepare the accounts nor took any effective initiative to set right the position. Moreover, there was no system of Internal Audit and performance appraisal to analyse the efficiency of these departmentally run undertakings. As a result there is no accountability of the management and government in respect of the public funds spent by these undertakings...."

The CAG then lists companies and the latest year for which their accounts are available. Remember, he is not commenting on their financial and physical performance – that is awful by every standard. Nor even on the veracity or otherwise of the accounts. He is merely on the most elementary requirement – whether they have cared to maintain even pro-forma accounts. It transpires that accounts for the Sisal Plantation Scheme have "not [been] prepared since inception" – in 1955/56. That the accounts of the Oriental Gas Companies' undertakings too have "not [been] prepared since inception" – in 1960/61. That the accounts of the Government Sales Emporia in Calcutta and Howrah too have "not [been] prepared since inception" – in 1951/52. That the accounts of the Government's Silk Reeling Scheme too have "not [been] prepared since inception" – in 1956/57. That the accounts of the Government's Training-cum-Production Centre – Mechanical Toys, Hooghly, too have "not [been] prepared since inception" – in 1972/73. That the accounts of the Government's Central Lock Factory, Bargachia, Howrah, too have "not [been] prepared since inception" – in 1972/73. That the accounts of the Government's Industrial Estate, Manicktola too have "not [been] prepared since inception" – in 1983/84. That the accounts of the Government's Industrial Estate at Saktigarh too have "not [been] prepared since inception" – in 1983/84. That the accounts of the Government's Kanchrapara Area Development Scheme too have "not [been] prepared since inception" – in 1975/76. That the accounts of *"bats"* under the management of the Government too have "not [been] prepared since inception" – in 1982/83. Fifteen other companies are listed – with accounts not being available for 3 years to a decade. Accountability! Governmental enterprises serving a "social purpose"!

Having given this shameful list, the CAG observes, "No action was taken by Government against the management of these undertakings for such gross failure and disregard of public interest."

His concluding words are worth putting as the frontispiece of reports of public sector enterprises. The CAG laments,

> "The lack of accountability arising out of the failure to prepare accounts by the departmentally run units for years on end is a matter of serious concern, as large amounts of public funds are involved coupled with the possibility of serious financial irregularities remaining undetected for long periods. Since these are departmentally run commercial units, responsibility for failure to ensure accountability of public funds should be fixed on the Heads of Departments. Government should re-examine the justification of continued release of budgetary funds to units without finalized accounts and without assessing their financial performance...."

That was written three years ago. Nothing but nothing has happened since then on any of the strictures. Not one person has been brought to book. The culture of not one unit has changed in any way.

Laws

Such being the facts, we can formulate "laws of public sector units":

❑ The more governmental an enterprise, the more unaccountable it is;

❑ The more unaccountable an enterprise, the more uncompetitive it is;

❑ The more uncompetitive an enterprise, the more certain it is to die the moment the artificial respiration from the governmental exchequer ends;

❑ The more certain it is to die, the more resistant its management and trade unionists, and even more so the politicians of the region will be of change, the more vociferous and minatory will those be – those sections of management, of labour, others – who have done most to bring the unit to its sorry state; they are the ones who will do everything they can to thwart the only steps that might save the unit and the jobs in it.

When we combine these laws – laws almost of Nature, I would say – with the empirical fact that the largest concentration of derelict, irremediable governmental enterprises lies in Bengal and Bihar, we come to see what is taking place. It is the political and trade union leadership of *these* states that is the most determined to block change.

That is what the country has to make up its mind about: should it mortgage reforms to those within public sector enterprises who have done most to bring them to the sorry state in which they are? Should it mortgage reforms to politicians and traders in unions from precisely those regions in which – because of the actions of these very personages and groups – the work environment has been worsened · the most?

3

Disentangling the Government

"Administration degenerates," C.M. Chang wrote in 1936, "into mere correspondence. The result is that politics too often ends where it should begin, with the assertion of intentio₁s. A clever magistrate is one who engages a good secretary who has at his command an excellent literary style which, like charity, covers a multitude of sins.... An old hand at the game knows that since the orders are so numerous, no one is expected to take them seriously." Hsu Dau-lin recalls that "Party resolutions were treated in the same way that government officials treated government documents: everything was done on paper only, and as soon as it was on paper it was forgotten."...

Unaccountable to forces outside the government, the officials tended to be concerned less with administrative goals than with bureaucratic means. "The Kuomintang," wrote Searle Bates in 1932, "seems to use most of its income and energy in making its own wheels go round, with little benefit in public service."....

"In China," Chiang Kai-shek remarked in 1932, "when something arrives at a government office, it is yamenised *– all reform projects are handled lackadaisically, negligently and inefficiently." Scathingly he told the officials that they were ruining the nation with their refusal to* shih-kan *– that is, to act so that there are real results. "Our work," he declared, "consists almost solely of the passing back and forth of documents. Stated simply, the documents sound good, but they are written negligently without regard for the true facts of the situation. With regard to practical work, Chinese either do not know how, or – if they know – they are slow in the extreme. It is not simply a matter of not completing today's work, but of putting off this week's work until next week, and indeed of putting off this month's public affairs until next month, and even of not doing this year's work until next year. This matter of amassing and delaying documents in this way can procrastinatingly ruin everything, causing deadly suffering for the common people.".*...

Nanking remained a Kafkaesque world of documents. Hsu Dau-lin, who knew the bureaucracy intimately from the inside, recalled that a document arriving at a provincial governmental office was transmitted through thirty-seven steps, each of which consumed from a few hours to a few days. As a consequence, "A reply after a half year's time was a surprise to no one. Not a few documents perished on their long and weary journey, buried alive in somebody's desk drawer. But just because of this lengthy processing procedure, mountains of documents were to be seen in every government agency."....

Perhaps the most characteristic aspect of yamenization *was the tendency of officials to produce documents of all kinds – plans, regulations, laws – that had little relation to reality and that had virtually no possibility of reaching the stage of implementation....*

Lloyd E. Eastman, *The Abortive Revolution,*
Harvard University Press, 1974

The Government's Advisors in the disinvestment of ITDC hotels – Lazard – were scheduled to visit Delhi's Samrat Hotel on 3 February 2001. Bidders naturally want to see the enterprise they are bidding for. The Advisors are to provide them every detail about the enterprise and its operations. They have therefore to make a thorough study of records. They have to inspect the site, the assets. This visit had itself been long delayed: it was taking place *four and a half years* after the process of disengaging the Government from hotels had commenced. The Advisors were in a restaurant of the hotel. Employees gathered. They started protesting, shouting, intimidating. This continued for half an hour. The Advisors could neither continue to sit because of the situation that had been created, nor could they leave as the entrance was blocked. Eventually they were escorted out through the kitchen of the restaurant. The site visit had to be aborted. The management personnel who were with them explained to them, ever so helpfully, that such protests were likely to spread to all the other hotels in Delhi.

Bidders and the Lazard people were next scheduled to visit Ashok Hotel – on 6 March 2001. At the penultimate hour the visit had to be postponed: on 5 March, the employees of the hotel – a hotel that was losing Rs.9 crore that year – gave the fullest evidence possible that they would "deal with" the visitors should the latter dare to enter the hotel compound the next day. The visit was rescheduled for 16 March. ITDC management was requested to make all arrangements to ensure that the bidders would not be scared away from the process. Nevertheless, disturbances were repeated that day. The visit had to be rescheduled once again – to 26 March.

The Advisors were compelled to inform ITDC that, in view of the incidents that were taking place, they would need to be guided as to what should be done about inspecting other properties that were coming up for privatization, and that "In view of such incidents, it will not be appropriate to conduct the exercise until stringent police security is provided for the safety of our team as well as the bidders."

The results were not long in hitting back.

Just two weeks later, on 19 April 2001, Advisors were shooed away from Ranjit Hotel in Delhi by the Union employees.

On 25 July, as the Asset Valuers reached Qutab Hotel, the Union leaders and their cohorts came out to intimidate and threaten them. The Asset Valuers had to leave the premises without completing the physical inspection.

On 9 August, the Advisors escorted prospective bidders to inspect the Janpath Hotel. Employees surrounded the room in which the meeting was taking place. They insisted that the Lazard staff leave the premises forthwith. They threatened them with dire consequences should they return to any ITDC property henceforth. They hurled threats at the hotel's executives – and threatened them against providing any information to Lazard or to bidders.

At the other end of the country, on 26 March 2002 bidders reached Kovalam Hotel in Kerala – a hotel that, in spite of its excellent location, lost Rs.3.5 crore that year, a hotel whose occupancy rate was a mere 24 per cent. While they were going round the property, they were attacked by a group. The Advisors immediately informed ITDC management about what had happened, and how the bidders had barely escaped physical harm. We will get back to you within half an hour, they were told. They heard nothing in the days that followed. On the eve of the next scheduled visit – on 4 April – the Advisors did not just alert the ITDC management in advance as they did in each case. With the experience of the previous visit ringing in their ears, they alerted the management twice, and requested it to seek the help of police or whoever could take charge of security at the site. The only thing that happened as a consequence was that the bidders and Advisors were physically assaulted at the site – by a posse of persons that included employees of the hotel. The visit had to be abandoned.

At each turn, in spite of specific requests to the contrary, senior personnel of ITDC broadcast to prospective bidders who had not been present that day information about the disturbances that employees had caused.

Talk of value-depleters!

That employees of a Government undertaking could disrupt a decision of Government with such impunity was bad enough in itself. But, as we shall see, intimidation and disruptions were the least of the obstacles that the privatization process encountered.

The first, most elementary ingredient

The process of privatizing ITDC hotels commenced in September 1996 – that is when ITDC was referred to the Disinvestment Commission. The Commission submitted its report on the Corporation in February 1997.

The recommendations of the Commission were then referred to the Committee of Secretaries, headed by the Cabinet Secretary. This group cleared the basic proposal in July 1997.

The proposal was now fit enough to be submitted to the Cabinet Committee on Disinvestment – the Committee is headed by the Prime Minister. The CCD cleared the proposal on 16 September 1997.

One full year had already gone by in reaching this stage, that is the approval in principle to begin the process.

At last we were ready to begin. But not quite. First we had to appoint the Advisor for the transactions. To do so, we had to float an international tender. To do *that,* we had to first issue advertisements requesting interested parties to file their Expressions of Interest. The applications had to be assessed first by the Inter-Ministerial Group. The recommendation of this Group about which of the parties should be selected as the Advisor had to be put to the Committee of Secretaries, headed by the Cabinet Secretary. The recommendation of the Committee of Secretaries had to be put to the Cabinet Committee on Disinvestment, headed by the Prime Minister.

The Advisor's appointment was eventually approved on 18 July 2000. Lazard, the well-known international consultants, were selected.

At last we were ready to begin the transaction – you might think. But not quite. First we had to get together the basic facts, the elementary records of activities and assets of the hotels that prospective buyers would need to know.

The first meeting of the Advisors with ITDC management was held in the first week of August 2000. We had counseled the Advisors that at this meeting they must submit a list of the data that would be needed. They did so. It was agreed on all hands that the information would be submitted by the ITDC management by the 3rd week of September.

On the 1st of September, I received a communication from Lazard informing me that till then just about 10 to 15 per cent of the information had been received from ITDC. My colleagues and I got on the telephones, we held meetings. Fervent promises were made.

It didn't require much insight to glean the objective behind this foot-dragging. Nor to foresee the certain consequence: by delays of this kind, the entire privatization process could be easily killed. Towards the end of September, therefore, we decided that we would *not* wait for information about all the 31 properties to become available. We would privatize in tranches: the hotels for which information was available, the ones which were less entangled in disputes about land, municipal taxes etc. would be privatized first.

Feet continued to be dragged – in slow motion.

Even the most elementary information – Capital Expenditure, Title Documents, etc. – was not received till the Inter-Ministerial Group meeting on 9 October 2000.

Visits to all properties had to be completed by November 2000. In fact, only the eight properties that were per force earmarked for being privatized in the first round could be visited – and that too with incidents of the kind that I have listed above.

Information, which was to have been provided by September 2000, continued to trickle in till December.

But by now, the Advisors and we learnt of the many disputes that ITDC had with state governments, with authorities like the Land and Development Office in Delhi, the New Delhi Municipal Committee, the Delhi Municipal Corporation. To say nothing of these issues being resolved, even information about these disputes, and that too relating only to the eight hotels that had been selected for being privatized in the first tranche continued to trickle in till February 2001.

Information – basic, elementary information – about hotels that were selected for the second tranche was not complete till June 2001.

Information

To say that information arrived by February or June is of course misleading. For "information" may be said to have arrived. But even the most cursory scrutiny showed that it was contradictory, it was incomplete, in instances it was illegible.

Documents made available to C.B. Richard Ellis, the consortium partners of the Advisors, showed that the total built up area at the Temple Bay Hotel in Mamallapuram was 6,585 sq. m. But in correspondence with Lazard, the Advisors, this area was put at 3,526 sq. m. The plans that were made available to Richard Ellis showed that the total land area of Hotel Ashok Hassan was 3.34 acres. Communications from ITDC, however, put this figure at 2.69 acres. One set of documents that reached the Advisors put the built up area of Bangalore Ashok at 13,521 sq. m. Another set put it at 12,905 sq. m. The built up area of the Ashok Hotel at Madurai was put at 4,212 sq. m. in one set of documents and at 3,871 sq. m. in another. One set of documents set the built-up area of the Lakshmi Vilas Palace Hotel of Udaipur at 11,000 sq. m.; another put this at 7,135 sq. m. The list that was given to the Advisors regarding Qutab Hotel indicated clearly that the tennis courts of the Hotel and the area and buildings of the Management Development Centre attached to it were part of the assets to be disinvested. Suddenly, a communication arrived declaring that these would *not* be part of the property to be disinvested – predictably that raised another issue: the Management Development Centre had no independent access, and the Lease Agreement contained a clause that prohibited the lessee from creating any easement on the leased premises!

Ownership of the land on which the hotels stood, the terms and conditions of lease, liabilities – on each of these elementary matters the information that was provided was incomplete, contradictory, plain wrong.

"In a meeting", "On leave"

In the Ministry of Disinvestment, every few days we would receive the copy of yet another distressing communication that the Advisors had been compelled to send ITDC management.

"Dear Mr. ....," began a typical letter, "This refers to the decision taken during the review meeting taken by Minister, Disinvestment on October 4, whereby ITDC were to approach Airports Authority of India to seek their consent to transfer the lease of the airport restaurant to the party selected for Hotel Ashok, Bangalore under the disinvestment process and that the outstanding amounts due to AAI from ITDC would be paid by the new party. I regret that despite being aware of the importance and urgency of the entire matter, ITDC's officials have not followed up the matter aggressively with AAI. As mentioned to you over the phone, I met Mr. ...., along with Mr. ...., ITDC last week on the matter to explain the need for immediate action by AAI. I also sent a letter (copy enclosed) providing the details of the proposed arrangement and the provisions incorporated in the transaction documents to safeguard the interests of AAI to Mr. .... immediately after our meeting. I have since been trying to reach Mr. .... and even left messages for him with Mr. .... However, I have not received any reply from him...."

And again, "*Re: ITDC – Building Plans for Lodhi, Ranjit, Janpath and Qutab.* Dear Mr. ...., This refers to my fax dated July 2 to Mr. .... (V.P.) and our discussions on the above subject. We have been repeatedly requesting you that the building plans for the 4 properties are required as part of the Data Room documents for the due diligence of the properties by the bidders. As you are aware, the due diligence for Lodhi Hotel has started today. However, we have not yet received the building plans...."

And yet again, "Dear Mr. ...., I refer to my earlier fax of 23rd December on our discussions with officials of Ashok Hotel, Delhi in relation to fixing meetings with them and discussing some key issues which are to be incorporated in the Information Memorandum. I must bring to your notice that despite our repeated reminders over the telephone, and a detailed questionnaire having been sent to your colleagues, we have not received any information, neither have you responded to our office for setting up these crucial meetings. The certain change of stance in meeting your officials at Ashok Hotel hinders our process and therefore delays all our deadlines. My colleague, ... has been trying to reach your office over the phone for the past few days without any luck and I tried both your offices today but was told that you were out of the office and busy. Could you please treat this matter as very, very urgent and respond to us immediately to enable us to complete our work within the deadlines set...."

And yet again, "Dear Mr. ...., This has reference to Lazard team's scheduled meeting with G.M. (Accounts) of Ashok Delhi on December 20. During the meeting the team was informed that the unit's Heads of Departments had received direction from their senior that they are not to interact with the Advisor's team directly. They were also told that any further information with regard to Delhi Ashok will henceforth be provided only through written communication through V.P. (Hotels). I understand that my colleague .... spoke with you on this matter and you confirmed the same to him. As you may appreciate that while significant information asked for can be compiled through written communication, nevertheless discussions and meetings with Heads of Departments are of utmost importance to understand the current and potential business of the hotels...."

On September 17, 2001 the Advisors were again writing to ITDC management: "We have not yet received the annual accounts for the first tranche of ITDC properties for the year ending March 31, 2001, and assets and liabilities pertaining to these units but not yet reflected in the books of the units. I would like to reiterate that this information is required for valuation of the hotel properties and replying to the bidders' queries. Please treat this as urgent...."

On 12 October 2001: "This has reference to my telecom with you and my fax dated October 10, 2001, whereby I had requested you to urgently provide us the status on the dues payable to various regulatory authorities by the properties included in the first tranche. However in spite of repeatedly calling you and leaving messages with your office we have not been able to contact you. We would request you to treat this as extremely urgent...."

On 22 October 2001: "Several pages of the audited balance sheet of the Hassan unit that we have received from you are not readable...."

November 19: a reminder listing the properties in regard to which queries had been sent, the dates on which they had been sent, the dates by which the data was to be received, and what the status was on 19 November – Samrat: "Not received"; Kanishka: "Not received"; Indraprastha: "Received"; Qutab: "Not received"; Janpath: "Not received"; Ranjit: "Not received"; Lodhi: "Not received"; Udaipur: "Received [answers] only [to] queries to be answered by the unit. Queries addressed to corporate office unanswered"; Varanasi: "Received [answers] only [to] queries to be answered by the unit. Queries addressed to corporate office unanswered."

27 May 2002: Answers to even elementary questions are not forthcoming. The Provident Fund Commissioner has filed a case against ITDC for not making any provision for Provident Fund during 1982-87: what would be the contingent liability on this count? Hotel Indraprastha has been demarcated: what are the outstanding liabilities to the Land and Development Office and other authorities? The 15th floor of Hotel Kanishka houses certain offices of Parliament Security. Will these be vacated after privatization?....

28 May 2002: "During the due diligence of Hotel Indraprastha, it was discovered that certain essential plans like ground floor plan and floor level plans had not been included as part of Data Room documents. These are essential for any bidder to make his estimate about the property. Accordingly, on the last date of Due Diligence, i.e. May 18, 2002, we had asked the Unit's Engineering Team to prepare sets of copies of the floor plans for the qualified bidders. However, one week has passed by and the plans have still not been photocopied. Bidders have been calling us frantically since their queries and technical evaluation of the property will depend on the availability of these plans. We have been following up this issue with the unit, but till today morning the photocopies had not been made.... Some of the bidders for Hotel Indraprastha are also interested in meeting Mr. ...., the General Manager of the Kanishka Shopping Plaza for specific questions relating to the Shopping Plaza. During the period of Due Diligence, the bidders could not meet him as we were given to understand that he was on leave...."

Sent up and down the official ladder

At every turn Advisors had to run up and down the official ladder. And as they were deflected, my colleagues, and on occasion I had to do the running.

To continue the instance I have reported earlier, not one of the hotels in Delhi had a Completion Certificate. To get the Completion Certificate "with retrospective effect", so to say, we were told to produce the Completion Plans. These too were not available. Therefore, they too had to be manufactured "with retrospective effect". But to do that, we were told, we must produce Completion Drawings. These too were not available. We were told that the way out was to prepare "as is drawings". But to prepare these, two architects had to be appointed. Fine, said both ITDC and the Central Public Works Department, but who shall pay for the architects? CPWD, said ITDC. ITDC, said CPWD. Each had its reasons: the hotels are in fact owned by CPWD, ITDC pointed out; but they are on long-term lease to ITDC, CPWD pointed out. But then what is to be done?, the Advisors and we inquired in exasperation. The matter may be referred to Secretary, Ministry of Urban Development, said both....

In accordance with the recommendations of the Disinvestment Commission, Government had decided that the Ashok Hotel in Bangalore would not be sold outright, that along with Ashok, Delhi and the Lalitha Mahal Palace, Mysore, it would be given on long-term lease. The Bangalore Ashok had been constructed in 1972. A part was added in 1974. But the sale deed of the land on which it stood had not been concluded. To proceed with the hotel's disinvestment, this document was needed. The Information and Tourism Department of the state government was contacted. A draft sale deed was prepared. That had to be vetted by the Legal Department. The vetted draft was then sent to the state Public Works Department. From there it would go eventually to the Sub-Registrar, Bangalore for execution and registration. Our Ministry had been after ITDC to have this process completed. The Company Secretary was in Bangalore for the purpose. He went to the Secretary, PWD's office. The Secretary was on leave. So, he was directed to meet the Acting-Secretary. From there he was directed to the Deputy Secretary – the officer who was dealing with the case. All issues have been resolved in regard to the sale deed, the Deputy Secretary was kind enough to say. In that case, can the deed be issued while I am here in Bangalore?, the Company Secretary inquired. It will take at least a week to issue the authorization letter, he was informed....

But that was just one of myriad issues to be sorted out. And just in one of 24 cases. The Bangalore hotel ran a restaurant at the city's airport. That restaurant had been taken on lease by ITDC from the Airports Authority of India. To transfer the lease to whoever would win the disinvestment bid required the consent of the latter. But formalities relating to the original agreement, it turned out, had not been completed: these included the point that the advance license fee and security deposit had not been deposited. ITDC owed about Rs.60 lakh to the Airports Authority for this restaurant. AAI maintained that they would not be able to give their consent to the lease being transferred to any other party till ITDC paid these dues. ITDC maintained that it did not have the money to discharge the dues! Government decided that the dues would be paid by the successful bidder.

But for Government to decide is one thing, getting its employees to implement the decision is another. "This refers to the decision taken during the review meeting taken by Minister, Disinvestment on October 4," began a communication of the Advisors to ITDC management three weeks after the meeting, "whereby ITDC was to approach Airports Authority of India (AAI) to seek their consent to the transfer of the lease of the Airport restaurant to the party selected for Hotel Ashok, Bangalore under the disinvestment process and that the outstanding amounts due to AAI from ITDC would be paid by the new party. I regret that despite being aware of the importance and urgency of the entire matter, ITDC's officials have not followed up the matter aggressively with AAI. As mentioned to you over the phone, I met Mr. ...., Executive Director (Commercial) AAI along with Mr. ...., Area Vice President, ITDC last week to explain the need for immediate action by AAI. I also sent a letter (copy enclosed) providing the details of the proposed arrangement and the provisions incorporated in the transaction documents to safeguard the interest of AAI to Mr. .... [the AAI official] immediately after our meeting. I have since been trying to meet Mr. .... [the Area Vice President, ITDC] and even left messages for him with Mr. .... [an ITDC official]. However, I have not had any reply from him...."

ITDC affirmed that they had indeed been "rigorously pursuing" the matter. But the result could hardly reassure the Advisors, much less us in the Ministry. "The undersigned," wrote the ITDC official, "after rigorously persuing [sic.] the Airport Authority and [sic.] was able to speak to GM (Commercial) of AAI Mr. .... and conveyed to him the urgency for communicating their decision on the matter of ITDC urgently. Shri .... acknowledged that they have received the letter from ITDC yet AAI would be in a position to communicate their decision only after the legal opinion is obtained from their legal department. He also showed his inability to communicate anything in writing to ITDC till the matter is decided at their end. However Mr. .... did mention that under the circumstances AAI may not agree for the same terms and conditions to be followed in case of change of ownership after disinvestment in the instant case."

Even as we were wading through this matter of the lease documents, the Advisors learnt that ITDC was about to enter into a contract with Indian Airlines to supply 40-odd rooms for two years to the airline at a rate one-third less than what was being realised. The contract was already in the draft stage, they learnt. That would certainly depress the valuation even further. Everyone had to give up everything else and first prevent such an obvious value-depleter....

An "issue" at every turn

That bit about "why should we pay for the two architects?" is typical of what administration has become: *anyone* can raise *any* "issue", and thereby secure a delay for weeks and months at a time, often he can in fact derail the Government completely from implementing its decision. At turn after turn, our Ministry had to contend with this feature.

ITDC had 32 properties. No one would want to buy all the 32. But to sell each separately, the properties had to be "demerged". In demerging one is obliged to protect the interests of shareholders. ITDC was owned overwhelmingly by the Government. TATAs held 10 per cent of the shares: but they said they would go along with whatever the Government decided. But still the demerger plans must be approved by shareholders, a Joint Secretary held.

And then, "What about the interests of creditors?," he demanded. They may feel that change of management will jeopardize the loans they had given to ITDC. It so happens that the courts have already settled how the interests of creditors are to be protected. The crux of their judgments is that, while the interests of creditors should be protected, they do not have the right to veto a demerger or amalgamation scheme. In any case, we were building the necessary clauses into the sale agreements. "No," the officer decreed. "Each sale must be approved by creditors in a separate meeting which must be held at the site of each hotel." That gave every chicken supplier who had not yet been paid by ITDC a say in the matter: for the Companies Act provides that such schemes must be approved by 75 per cent of the creditors present and voting. But, the moving finger having writ, there was no way round the meetings. The Joint Secretary insisted that the approval could be obtained only by convening the meetings, that it could *not* be obtained by circulating the resolution among shareholders and creditors.

All right, meetings. But who has to be called to them? ITDC said that they did not have the list of creditors handy, preparing it would naturally take time....

The result was what had been predicted: a few small creditors attended the meetings, and in three cases they defeated the demerger resolutions. In the end, the powers that be agreed to dispense with this farce of holding meetings, and settled instead for the alternative that was obvious and flowed from the court judgments themselves: that is, ITDC would provide corporate guarantees to protect the interest of the creditors. Even that proved insufficient. Governmental bodies – the Municipal Corporation of Delhi, the NDMC, the Land and Development Office, the National Buildings Construction Corporation – declared that they could not be satisfied with guarantees of a body that had defaulted so blatantly on dues to them. Therefore, we provided that the successful bidder would defray the dues. We had also to provide severe penalty clauses: that if the purchaser failed to discharge dues to the creditors within specified periods, the Government would be entitled to buy back the shares at one-half the price that the bidder had paid to Government....

Any one at any level at any stage

The scheme for demerger was prepared by the Legal Advisors for the transaction. It had then to be put to the Inter-Ministerial Group for approval. Then it had to be filed with the Department of Company Affairs for *its* approval. And then it had to be put to the Board of Directors of ITDC.

And every one at every level was free to question everything. The Cabinet Committee had approved the demerger scheme. Eventually, the Board of ITDC met. It approved the demerger of 22 properties, but not of the 4 properties that were to be given on lease-cum-management contract. The Board maintained that it had yet to understand the advisability of demerging these properties, and, pending such understanding breaking out, it naturally withheld approval from the scheme. So much for the scheme that the Cabinet Committee presided over by the Prime Minister of India had approved!

And at every step esoteric issues got raised. Shall the shell companies that would be formed to "own" the individual hotels for the few weeks before privatization be public limited companies or private limited companies?... Reasons why the word "Ashok" cannot be used in the names of the shell companies.... The manner in which accumulated losses of ITDC must be shared between the new shell companies.... The affidavit about the schemes contained the declaration that "the information is true and correct". This should have read, said the authorities concerned, "the information is complete, true and correct." And there should have been a separate affidavit for each property, not a portmanteau one covering all of them.

The result was that the demerger process which had been started in October 2000, did not get completed till the end of 2001: the matter had to go up for the approval of the President of India, it had to be considered by the Cabinet Committee on Disinvestment thrice. By mid-November 2001, the Cabinet Committee on Disinvestment had approved the bids for the hotels at Bangalore, Madurai, Bodhgaya, Hassan, Mamallapuram and Agra. But we could not complete the transactions as motions regarding the demerger scheme were still being executed.

Another six months were eaten up by another "issue" – the appointment of the Asset Valuer. ITDC started the process in January, 2001. It prescribed certain conditions and set out the scope of work. It invited offers from 71 parties. Arguments broke out between departments, and with the Advisors as it was alleged that the scope of work was being redefined from step to step. Eventually a valuer was selected. He was asked to reduce his fee. He didn't. In the meanwhile, another Department ruled that, by a provision of Company Law, a company could not pay for activities connected with its own privatization. As the Disinvestment Ministry was to pay the Asset Valuer, it began the process of selecting one. ITDC said that it had already completed the selection. Could you then send us the relevant file?, we inquired. It has been sent to our Minister, we were told. The whole thing had become so acrimonious that I had no alternative but to cancel everything, and start all over again. It was not till the end of June 2001 that the Asset Valuer could be appointed.

The same "issues" – who will pay for their services?, can they be selected by limited tender? – were raised in regard to, and thereby dogged the appointment of other intermediate advisors: chartered accounts, lawyers. The process of appointing them began on 1 August 2000, and could not be completed till the end of January 2001.

ITDC officials now raised another "issue". The hotels had been making losses, they began. These losses had been met by other divisions of ITDC. Therefore, before privatizing the hotels, the Ministry of Disinvestment must reimburse the other divisions of ITDC! Detailed indents – hotel-wise! – were sent: November 2000 to March 2001 – Rs.7.55 crore; April 2001 to September 2001 – Rs.10.52 crore. Soon a reminder arrived. The correspondence became more strident with each exchange.

Even as this was going on, the Land and Development Office put in its spoke. Officials who had neglected inspecting the hotels properly for decades, suddenly went round, spotted a host of violations, and intimated that they would send lists of unauthorized constructions, misuses, illegalities, the works, and issue show-cause notices. What effect that would have on valuations required no imagination: such lists and show-cause notices would immediately become parts of the Data Room, and contribute to scaring bidders away....

All this apart, there was a dark overhang to everything: the Corporation and these hotels, as we have seen, had not been discharging even their statutory liabilities. Provident fund contributions had not been deposited. Property taxes had not been paid. Lease dues had not been cleared. Electricity charges had not been paid. Water charges had not been paid. A rough estimate put these statutory, obligatory dues at around Rs.90 crores. Naturally, the bidders would not proceed till the quantum and status of these liabilities were settled; till they were told conclusively who would be held responsible for the dues not having been discharged in the past – the original managers, etc., or the successor company – and who would be responsible for discharging them after privatization. But to do that required discussions – "negotiations" would be the better word – with a multiplicity of authorities: from the departments of law, company affairs, labour, etc., to the Cantonment Board of Agra, the Municipal Corporation of Madurai.

Sorting out an "issue"

Each authority in turn had to go through loops of its own entwined in loops of others. The land for the Ashok Beach Resort at Kovalam had been transferred in six phases – over the previous thirty years. The figures that the Advisors were supplied by ITDC added up to 78.61 acres. But the statement from the hotel itself put this figure at 64.5 acres! To sort out this single anomaly required the hand of ITDC, of the Ministry of Tourism, of the Department of Tourism, Government of Kerala, of the District Collector, of the Village Officer, Vizhinjam. A single, sample communication will indicate the state in which things were, and what had to be done to get over even such an elementary problem. The communication was sent by the General Manager, of the Kovalam Ashok Beach Resort on 22 April 2002. Here it is:

"Enclosed please find the Possession Certificate issued from the Village Officer, Vizhinjam which is a self-explanatory [*sic*]. As far as Thandaperu record is concerned, we are in possession of 25 hectares 78 ares [*sic*.] and 40 sq. mt. During the due diligence most of the parties wanted to have clear possession certificate less the encroachment as well as disputed area. "I talked to the District Collector about the same. Mr. T. Balakrishnan, IAS, Secretary (Tourism) called a meeting of the Collector as well as Tahasildar etc. Mr. Amitab Kant, IAS, Joint Secretary also followed up from Delhi and asked Mr. Balakrishnan to expedite this particular problem. During the meeting, this problem was discussed and it was decided that barring the adverse possession area, a clear possession certificate would be issued for the balance which is with us. Basically, there are two areas which are under dispute.
  1. KTDC
  2. Udaya Samudra
"As far as Palace and land surrounding the same, there is no record of transfer of land and payment from the State Govt. to ITDC. Even the State Govt. also does not have the record of the same. This land was not acquired land and this particular piece of land was owned by Kerala Govt. and has been transferred to ITDC at some point of time. We are not able to

trace out the record of the transfer nor Kerala Govt. also [*sic.*] does not have any record of this particular transaction. However, mutation has been done in the record and the Palace & surrounding areas are our property. Even the taxes have been paid for the complete land in spite of adverse possession.

"Since Govt. of Kerala is not very sure with regards to the mode of transfer, they also marked this area as adverse. Hence, after working out the complete adverse area, 16 hectares 47 ares [*sic.*] 95 sq. mt. of land has been given as clear possession and the balance land i.e. 9 hectares 30 ares [*sic.*] 45 sq. mt. has been given as adverse possession.

"Submitted please...."

But getting the extent of land sorted out was just the beginning. There was a long-standing dispute between ITDC and the Kerala State Tourism Development Corporation over 5.80 acres. And there was an equally ancient dispute about a structure right in the middle of the property – the Halcyon Castle. At long last, ITDC proposed a *quid pro quo:* ITDC would hand over the disputed land in the northern corner of the property; in turn, it requested that the state Government cede its claim to the Castle. Fine, said the Tourism Department of the state. But, it said, as this was a major decision involving transfer of land, the matter had to be referred to the state Cabinet....

Property-specific loops

Vaulting over such walls did not mean that we were now free to proceed. It just got us as far as the next wall. Each property had impediments of its own.

Bidders naturally must know the court cases in which the property is entangled. But there was no central list, to say nothing of any estimate of what the financial liability was liable to be in the event the judgment went against the hotel.

Collating even the basic information – just the cases that were before the courts, and the point that was in question in the case – took a good bit of time. It turned out that the hotel establishments were embroiled in 339 cases.

Several of these involved other governmental agencies: the state electricity boards – about billing, about dues not having been discharged; several involved disputes with local municipal and zonal authorities – about property taxes, about illegal constructions; several involved disputes with tax authorities. There were numerous cases that employees had filed against the hotels – for wrongful termination of services, for ignoring seniority, for denying promotion on grounds that the employees claimed were unjustified; several that hotel managements had filed against employees – for absenteeism, theft, molesting a guest, drunkenness, negligence, habitual unpunctuality, allowing credit that was as good as writing off the amounts to guests/ suppliers/contractors. There were a host of cases against contractors, suppliers, tour operators – about unpaid bills, about leasing of restaurants, travel counters and other facilities. Similarly, ITDC had agreed to refer some of the disputes to arbitration, and then filed appeals against the awards of the arbitrators. There were appeals against verdicts of labour courts. There were cases against the local community: about cremation and burial grounds, about dwellings that had been set up illegally on the premises of the hotel....

The cases were in High Courts, in local courts, in labour courts, before arbitrators. The problem was not just that the information had to be collected. The problem was that in many instances, the Legal Department did not know where the case stood at the time.

But gathering and compiling the information was but the first step. It soon became evident that whoever won the bids would have to contend with this heap of litigation for an indefinite future, and with uncertain liabilities. The Hotel Temple Beach Bay at Mamallapuram, to take one instance, was involved in a dispute with the local fishermen. The latter had set up cremation and burial grounds at three different places encompassing 2.36 acres. They had also constructed their dwellings on property that belonged to the Hotel. True, the Sub-collector, Chengalpattu had given an order – in 1998 – permitting ITDC to construct the compound wall that it had proposed to screen off the burial and cremation grounds. But the people of the area had prevented it from doing so. The order of the Sub-collector too had been a conditional one: ITDC may construct the wall, he had decreed, but if the religious people of any community object to locating the cremation and burial ground at the new site that ITDC had proposed, ITDC will have to shift back one of the cremation and burial grounds to the eastern side without any protest. When contacted, the management at the site explained that land for the new cremation and burial ground had not been handed over, that the fishermen had refused to stop bringing dead bodies for cremation and burial "in front of our guest cottages". ITDC put the onus on the revenue authorities who, it said, were not able to convince the fishermen. The authorities said they were not able to do so because ITDC had not filed the necessary written commitment. On top of this, we learnt that the new lobby, kitchen, a new block of 12 rooms, another set of 7 duplex rooms, all fell within the prohibited "200 meters from the high tide line" zone, and ITDC had in fact received demolition notices in regard to these from the Mamallapuram New Town Development Authority....

Two kms from the site, ITDC operated a restaurant. It was spread over 4.5 acres. But it was not clear who owned the land. The Advisor had to first persuade ITDC to locate the actual owner of the land, and execute a transfer deed with him.... In fact, inspection disclosed that the Hotel owned yet another 7.05 acres – for which too the transfer deeds were not available. Here too ITDC had to first determine who the actual owner had been, and execute the deeds.

The sale deed for the land on which the hotel at Khajuraho stood had not been registered. Internal correspondence, as we have seen, disclosed that, in fact, in the local land records the property still stood in the name of the original owner – Maharaja Bhawani Singh. In addition, it turned out that there was a dispute in regard to the land on which 16 of the rooms, the chef's residence and a portion of the swimming pool of the hotel stood. A private party claimed that this land belonged to it, and ITDC had usurped it. The Additional Commissioner had held against ITDC. On the other hand, the private party had encroached upon the southern portion of the plot belonging to ITDC....

The Hotel at Udaipur, the Laxmi Vilas Palace, had leased 7.78 acres of land to Hindustan Zinc Ltd. for 99 years, at around Rs.1 lakh a year. HZL had constructed houses for its staff on this land. In turn, HZL had constructed 12 staff quarters at its cost for ITDC, and leased them to ITDC at Rs.25,000 a year.... Talk of cross-holdings!

Calcutta: for *thirty years* a dispute had been raging between ITDC and the Airports Authority of India – this one was about the lease rent to be charged. It was now lying with the Ministry of Law. For *twenty-two years* another dispute had been raging between ITDC and AAI – the lease rent to be paid for the restaurant ITDC was operating at the Airport. The matter was now lying for arbitration with the Joint Secretary and Financial Advisor, Ministry of Civil Aviation. Because of these disputes the lease and license agreements had not been signed either for the hotel or the restaurant....

We could not proceed with the Hotel at Aurangabad for quite a different sort of reason. ITDC had purchased land from Southern Railways in 1980, and had paid Rs 9.94 lakhs to the latter. That much was established. But for *twenty-one years* since then there had been a dispute about the *extent* of land for which this payment had been made: ITDC maintained that the amount had been paid for 24.72 acres; the Railways maintained that the amount had been paid for only 12.44 acres. ITDC had taken Southern Railways to court. The Railways claimed first that ITDC must pay another Rs.4.13 crores to it for the extra land. Soon, they upped the amount to Rs.5.94 crores. Pradip Baijal, Secretary, Disinvestment devised a formula for an out-of-court settlement: two bids would be invited – one for 12.44 acres, and another one for the entire land; in case Government finally accepts the bid for 12.44 acres only, Railways would get Rs.1 crore; in case it accepts the bid encompassing the entire area, Railways would get the entire incremental amount. But at the last moment another complication erupted: with just 3 weeks to go for the financial bids, an advertisement appeared in *The Economic Times* – a lady claimed that the entire land was part of the estate she had inherited....

The Department of Tourism and the Land and Development Office under the Ministry of Urban Development were engaged in a long, and vigorous battle about the ownership of the land on which Delhi's Lodhi Hotel stood – and had stood for *thirty-seven years!* The Department of Tourism insisted that the Land and Development Office, Ministry of Urban Development had transferred the land to it. L and DO insisted that the ownership continued, on behalf of the President of India, to vest with the Ministry of Urban Development. The *shastras* were brought out – by each side. One claimed that the land had been transferred by the Under Secretary, Ministry of Urban Development to the Department of Tourism at cost for its use. The other claimed that the latter had acquired it at a premium....

Almost all properties had constructed unauthorized structures. These had not been regularized. The amounts that would have to be paid to compound the violations – assuming that the local authorities would condescend to regularize them and not press the show cause notices that they were now issuing – were anybody's guess....

And that is just one enterprise

Problems – equally frustrating, equally silly, problems just as divorced from the tasks that the enterprise had been set up to execute – dogged every single transaction.

In fact, the hotels in many ways had been transactions that it had been possible to complete in record time!

Jessop and Co. had become sick by the early 1970s. With the delusions of those days, to save it from extinction, the firm was nationalised in 1973. Its losses mounted. It was given reliefs upon reliefs – by January 2002, it had been given reliefs of *Rs. four hundred and sixty six crores*. But its losses continued to mount. Its net worth became negative – hugely negative. It was referred to the Board for Industrial and Financial Reconstruction in 1995. While the Board considered schemes after schemes for putting it on its feet, the net worth of the company fell to *minus Rs. 290 crore*. Its accumulated losses rose to *Rs. 372 crore*. The Board kept on deliberating.

The Government announced that it would turn the enterprise over to a private party: that was on 30 January 1997.

BIFR sanctioned a revival scheme in May 1998.

After two years of efforts had not yielded any partner, the Ministry of Heavy Industries transferred the case to the Ministry of Disinvestment – that was in February 2000.

BIFR appointed SBI Caps as the Operating Agency – to finalise a scheme to enlist private partners for converting the company into a Joint Venture.

In August 2000 BIFR passed an order that would have hamstrung the efforts at disinvestment.

The Operating Agency issued advertisements in September 2000 inviting private parties to form a Joint Venture for running the company. It received no response at all.

Government filed an appeal against the order of BIFR before the Appellate Authority for Industrial and Financial Reconstruction in November 2000.

This authority took till January 2001 to affirm that there was no bar to the Government submitting to BIFR a scheme for disinvestment as a possible way of reviving the company.

The process for disinvestment could be begun only thereafter – in February 2001.

Given the procedures that had been prescribed, the bids could be invited, and finally approved by the Cabinet Committee on Disinvestment only on 27 February 2002.

In other cases, that would have been the end of the road. But this was a BIFR case. So all that could be done was to submit to the BIFR – a body headed by an itinerant IAS officer – a scheme that had been approved by the Cabinet Committee headed by the Prime Minister.

The BIFR thereupon referred the scheme to its Operating Agency for the case – as a result sundry employees of a subsidiary of the State Bank of India now commenced sittings on a scheme that had been approved by the Cabinet of India!

The Operating Agency could not find time to hold a meeting – its first meeting – for a month.

Two months later, BIFR concluded that its Operating Agency had found that transparent procedures had indeed been followed in inviting and approving the bid!

As the BIFR had still not passed any order, and two and a half months had gone by, our Ministry wrote to BIFR requesting it to come to a decision.

The Operating Agency now convened yet another meeting.

Eventually, *four months after the Cabinet had approved the bid,* the Operating Agency gave its report to BIFR. Ostensibly, what it submitted was a scheme that the Agency had prepared. In fact, the "scheme" was just a rewrite of what the Cabinet had approved. But four months had gone in the rewriting.

BIFR decided to circulate the scheme of the Operating Agency, and gave parties another three weeks to file their objections or comments.

When that hearing was held – by now *five months* had passed since the Cabinet had approved the bid – BIFR directed the Government of West Bengal to give their final views about their proposal that a bank guarantee be sought from the bidder that he would discharge the loan which the state Government had given to Jessop to cover its sales tax dues!

But along the way the company's Staff Association had filed a writ in the Calcutta High Court against the disinvestment of Jessop.

The Court passed an interim order: while BIFR may proceed with hearings on the proposal submitted by the Government about inducting a strategic partner, the Government should not act on the orders of BIFR without obtaining leave of the Court.

Hearings followed hearings.

Jessop of course continued to hemorrhage.

The writ on Jessop was just one of *thirty-one* writs that had been filed against disinvestment by July 2002 – right up to the Supreme Court. Each of them required the help and time of a host of individuals and agencies: from the Attorney General and Solicitor General to local lawyers, from the Departments of Law, Company Affairs and the Administrative Ministry to the management of the particular enterprise.

Lessons

1. What we had to wade through, a glimpse of which I have given above, is not special to disinvestment: on the contrary, disinvestment is but a prism through which we get a glimpse of what has become of administration, of governance in general.
2. At this pace there is just no way by which we will be able to keep up with the rest of the world.
3. The element that is most urgently needed as part of the "second generation reforms" is the reform of processes – and that includes decision making within the Executive; the ambit of cases that the courts will entertain as well as the dispatch with which they will deal with them; and also the loops through which necessary legal changes will have to pass in legislatures before they will become law.
4. As for expediting administrative decision-making, we must learn from the fate that has invariably befallen attempts to speed things up. Remember how many committees were established to expedite import and industrial licensing? Remember the "single windows" that were instituted? The single-point Secretariat for Industrial Clearances? Things reverted to the *status quo ante* within months of each initiative. It is only when the function itself was jettisoned that the improvement came about.

A coral reef

4

Regulators, licenses, technologies

At a seminar in Delhi recently, the Chief Technical Officer of Motorola – she is an Indian, Padmasree Warrior, a graduate of the Delhi IIT – disclosed that soon Motorola will be coming out with a new instrument. When you reach your home, this instrument will function as a cordless phone. When you step out of the house, it will function as a cellular phone. When you reach an area that is not covered by cellular services – the mountains, say, or the Arctic – the instrument will function as a satellite phone.

But in India the cordless phone that you use within your house works on the network of a Basic Service Provider – the one who provides fixed-line service. To provide cellular service – over which you may use your cell-phone – an operator has to get a separate license, through an entirely different process of permissions, regulations, fee-structures. And to use a satellite phone, you as a consumer have to seek special permission that only the Department of Telecommunications can give. In a word, to use that one instrument you will not just need access to service providers who have set up business in three strictly separated silos, you will have to

---

This essay describes the licensing system as I found it when I was given charge of the Ministry of Communications and Information Technology. The sector was mired in litigation, and in acrimonious allegations. Lobbying ministers and officials was the order of the day – the core competence of many an entrepreneur, as well as the feature that made the Ministry so attractive for potential ministers and officers. I realized soon that the only way out was to as far as possible scrap the licensing requirements altogether, to permit operators to do what technology enabled them to do. The tortuous course of disinvestment decisions had already taught me that I would be ensnared in the webs of different ministries were I to propose one improvement at a time. The Prime Minister approved the proposal to set up a Group of Ministers to consider the entire range of issues in one go. The Group endorsed the diagnosis underlying in this essay, and the proposal for a single, unified, quasi-automatic Universal Access License. The Cabinet approved the recommendation of the Group of Ministers.

get the Department of Telecommunications to anoint you among the select handful who are allowed to use satellite phones.

But we don't have to wait for tomorrow. Our regulations for apportioning the amount that the customer pays between the different service providers who come into play when you phone someone – the fixed line service provider in Delhi who has provided your phone; the provider of the network over whose lines, etc. your call travels to Kanpur; the owner of the cellular service whose network your friend in Kanpur is using – is based on a host of distinctions: transitions, handover points, gateways, etc. But with the changeover from the circuit switched network to packet switched network, these distinctions are erased. The network becomes seamless as well as ubiquitous. The same thing holds at your end – that is, that of the consumer. It is already possible to have a single socket in your house deliver voice, data, Internet, as well as radio and TV broadcasts. But our licensing system insists that each of these be a separate service.

Even a single mode can now do many things. We make a sharp distinction between telephony and broadcasting, between radio and TV. But mobile instruments are now available through which you can receive radio programmes, through which you can transmit and receive videos or movies, through which you can transmit TV programmes that you have recorded, through which you can surf the Internet.... Soon, they will be able to receive videos and TV broadcasts. I was invited to inaugurate a new service of MTNL. We were at Ashoka Hotel. At the MTNL headquarters, they started a film on Begum Akhtar that they had financed. The film was received at Ashoka Hotel in an ordinary phone, that phone in turn had been connected to a computer, and the entire film was projected on to the full screen – as it would be in a cinema hall. Was this telephony, or broadcasting, or a cinema-show?

A sharp distinction is made today between cellular and WLL services. The former uses GSM, the latter uses CDMA technology. Ferocious litigation has been going on between the two sets of operators. TDSAT has directed Government to keep the services distinct. And that because that is how the licenses were given. What is the position in technology?

❑ The infrastructure of one can provide all the services that the infrastructure of the other can provide.
❑ At the other end, the consumer can now buy a handset that gives him the freedom to access both CDMA and GSM services.
❑ Competition has ensured that tariffs too have converged.
❑ Each of these two technologies can provide either type of service: mobility within a limited area or over an unlimited area.

But our licensing system insists that the operators using CDMA technology ensure that the person is able to use his handset only within a *tehsil*. Make sure that this bolt of lightning stops at 17½ kilometers, it says in effect!

Remember what happened when cordless phones first came out. They were illegal – for they were wireless instruments, and transmissions without wires were governed by the Indian Telegraph Act. Of 1885, thank you! But once a thing becomes available, people adopt it, and the law has to reconcile itself to the new state of affairs. That is what happened. People installed the cordless instruments in their homes, and eventually the law succumbed – and pronounced their use to be legal.

The same sequence has been repeated again and again. Till two-three years ago, youngsters were being arraigned by our enforcement authorities because they were calling their friends over the Internet: the Internet is meant only for data, not voice, said our licenses. But in mid-2003, Government allowed Voice over the Net.

In that allowing too there is a lesson. Voice over the Net was permitted, but only for international traffic, not for calls within the country. Even that distinction does not tell the whole tale: Voice over Net was allowed for international traffic – but only for incoming international calls!

Such recognition of reality-in-singles doesn't end the complications, of course. Consider that last example for a moment. The Internet makes no distinction between your calling someone in the city in which you are, or someone in Mumbai, nor indeed someone in distant New York. You are charged a standard rate for accessing the Internet. But under our regulations there is a strict demarcation between local calls, national long distance calls and international calls. In rates of course. But also in permissions. Among the most contentious issues in the telecom sector has been who shall get a license for "national long distance" telephony as distinct from telephony within a city, who shall get a license for "international long distance" telephony as distinct from long distance calls within the country. Thus, while calls over the Internet are much cheaper, Basic, Cellular "National Long Distance" service providers are not allowed to provide telephony through this medium. Only those with Internet Service Provider licenses are allowed Internet telephony – and that too only for one category of calls.

Nor is that the end: those who have licenses as "Internet Service Providers" have to pay no license fee for Internet telephony; those who have licenses as "International Long Distance" service providers have to pay 15 per cent of their Adjusted Gross Revenue as license fee. Not just that. The Internet Service Provider is not required to pay any entry fee. The International Long Distance Service Provider is to pay an entry fee of Rs.25 crore!

The consequences are obvious:

❑ When technology enables people to avail of or provide a service and licenses prohibit it, the licensing regimes will be violated. The State's first reaction will be to set enforcers on to users of the service and its providers. That will just foment corruption. And further technical sophistication – improved technology will make policing more and more difficult.

❑ When the same service can be provided through alternative technologies, but the rate structure is such as to make service through one route more expensive than through the other, a "grey market" will arise. People will just by-pass the more expensive route – it is reported that VSNL loses up to *forty per cent* of long distance traffic to this grey-market. All concerned agree that the operators who provide this by-pass are violating the law. Posses sally forth to catch the culprits. The occasional violator is caught. But that has no real impact on the scale of the diversion.

❑ What is round the corner is manifest. Those who got licenses only for national long distance or international calls, for instance, will find their business drifting away as more people acquire access to

Internet and as the "Voice over Net" technology improves. They will then either have to reconcile themselves to go on losing business, or invent ways to provide the same service surreptitiously, or – our usual option – use the State apparatus to somehow delay Internet telephony.

❑ In the end, our regulations will adjust to the new reality – but after forcing the country to lose years, after entangling everyone in coils and coils of litigation.

❑ There is the economic cost also. Not just for the consumer. Not just for the service provider. For the country itself. In the licensing system as it stands, separate licenses are required for "Basic", "Cellular Mobile", "Global Mobile Personal Communication System", "National Long Distance", "International Long Distance", Internet, VSAT, Paging, as well as each of the other services. As a result, operators providing each of these services use separate infrastructure, the Guidelines require them to maintain separate accounts, and to bill customers separately for each service. Avoidable expenditure has thus got incurred on duplicating the infrastructure, and on support services. The customer is inconvenienced – he has to deal with a multiplicity of service providers.

But the worst consequence is different. It is the habit that such structures and mental mores engender. Of shunning change. Of frightening the lay public of every new prospect. Of convincing ourselves that the opportunity that has erupted before us is actually a snare.

A coral reef

The drag that such regulations impose on the adoption of technology is one aspect of the matter. The other feature, from which several consequences – from litigation to lobbying – flow is that licensing systems are coral reefs. They grow bit by bit over the years. As a result, every system of this kind is riddled with incongruities entangled into incongruities.

Recall the differences listed above in the entry fees and license fees that have to be paid for international calls by the Internet Service

Provider and the International Long Distance fellow. Now, consider the area of operation.

If you are in Ganganagar, Rajasthan, and make a call to Udaipur, also in Rajasthan, or from Surat to Bhuj in Gujarat over your fixed phone, the call counts as a long distance call, and is charged accordingly. On the other hand, if you make the same call over your cell phone, it counts as a local call, and is charged accordingly! Reason? For cellular services, a state is a local area. For basic services – those of the BSNL, for instance – the unit of measurement is a construct called an "SDCA", a "Short Distance Charging Area". This is generally coterminous with the boundaries of a *tehsil*. So, under our regulations, if you have a cell phone and call anywhere within the state in which you are, that is a local call. But if you call over the fixed phone from your home beyond the tiny *tehsil* in which you are, it is a long distance call.

What if you call a cell phone from a fixed line phone in Udaipur? The charge then comes to depend on an altogether different concept: a Point of Interconnection. The call from your fixed phone is handed over at some point to the cellular network. If that Point of Interconnection is more than 50 km distant in another SDCA the call is charged as a long distance one; but if it falls within the same SDCA, and even though it is more than 50 km away, the call will treated as a local call, and the long distance tariff will not be applied.

But, as always happens in regulations, the SDCA is not always just a *tehsil!*

In Maharashtra, for basic operators, Goa and all of Maharashtra, including Mumbai, are one service area. For cellular operators, Mumbai, Navi Mumbai and part of Kalyan are one service area for the purpose of licenses. The rest of Maharashtra is another service area. In Tamil Nadu, for basic operators, the entire state – including Chennai – is one service area. But for cellular operations, Chennai plus Mahabalipuram plus Malaimanar are one area, and the rest of the state is another area. In West Bengal, for basic operators the entire state is one area. For cellular services, Kolkata is one area, and the rest of the state is another.

In these states, therefore, there is one license for basic operators, and two for cellular operators. In Delhi, the position is the opposite.

As far as cellular operators are concerned, the service area includes Delhi, Gurgaon, Faridabad, Ghaziabad, NOIDA including Greater NOIDA. But for Basic Service Providers, these five areas constitute four different SDCAs in what are by the other reckoning three service areas!

Ghaziabad, including NOIDA and Greater NOIDA, is a curate's egg by itself. It is a part of the UP (West) service area for Basic Services but a part of the Delhi service area for cellular services. As a result, if a subscriber residing in a house in Ghaziabad uses his fixed phone to dial a cellular phone in the same house, the call is taken to be an inter-circle call, and is charged accordingly.

In a word, in Delhi, for basic operators the Delhi metropolitan area, which is one SDCA, is the service area; for cellular operators the metropolitan area plus several adjacent areas are one, single service area. In Maharashtra, West Bengal, Tamil Nadu, the position is the exact opposite!

That the consumers – and readers, to say nothing of sundry ministers looking for the rationale of these distinctions – are left confused is the least of the consequences. Given that calls within a state are long distance calls when fixed phones are used but local calls when cell phones are used is certain to induce migration of vital business from an organization like BSNL – one that is providing the basic service. Second, there is the disjunction: wireless signals cross *tehsil* boundaries but the licensing system requires them to be bottled within silos! That is one of the spurs to the interminable litigation between telecom operators that has become as much a hall-mark of the telecom sector as rapid growth.

Today it is almost impossible to take any step in this sector – even on the smallest matter – without being accused of doing so to surreptitiously help one side or hurt another. Ahmedabad and Gandhinagar in Gujarat are a continuum. Persons living in one part work in the other. Similarly, Mohali, Panchkula and Chandigarh in Punjab, and Mumbai and Navi Mumbai in Maharashtra are in effect single conglomerations. But in each instance they are separate SDCAs. Therefore, they have different STD codes – though even in that there is a difference: BSNL has been allowed to treat them under one common numbering scheme; private basic operators, however, have been tasked to treat them under two distinct numbering schemes! Leaving that aside, businessmen as well as important political leaders asked me to see why the areas could not have one common STD code. The staff in the Telecom Department on the other side have been warning me that, should the areas be treated as one common charging area, we will be accused of deliberately enlarging the SDCA to help the WLL operators – they are allowed to provide mobility only *within* an SDCA, and by permitting a common numbering plan, we will be allowing these operators to extend their service into the adjacent areas!

Here is another gem. Today basic and cellular operators are not allowed to connect to each other at the boundary of two service areas. Thus, if "X" has got a license for providing cellular services in UP and in Haryana, he can lay his network up to the border point of UP on one side and up to the border point of Haryana on the other. But he cannot join them! So, if one of his customers in UP calls someone in Haryana, even though the latter is also his subscriber, he cannot take the call over his network. He must "back-haul" the call to a designated point and hand it over to a National Long Distance Operator who, in turn, will carry it to Haryana! The fact, the cognoscenti tell me, is that "integrated" operators like "X" are in fact carrying the long distance traffic over their own network. The small operators have to depend on the "National Long Distance Operators" and pay the charges that have been prescribed by TRAI. But the moment you try to remove this anachronism – because it is being violated in practice; because the violation is almost impossible to police; because the step would make regional calls cheaper – someone or the other from among the "National Long Distance Operators" will insist that his interest is being hurt, and he must be paid a compensation! Else, courts, TDSAT, TRAI, plants in newspapers....

Every licensing regime thus leads to interests getting vested in maintaining things as they are. The moment you try to improve it, someone is bound to take you to court – and that happens even when the change is not liable to hurt the person particularly: keeping the other fellow from benefiting is an even stronger spur in India than wresting a benefit for oneself! Hence the mountain of litigation that has accumulated in this sector in the last five years. The litigation in turn foments uncertainty, and it encoils everyone in insinuations of the worst kind. Together, they deter further investment.

Different vintages

The mal-effects are made all the more certain by the fact that bunches of licenses have, necessarily, been given over time – one appurtenant after another pertaining to each vintage differs, as it invariably will: for in the meantime requirements, technologies, perceptions are bound to change – specially in a sector in which products replace each other by the month, technologies by the year.

If you got your license before the New Telecom Policy of 1999 to provide a Basic Service, and you shifted to the NTP-99 regime, till the shift you would have paid a license fee between Rs.29 crore and Rs.532 crore depending on the service area. The amount was determined by competitive bidding, and it was for a period of up to 22 months. If, on the other hand, you had bid for a cellular mobile service, you would have paid a license fee between Rs.38 lakhs and Rs.512 crore depending on the service area – this too by a bidding process for a period of up to 43 months.

Those were the license fees you would have paid if you had got your license *before* NTP-1999. If you got it *after* NTP-1999 was announced, for the Basic Service you would have paid an entry license fee ranging between Rs.2 crore and Rs.115 crore depending on the service area. And this fee was fixed, not by bidding but by the Government. For the cellular service the entry fee was between Rs.1.1 crore and Rs.207 crore. And this fee was *not* fixed by Government but by bidding. HFCL paid Rs.177 crore to provide the basic service in Punjab. Reliance got the license for Rs.20 crore. A gain for Reliance. In Gujarat, Reliance paid Rs.179 crore for providing the basic service. Tatas got the license after 1999 for Rs.40 crore. Everyone is therefore able to produce "proof" that he has paid more, and that Government must "compensate" him before he will allow it to take the next step.

But in addition to the license fees, there is an annual fee. If you were providing the Basic Service, you would have to pay 8%, 10% or 12% of your "Adjusted Gross Revenue" – there are points of high scholarship regarding that chimera too, but we will ignore them for the moment – depending on whether your Circle was Category A, B, or C. If you were providing a cellular service, however, you would have to pay an annual fee of 15% of the "Adjusted Gross Revenue". But soon enough the basic operators were allowed "limited mobility"; that is, their cordless phones, so to say, could operate beyond houses – hence, "mobility" – but within that construct, the SDCA – hence, "mobility" albeit "limited". As a compensation, that annual fee for cellular operators was reduced from 15% to the 8, 10, 12% levels as in the case of basic operators.

As a basic operator, before NTP-1999 you would have to contend in a circle with competition from just one more operator. NTP-1999 and the "migration package" lifted the limit: henceforth you would have to contend with as many operators as chose to set up operations in that circle. In the case of cellular operators too the earlier limit of two operators in a service area was lifted – but it was decreed that there would be no more than four operators in a circle.

If you intend to provide Internet Service, or a radio taxi service, or any other service connected with telecom, you just have to pay the entry fee, and begin. If, as we just saw, you want to set yourself up as a basic operator, even then all you have to do is pay an entry fee, and begin. But even if you pay the fee, you cannot begin a cellular service – not unless in a particular telecom circle there are fewer than four operators. Why is there a limit on competition in cellular services, but none for other services? The reason given is that cellular operators use spectrum, and spectrum is a limited resource, and therefore the number of providers has to be limited. Now consider what has happened to that rationale. Every basic operator has been allowed to commence a "limited mobility", WLL service. But that service too uses spectrum! So, if more entities come in and set themselves up as basic operators, our licensing regime shall allow them to commence service. But if more want to enter the cellular field and provide competition to existing operators, they shall *not* be allowed – even though now both sets – basic as well as cellular – make demands on the same scarce resource, the spectrum!

The original old basic operators were allowed to use spectrum up to 8+8 Mega Hertz, while the old cellular operators were allowed 4.4+4.4 Mega Hertz. When the old basic operators were allowed "limited mobility", their allowance was cut to 5+5 Mega Hertz. The old cellular operators were allowed to raise their usage to 10+10 Mega Hertz.

But that was the difference between the "old *basic*" and the "old *cellular*". The *new* basic licensees were allowed a maximum of 5+5 Mega Hertz, to be released in steps beginning with 2.5+2.5 Mega Hertz. The *new* cellular operators were allowed 6.2+6.2 Mega Hertz. This latter allowance was later raised as in the case of "old cellular" to 10+10 Mega Hertz.

Then there are obligations that go with the license. These too are of two types: a "roll-out plan", that is the pace at which you will extend your network; and a separate "universal service obligation", that is the pace at which you will cover areas like villages that are liable to be unprofitable. The precise content of each of the two categories of obligations differs depending on whether you are an old licensee or a new one, and whether you are a basic operator or a cellular one.

If you are a basic operator and you got your license *before* NTP-1999, Government would have specified the number of villages in which you must set up public telephones as well as the number of "DELs" – Direct Telephone Lines – that you must install. If you are a basic operator but you got your license *after* NTP-1999, your obligation has been specified as the proportion of rural, semi-urban and urban SDCAs you must cover.

If you are a cellular operator, the obligation is of yet another caliber: for operations in a metro, you must cover 90% of the service area within one year; at least 10% of the District Headquarters within one year; and 50% of the District Headquarters within three years.... The latter was subsequently amended to "cover any other city/town in a district in lieu of District Headquarters".... Unlike the basic operators, in this case whether you are an old or new cellular operator does not make a difference.

Such discrepancies are inevitable: technologies change, priorities change, governments learn what is possible, what will shoo-away investors.... Inevitable, but not without consequences. In attempting to freeze time, so to say, at what it was when the licenses were issued, the discrepancies hamper the adoption of new technologies. They foment a sense of having been wronged – in all participants. Each side believes that the other fellow has been given undue favours – favours in lieu of which *it* must be given yet another concession. And each can produce "proof": the cellular operators argue that they were made to pay higher license fees than the basic operators – and they have the figures to show that; the basic operators argue that *they* have been made to pay more by the yardstick that matters, namely the fee per unit of spectrum they have been allowed – and they have the figures to show that. Grievance leads to litigation – of course, given our creativity, we do not necessarily need a grievance to litigate.

A temptation? A compulsion? A compelling temptation!

There is another, an even deeper consequence. As much turns on the precise wording of the license, entrepreneurs are under the greatest temptation – they would say, under the greatest compulsion – to induce, cajole, bend functionaries of the State who are writing the licenses. In the alternate, after the license has been written, the entrepreneur tasks his lawyers and engineers: technology allows me to provide a seamless, boundless service, he tells them; now, read this license and devise a method by which I can provide the maximum that technology enables me to furnish, without violating any specific provision of the license.

A hardy perennial of this sector, and an aspect that is currently in the news will illustrate what happens.

Each time a session of Parliament begins questions stream in about telephones in rural areas, and the "failure" of Government to compel private basic operators to establish these. Now, if you see the licenses that were issued originally, they do impose an obligation that requires the operators to establish the phones – the obligation, as I noted earlier, was in terms of both: each basic, fixed line operator has to install a certain number of direct connections, and a certain number of public phones in the villages. And if you see the record, not one operator has installed what he had committed he would: together they had committed to establish public phones in about 98,000 villages; they have in fact covered only about 12,000 villages. What comes in the way of imposing penalties so severe that the operators would just *have* to live up to their commitments?

One impediment is a sentence that made its way into the licenses: after saying that the operator would have to provide those village public phones, the clause recorded, "If all the villages in the service area have been provided with at least one public telephone by the DoT (the Department of Telecommunications) or the private operator, in such cases this obligation will cease to be applicable."

The result? If you could get the government department – or its successor, the BSNL – to take up your area, you would be liberated from the obligation. That is the argument of the operator who has not installed public phones in Punjab: all the villages there have already been covered by BSNL! That is also the grievance of the operator who has not provided the public phones that he was to set up in Madhya Pradesh: "We have gone out of our way to provide service in God-forsaken places," he says. "Just because BSNL has been concentrating on Punjab and has neglected Madhya Pradesh, why should *we* be penalized?"

And *both* have another grievance together! Look at the basic operators who were given licenses later to provide the "limited mobility" service, they say. These Jhonnies were not required to install *any* direct lines into private homes, nor were they required to establish any public phones in the villages. They were asked to establish only "Points of Presence" in district and *tehsil* headquarters. On the other side, the WLL(M) people argue that they can't go about forcing mobile phones on individual customers. Theirs' is a service over the air, so to say. All they can do is install transmission stations to cover the area, and offer the service to those who subscribe for it....

Of course, penalties were listed in the licenses: for instance, if your circle is of "B" category, you have to pay Rs.4 crore if you don't install that many direct connections, another Rs.4 crore if you don't install that many public telephones. It was so much easier for the basic operators to pay the amounts – a mere Rs.53 crore in all – rather than install the connections and public phones.

Notices for non-compliance.... Stay orders by courts.... Assertions by each side that the other has been favoured.... Demands for compensation to make up for concessions given to the other....

To freeze time

Our industrial progress was set back a generation, perhaps by more because of the industrial and import-export licensing systems. The licenses used to be user specific, they used to be use specific, they used to be technology specific, they used to be product and input specific. An entrepreneur was allowed to produce commodity 'A' at a factory located in place 'B' by using process 'C' deploying machine 'D' imported from country 'E' by inserting raw material 'F'. Often the price at which he could sell the resulting product too was specified. If he departed from any one of these conditions in the slightest, he was guilty of violating the law, and was thereby liable to be prosecuted.

And who was to determine what the entrepreneur was to produce, where, how, etc.? Personages ensconced in government offices: the Comptroller General of Imports and Exports, the Directorate General of Technical Development, the Planning Commission.... The premise was that the licensing authorities were better judges of what should be produced, by whom, with what equipment, etc. than the entrepreneur who was putting in his money. The authorities surrounded their work and processes in much mystery. But when at the height of their power and reputation in the mid-sixties I examined the record – including their internal worksheets! – I had little difficulty in showing that nothing more than rules of thumb formed the basis of their decisions. [For a sample of what I found, see, "Controls and the current situation: Why not let the hounds run?," *Economic and Political Weekly*, 1973, Volume VIII.]

That system has been dismantled in most sectors of the economy. But ironically, the telecom sector – one of the sectors in which technological change is the fastest – is one of the remaining bastions. A bastion of both – the service/user/technology specific licensing regime as well as the mind-sets that go with it – among private entrepreneurs as much as in the governmental set up!

Changes in technology strain this regime at every turn. On the other side, as those who got licenses used to do in the sixties and seventies, entrepreneurs try everything to use the licensing regime to ensure that new technologies do not affect their turf for as long as possible.

But today new technologies are born every two years, new products are born every three months. Decades ago, Arthur C. Clarke formulated two axioms about the advance of technology:

❑ Whatever is thought possible – and much of what could not even be conceived – comes to pass;
❑ It comes to pass sooner than anyone had thought possible.

To these we can add lemmas from our own experience:

❑ The change comes to have effects that reach farther than anyone had imagined;

❑ The new developments come as jolts even to entrepreneurs – for changes are ever so often triggered by mavericks experimenting away in their garages; in any event, civil servants, judges, to say nothing of ministers are least equipped – by their training, their aptitudes – to anticipate the technologies that will break out, and the consequences they will unleash.

We see the resulting tremors in the telecom sector every other day. On the one side the new technologies enable participants to digitize all data; they enable them to compress reams upon reams of it into unimaginably minuscule magnitudes; they offer ever-new algorithms to "code" it, to "packet" it. On the other, bandwidth capacity to transmit this data is widening by the month. The two developments together enable different services – TV, radio, Internet, telephony – to be provided through the same infrastructure. And to be accessed by the final consumer through the same instrument – the TV set, his desktop, his hand-held device, his "telephone".

The system – licensors, enforcers, regulators – can strive either to block such new capabilities or facilitate their being adopted swiftly:

❑ We charge heavy entertainment tax from cinema halls. But movies are now offered directly to the viewer from satellites. Soon, we won't need even our TV sets to see them: computers, hand-helds, even phones will receive them directly via wireless networks maintained by the traditional telephone companies. Will the transmitters be evading entertainment tax?

❑ Recently the Digital Library of India has been launched. 30,000 books have already been included in it – you can download each of them directly via the Internet. Within a year, a million titles are to be digitized and made available through this site. Is the programme to be halted because, in a sense, it enables providers of those books and readers to evade sales tax?

❑ The country's Wireless Advisor has allocated 1452-1492 Mega Hertz frequency band for digital audio broadcasts from 2004. Assume a company uses that band to receive the records of a hospital in Germany, and transmit back the data after processing it. Is the company violating the law? But in the new technologies, "data" in the traditional sense – a string of numbers or text – is indistinguishable from voice – both are transmitted in the same form. And if the rate that is charged for the use of the former frequency band is lower than for the latter, the firm *will* use the cheaper band. Will we then bring the rates in line or will we set the CBI after the firm?

❏ Today you can read almost all our newspapers on-line. When text-to-voice software improves a bit, you will be able to hear them. Would that be "broadcast" or "print"?

❏ The distinction between "broadcast" and "telephony" used to be that the former was one-way: as listeners we just received voice or images; telephony on the other hand is "interactive". But even today broadcasts – over both the radio and TV – can be interactive: listeners participate in quiz programmes and discussions by ringing up the studio even as the programme is on air. Soon, you won't need your phone to do so; you will be able to talk directly through your TV set. Will that be "telephony" or "broadcasting"? Accordingly, will it fall in the jurisdiction of the equivalent of a Broadcasting Commission or the telecom regulators?

❏ We have recently seen the spat over whether the set-top box must be used or not. Soon the "dish" for receiving signals directly from satellites will become so cheap – a TV company is already offering the dish at Rs.100 a month – indeed the capability will be routinely built "free" into the standard TV set and computer, that people will not have to go through cable operators at all. Will we stall the introduction of those TV sets or computers so as not to "discriminate against" those whom we have pushed into investing in set-top boxes? Or because the new capabilities will drive cable operators to bankruptcy?

❏ We do not have to wait till tomorrow for the converse case. Cable operators in the US, and even in the so-much-slower UK, have upgraded their networks so that they can offer telephony, and provide access to the Internet. In India we look upon telephony, internet, TV-through-cable as distinct. Should we therefore prevent such upgradation?

That is the basic difference. Should we block the introduction of a new technology or practice because it violates existing laws and regulations? Should we clutch on to those laws and regulations till they are disregarded into complete meaninglessness – as happened with those extortionate tax rates, with those elaborate industrial and import licensing systems? Or should we put the new possibilities to work? Today there are 90 million TV sets in the country. There are only 60 million phones. There are only 9 million computers through which the Internet can be accessed. We are constantly hectoring governments to increase teledensity, to ensure greater access to the Internet. And governments are in fact spending enormous amounts to set up the infrastructure to do so. But surely, the quickest and cheapest way to increase teledensity and Internet usage is to encourage the technology that will enable the TV set to provide telephony and Internet access too.

Orientation

Nor are our laws and regulations the only impediment. Even more formidable a hindrance is the *orientation* of our regulators.

Almost all of our regulatory and dispute resolution bodies – from the Inter-state Water Disputes Tribunals to TDSAT – are headed by sitting or retired judges. The function of these bodies is viewed as being akin to that of courts. It is "quasi-judicial", we say. Similarly, if one calculates the proportion of the total time of the hearings of a typical case in these bodies that has been taken up listening to the arguments of lawyers, and contrast that with the proportion that the body has spared for listening to, say, technologists or engineers, the former would far outweigh the latter. As a result, these bodies approach every problem the way courts do – that is, by examining affidavits, interpreting sections of laws, regulations, rules, sub-rules, circulars. Seldom do these bodies search for what management experts call "design solutions" – the way by which the total quantum of the good in question – water in the reservoirs, the market for telecom services – can be multiplied so that *all* the contenders would have more to work with. The entire approach is to assess "legality". The premise is that the matter is yet another zero-sum contest – what one contender gets, the other will necessarily forfeit.

The result is made all the more certain by the task that is set for the regulatory body. Thomas Balogh compared "mathematical economists" to a child who, having just discovered a hammer, suddenly finds everything worth pounding. The simile applies to governance too. When you set up a Human Rights Commission, for it human rights are the over-riding desideratum that has to be ensured. Those rights, in fact the alleged violations of those rights by organs of the State are its reason for existence. What the conditions in Punjab were at the time – how the judicial machinery, for instance, had itself evaporated – is no concern of the Commission. In the telecom sector today, ushering in new technologies is not the objective for which TDSAT etc. have been constituted, the courts even less so. They have been constituted to resolve disputes, to adjudicate between contending competitors and their lawyers, to ensure "level playing fields".

The background and life-long training of the heads of these bodies, the specializations of the persons they listen to, the very mandate for which the bodies have been constituted all work to ensure that those "design solutions" are kept far away. The license says this, the regulation says that, in his letter X said this on date Y but in the circular of date Z the department said....

The basic determinant is thus the *orientation* of the regulator. Does he view his task as being to enforce word X over word Y in some circular or license? Or does he perceive his task to be to use every dispute to nudge the system towards the next technological advance, to use every occasion to maximize competition? Today, the orientation is the former. That is why the bodies become a brake on technological progress.

Lessons

The lessons are manifest:

❑ Regulatory bodies, especially in sectors in which technological advance is rapid, should have persons who are well-versed in technologies.
❑ Regulators must be on the look out for prospective changes in technology, they must assess what impact their decision is going to have on the adoption of new technologies.
❑ They must devote a greater proportion of their time listening to technology experts, to inventors, and less to lawyerly arguments.

An effective way to induce this reorientation would be to place at the hands of the regulator a fund to sponsor and reward inventions and their adoption in the industry. Members of the regulatory body would then *as part of their mandate* be on the look out for inventors and inventions. They would be continually receiving information about what is round the corner. They will be coming into contact with persons who are different from lawyers and accountants – and also from columnists!

In addition, regulators must bear in mind the habit, and the great skill of many of our entrepreneurs in using the licensing system and our courts to keep competition at bay. That habit and skill will be deployed in using regulators for the same purpose.

There must equally be a certain reticence, so to say:

❑ A regulator who tries to fine tune the flood of technological change, who attempts to ensure that every detail is in order, will tie the sector in knots. Many today demand that TRAI step in and "end the confusion," that it "bring order" to the multiplicity of "packages" that the telecom companies are holding out to consumers. But there are close to *six hundred* price-cum-credit-cum-security-cum-service packages on offer in telephony. How many can the regulator assess and police? Can he inspect every package to ensure that it is not "predatory"? Instead, should he not go by some rule? For instance, that an operator who offers a low price shall not revise it upwards for three years – that the operator may lower it further, but he will not raise it? Will such a general rule not ensure that he will not offer a price just to kill competition, and then, once the competitors have been eliminated, raise it?

❑ Such efforts to monitor and regulate every detail can only end in a wild goose chase. Assume the regulator decrees the price below which a cellular operator shall not peg his charge-per-minute. One operator circumvents this by offering handsets free. The regulator bans that or specifies the minimum that the operator must charge for the handset. The operator then keeps the charge for the handset at that level but adds features on to it. Or he offers a deferred-payment plan. Or he ties up with an insurance company and declares that anyone subscribing to his service can get the insurance policy at a concession.... These are normal marketing devices today. How many will the regulator plug? And will it be the case that such practices will be outlawed in the telecom sector but be allowed in, say, the marketing of newspapers? After all, they are already common place in the latter.

❏ Regulators like licensors must not set out to decide what technology the entrepreneur is to use to provide which service. Nor is it their job to protect entrepreneurs from the consequences of the latter's wrong decisions in regard to either.

Each of us can help the work of regulators: by subjecting their rulings to intense professional scrutiny. Such scrutiny is the hallmark of the American and British legal systems, and it is one of the principal reasons for the higher quality of their verdicts. In India, there is next to no analysis of judgments. The judgments are scarcely read. Has it gone in favour of or against the Government? That is about the extent of interest. Even our lawyers tend to head-note jurisprudence! Just the convenient sentence or two from a judgment!

Lessons for licensing systems are just as clear:

❏ Minimize licenses.

❏ Where you must have them, let the licenses not be "contracts" between the licensor and the licensee. Let them be as close to automatic authorizations as possible. Contrast the licenses that were given to the basic operators – basic operators will provide X number of public telephones in villages – and the pattern even in India in regard to the Internet: you pay the fee and commence the service you want to provide.

❏ When you have to give a license or an authorization, give it in the open, in full.

❏ If contractual conditions just have to be included, ensure that there is no ambiguity in the drafting. And that penalties for non-compliance are so stiff that the licensee will violate them at the pain of extinction.

❏ No license, no policy – how often we are told, "But the NTP-99 did not say this...." – should be viewed as having been writ in stone. On the contrary, every "policy", every license condition, like every law must have a "sunset clause" – that it will expire after X years unless it is renewed, and that only after due deliberation.

Of our organizations, it is the Reserve Bank under Dr. Bimal Jalan that set up a sort of Regulation Review Authority: a ginger group of young officers with a Deputy Governor as the distant head. It was given freedom to examine *ab initio* each form, each regulation. When those young, fresh minds could not find a manifest reason for its continuance, they would ask the concerned division to show cause why the rule, etc. should continue....

❏ Dr. Y.B. Reddy, the new Governor of the Reserve Bank, advocates that such sunset clauses should be incorporated not just in every law to be passed in the future, they should also be enacted for every existing law and regulation and form – that unless it is consciously enacted to continue within the next five years, it will lapse.

❏ The faster technological change is in a particular sector, the shorter must this time-to-sunset be.

❏ In these sectors, when a technological advance enables a person or induces him to step beyond the existing regulation, the presumption must be the opposite from what it now is – not that he must be arraigned, but that the regulation must be re-examined.

❏ One way, Dr. Reddy suggests, for shifting the balance of presumption is to examine in each instance whether for that regulation and licensing condition one can build in a compounding clause.

Deeply ingrained attitudes

For such reorientations – of those who draw up licensing regimes, of regulators – to come about, three attitudes that have got lodged deep into our heads need to be exhumed.

The first is the notion that unless an activity is regulated, there will be chaos, that growth has to be "managed". We still have not seen the basic truth that is all around us, the truth that Professor Hayek used to emphasize: order *does* come about through human actions *without* human design. From language, to the organization of society, to the rituals and mores of daily life, to the Internet – each of these has grown by human actions but *without* human design. For each of these, rules of conduct have evolved without premeditated design, certainly without governmental design. We have recent examples in the IT and cable industries: they have grown so swiftly precisely because governments were not alert enough to step in and "regulate" them! When activities develop like this, when order comes about spontaneously, before stepping in, governments must first answer, "*Why* should this activity be regulated? *Why* should another order be superimposed in this sphere on the order that has grown spontaneously?"

The second fixation is the excessively-expansive view we have developed about the responsibilities of the State. One of the great strengths of our civilization has been that our *society* takes care of many of the setbacks and misfortunes that are the inevitable part of life – misfortunes that in other civilizations fall upon the State. Our parents rely on us to serve them in their old age. We rely on them. Were I to be disabled from earning a living tomorrow, I know that I will have my parents' house to continue to live in, that I would be helped by my brother, sister and a host of relatives and friends. Anita and I know that were we to drop dead tomorrow, her sisters and friends would look after our Adit. In India our families, our society are our safety net. They are our social security system. In western countries the State has to perform these functions. Forgetting the strengths of our civilization, we are insisting that our State take over these functions. The State has neither the resources nor the competence to do so. But we are thoughtlessly going on piling more and more of such tasks on it.

We need no seer to foretell the result. Our families and communities will be weakened – for the bonds that are nourished by actual service to each other, by devoting time and resources to caring for each other will atrophy by disuse. On the other side, the State will not be able to fulfill the tasks that would have been loaded on to it. The quotient of resentment – in particular, against the State – will mount.

This is dramatically evident, and most immediately ruinous in spheres in which technical change is rapid. A license is given. Technological advance enables the service to be provided at lower cost. Competitors are eager to enter. The license holders insist that first the State "compensate" them. We had invested on the assurance that there will be no more than four operators in a circle, they say, if you allow a fifth.... The paging industry demands that it be provided a relief package because it has been well-nigh wiped out by the permission that has been given to the cellular industry to provide the short messaging service; the cellular industry demands that it be provided a compensation package before it will allow you to move to the universal license regime that technology so clearly dictates.... It is no job of the State to shield entrepreneurs against technological change, against the gusts of competition. It is certainly no job of the State to shield them from the consequences of their own wrong decisions.

The third attitude is, if anything, even more deeply ingrained in our heads. It is the place we have accorded – in our discourse, in our policies – to "equity". Everyone is convinced that the system is in some special way unfair to him. Those for whom reservations have been decreed are convinced that our society has always been, and most certainly continues to be unfair to them. The rest are convinced that those reservations have squeezed them out. The cellular operators insist that they must get further compensation packages, that the WLL fellows should in fact be kept at bay because the latter have been allowed to "enter through the backdoor"; because *they* – the cellular operators – are the ones who developed the market.... The WLL operators insist that they are being unfairly kept down because the cellular fellows have already reaped the advantages of early comers – "Were they not the ones who used to fleece consumers by charging them Rs.16 per minute? Is it not our entry which has ensured that rates have fallen below Rs.2 a minute? Is *that* not what has led to the explosive growth of telephony that all of you claim credit for today?"; the cellular operators, they say, were given a bail-out package whose net present value is Rs.30,000 crore....

Thus, every social group, every corporate entity is convinced – that *it* is being dealt with unfairly. The conviction is coupled with special ability! Each social group, each collection of corporates is able to dress up its special interest in principle! "Equity", "fair play", "level playing field"....

Today we are beset on one side by this combination – of conviction and ability – and a weak State on the other. A State that has been weakened by fragmentation – of the electorate, hence of legislatures, hence of the Executive. A State that has lost legitimacy in its own eyes

– in part because of this very factor, this barrage of egalitarianism, contrasted with the inevitable failure to deliver absolute fairness.

The result is predictable. The State lurches from one concession to the next, from yielding to the group that is insistent today to the one which is disadvantaged by that new concession....

Policy is buffeted. Growth is retarded. Every measure that is taken to alleviate the grievance of one group causes the other to feel that yet another injustice has been heaped on it....

To arrest this spiral we have to throw those attitudes out of our heads, and realize:

❑ Growth and order do not need governmental direction and regulation as much as they need free-play.

❑ Every change, every rule will benefit some and disadvantage some.

❑ The faster that technological change is in a sector, the more the relative positions of participants will alter.

The State just cannot keep providing "compensatory packages" to those who are disadvantaged by each wiggle of technology or fortune.

An institution

5

"A parking lot"

The tasks which the Planning Commission used to perform have much less relevance today.

Much of what it does even on those matters is more or less mechanical, a going through the motions: the Plan model and its relation to allocations, for instance; the Annual Plan discussions with Chief Ministers, for another.

Even after going through these motions, what the Commission says or decides on even those traditional functions, carries much less authority:

❑ In part because as an institution it has no greater expertise on those questions than other institutions: the operational ministries, for instance, or the better-run states;

❑ In part because, with the weakening of the political class, more and more of its allocations have become formula-based: just two factors – last year's allocation, and assorted formulae – are estimated by senior officials of the Commission itself to determine nine-tenths of the annual allocations to central ministries and to states;

❑ In part because, having become and having come to be seen as but a limb of Government, the Commission has got into the habit of not speaking the whole truth;

❑ In part because – what with the progressive weakening of the Commission *vis-à-vis* central ministries, and of the Centre *vis-à-vis* the states – it has adopted "going along" as its operational philosophy: knowing that eventually the Commission will fall in line, knowing that what it has to say it will confine to files and

---

This essay describes the Planning Commission as I found it when I was assigned Planning among other ministerial responsibilities. The Commission continued as it was, and had long been.

closed-door meetings, neither the ministries nor the states take the Commission's advice as seriously as they used to.

It is just a sort of way-side shrine, one in much disrepair, towards which one might as well nod – primarily because that is what one's forbears did in times past – and proceed. This state of affairs has several consequences:

❑ A great deal of time and money are being expended, in effect on keeping up appearances;
❑ Tasks which require to be done remain not-done;
❑ The self-image of the Commission, specially at the senior levels, has fallen very low indeed.

In their meetings with me, senior officials characterized the Commission as

❑ "a *Gaushala*"
❑ "a *Pinjrapol*"
❑ "a parking lot"
❑ "a doormat"
❑ "an appendage, a subordinate office of the Government"
❑ "a facilitator of what Government wants to do"
❑ "an irrelevance – at least in regard to the way it is working"
❑ "a limb the Government used to use to do and say things it did not want to say and do directly, but a limb which has by now atrophied too much to do even that much."

This feeling of irrelevance is reinforced by two facts – facts that are in a sense twins. On the one hand, massive changes have taken place in economic and financial policies over the last decade – the Commission has not been, and does not see itself as having been a prime initiator of any of the changes: quite the contrary – it has had to adjust its sails, and its prose to the policies that have been announced from time to time. Even where great changes have not been involved, the position is no better. Adviser, Irrigation, gives a telling and typical illustration. There are nine inter-state water disputes. They cover 9 million hectares, 4 to 5 per cent of hydro-power generation, and an investment of about Rs.40,000 crore. Only three of these disputes are before Tribunals. The Commission "is no where in the picture" –

either in resolving the disputes or in awakening people to what the design-solutions could be to the disputes. He reports that some notes *have* been given on these disputes, but that "what has happened to them is not known." To the query, "Why does the Commission not do something on its own?," he explains, "Because we work in a system." If a study is done, he says, it would travel up the ladder to senior officers; assuming they approve of the idea, it will be put up to the Deputy Chairman; he will send it to the PM – which means that it will go to an officer in the PMO; he in turn will either sit on it or send it to the ministry – "for comments"... Policies and problems apart, various issues loom on which it would be natural for the Commission's counsel to be sought. It is not.

On the other hand, when Government, in particular the Prime Minister has felt the need for new ideas, the Commission is not the body to which the Government or the PM has instinctively turned: quite the contrary, again. All the groups for financial sector reforms, for instance, were set up by the Finance Ministry with little contribution from the Commission; similarly, the very fact that the PM has felt the need to set up Task Forces, and that in these, apart from the Deputy Chairman being a member as an individual, the Commission has had little role, shows that the PM was not receiving from the Commission the policy advice he needed.

It has been put to me – but only by one officer – that the self-image is not as negative among the middle and junior levels of the staff. At those levels they do see, of course, that the Commission is not what it used to be, the officer explains, that it is not doing the things it could be doing. But they see this state to be primarily a consequence of "leadership failure" – that is, of the fact that the senior operational levels of the Commission are now manned by persons who have little or no expertise in the subjects over which they are presiding, and are therefore neither motivated nor equipped to get the staff to produce first-rate stuff on them.

Till a few years ago, these middle levels officers recall, specialists led sectoral divisions. Generalist officers were confined to handling state plans. As the Commission came to be used as a parking lot, more and more senior officers came to be parked here. The state-related work they were assigned was seldom enough. They therefore came to be put in charge of sectoral work also.

This single fact by itself accounts for much of the demoralization that an outsider senses, officials explain. It has also had several other consequences:

❑ The quality of sectoral and policy work has deteriorated;
❑ Career prospects of middle level officers have been blunted;
❑ The seniors themselves have come to look upon posts in the Commission as temporary punishment: in the last year and a quarter, the present Principal Adviser on Agriculture is the *third* one to occupy the position.

The resultant atmosphere of mediocrity has meant that – career prospects apart – there is no peer group pressure for excellence, and consequently none of the sense of fulfillment that would come from working among and for persons one respects.

I should mention that the cynicism now covers exercises of this kind – that is, exercises for reorganizing the Commission! And that because the Commission has good "institutional memory"! Officers can at short notice recite the fate of exercises to recast the Commission.

❑ 1964: a Staff Reorganization Scheme was prepared. The net result was that the total "technical" strength (from the level of Investigators to that of Advisers) increased from 285 to 327.
❑ 1967: the Administrative Reforms Commission submitted its report on the Machinery for Planning. Some posts were abolished. Some units like the Joint Technical Group on Transport Planning and Construction Economics were wound up.
❑ 1968-71: an Internal Reorganization Committee under the Chairmanship of a Member, B Venkatappiah, submitted two reports. As a result, 72 additional posts were created at various levels. The Finance Ministry went along with the enlargement – but with a stipulation: the staff strength of the Commission would be examined by the Staff Inspection Unit at an appropriate time. The Management and Project Evaluation Division was renamed as the Monitoring and Information Division. A Multilevel Planning Unit was set up in the Programme Administration Division – later this was renamed as the State Plans Division.

❏ 1975: there was a much-publicised effort to induct outside expertise into the Commission. It yielded one main result. There had been two divisions – the Power Division and the Industry and Minerals Division. Coal and Petroleum were taken out of the latter and put into the former; and a new name was given to the Power Division – it would henceforth be known as the Power and Energy Division.

❏ 1975/76: as stipulated by the Finance Ministry in 1971/72, the Staff Inspection Unit undertook studies of staff strength. They suggested the amalgamation of some posts, their redesignation, etc. As a result, the total number of "technical" posts was reduced by about 90.

❏ 1985: the Staff Inspection Unit conducted another study – this time of four Divisions. A few minor adjustments of posts followed.

❏ 1986-92: reorganizations continued in bits and pieces – as a result a few posts were transferred, a smaller number were abolished, and a few more were created. A few new Divisions were also created, and a few new "units" and "cells", and work was partitioned and joined into them – by transferring functions and staff from some existing ones. The Commission's role, functions, nature continued unchanged.

❏ 1991: a Task Force for Restructuring the Planning Commission was set up under the Chairmanship of a Member, V. Krishnamoorthy. Its mandate was to suggest the new role of, and a new structure for the Commission in the context of economic reforms that had been initiated. In its Interim Report, the Task Force recommended that a few specified posts be surrendered, including 100 non-technical posts. The proposal was submitted to the Deputy Chairman. He directed that it be re-examined. And then that there was no need for Lower Division Clerk or Class IV posts to be surrendered. Nor for surrendering any post of Upper Division Clerk, Assistant, Section Officer. A while later, the Task Force submitted its Final report. It contained a number of recommendations. Eventually, about 5 months later, 5 Joint Secretary level and higher posts were abolished. As for the rest, the Commission continued more or less as before. About a year after the Final Report had been submitted, on 23 July 1993, a full meeting of the Commission was held to consider the Report. The Prime Minister directed that a presentation of the Report be made at a separate meeting, and that the Commission organize a meeting of the Commission for this purpose at the earliest. No presentation seems to have been made after that directive. In the meanwhile, Service Associations of officers who were liable to be affected made representations against the proposed reorganization and possible reductions. Government set up a Group of Officers to look into these representations.

❏ 28 August 1995: almost exactly three years after the Task Force had submitted its Final Report, orders were issued abolishing four more posts.

❏ 1997/98: the new Strategic Management Group completed its study of how the Commission should be reorganized in view of the recommendations of the Fifth Pay Commission. It recommended that the Annual Plan exercise in its present form be abolished; the core functions of the Commission should be Perspective Planning, Medium Term Planning and Resource Planning; the Commission should be made into a fully autonomous body instead of being an agency of Government: for this purpose it should be constituted under an Act of Parliament like the Atomic Energy Commission and the Electronics Commission – in the circumstances, farcical examples: the Atomic Energy Commission owes its functional autonomy not to the fact that it has been constituted under an Act but to the fact that successive Prime Ministers have allowed it operational freedom; as for the Electronics Commission, the Department of Electronics was converted into the Electronics Commission in 1971, and the Commission was summarily disbanded in 1989 and "reabsorbed" into the Department!

❏ Mid-1998-January 1999: Deputy Chairman sent proposals to recast the Planning Commission. The Prime Minister's Office asked that views of Cabinet Secretariat be obtained. The proposals were recast in the light of comments....

If truth be told, the only result of these exercises was that some posts were foregone, some new ones were created, some boxes were redesignated, others shuffled, a few regrouped on the organization chart. But that was all. None of the exercises made any difference to the way either the Commission or the Government perceived its role, or to the way the Commission functioned.

Such factors – internal to the Commission – are naturally uppermost in the minds of the staff. The principal reason for the progressive irrelevance of the Commission, however, is different: while the policy environment in which it has to function has undergone a sea-change, while altogether new tasks cry out to be done, the Commission has persisted in doing – "doing," as we shall see, in a manner of speaking – the old tasks.

Vital Tasks

Yet, there are vital functions to be discharged, and the Commission is the natural body to discharge them:

❑ With the press of more and more urgent problems, ministries spend more and more of their time scotching fires: removed from immediate operational responsibilities, the Commission can take the long view;

❑ With the splintering of ministries, the likelihood dwindles that even a sectoral view will be taken of a policy issue even in relatively well-defined sectors like power or transport: the Commission is naturally suited to taking a view that transcends the narrow ambit of a ministry;

❑ With different political parties being in power in different states, and at the Centre, and with the pace at which power passes from one set of parties to another, the need in a federal structure for an institution that will be seen as impartial is all the greater;

❑ With economic development in general and financial resources in particular being more and more market-driven, the need is all the greater for an institution which will safeguard the interests of regions and sections that get left behind;

❑ Decisions are announced every few days by different ministries – opening sectors to foreign investors, disinvestments in public sector units; each ministry is proceeding more or less on its own; the Commission would be the natural body to examine each of these questions as a whole, as well as to draw up a rough calendar for the sequence of steps – so that, to take one example, adequate

preparations can be made for likely reactions of trade unions in
that sector or unit;
❑ With thinking within governmental structures becoming more and
more governmental, the need is all the greater for an entrepreneur
of ideas;
❑ With governments, and the political class as a whole finding it
costlier to urge measures which are liable to prove "unpopular",
the need for a body that will prepare the ground for hard
decisions is all the greater.

I believe that the fiscal bind towards which the states and the Centre
are hurtling is just the opportunity that can be used to at last take those
steps from which governments have been shying away.

The Commission is the body which should work out those steps in
detail so that, when alternatives vanish, the blueprint of what ought to
be done is ready at hand. The Commission is the body which should
condition people to the necessity of those steps.

Routinization

The five most conspicuous functions of the Commission are:

❑ Preparation of the Five Year Plan document and the Mid-term
Review;
❑ Allocation of Plan funds to central ministries and states;
❑ Assessment of schemes and projects of central ministries and
states;
❑ Annual Plan discussions with central ministries and states; and
❑ Evaluation.

Plan preparation and Mid-term Review

As a review of these documents will necessarily have to be very
detailed, I am not commenting on them in this note.

Allocations

In theory, there is a model. By deploying it the Commission estimates

❑ Resources
❑ Hence the overall outlay
❑ Thence sectoral demand

❑ Thence *via* sectoral capital–output ratios, sectoral outlays.

In fact

❑ The data is tenuous, and so also the relationships – of resultant
· demands, of required investments;
❑ There is no direct correspondence between "investments" that
flow from the model and the "Plan outlays" which the
Commission decides. And this at three levels:
  ○ The classification of expenditures is such that "Plan outlay" does not
  correspond to asset creation;
  ○ "Sectors" do not correspond to ministries;
  ○ Plan allocations to a state are not built up from allocations to sectors
  in the state.

In a succinct note, Adviser, Perspective Plan, has set out the steps that
are traversed from running the model to allocations. This is his
account of the steps:

* * *

A Note on Economy-wide Modelling and Sectoral Outlays

1. Public expenditures however are not classified on the same basis as the
National Accounts. The budgetary classification followed by both the
Centre and the States is on the basis of 12 "major heads of development",
which do not entirely correspond to the economic classification. It
therefore becomes necessary to translate the investment required by
economic sectors to the budgetary classification given by the major heads
of development.

2. A second level of problem arises from the fact that outlays as given in
the budget include both investment and current expenditures. The
classification between investment and current expenditures is also very
different depending upon whether an economic or a budgetary view is
taken. The budgetary classification between capital and revenue outlays
does not depend upon the use to which the funds are put. For instance,
a grant which is meant for physical infrastructure would be classified
as revenue, whereas a loan given for current expenditures would be
classified as capital. The economic classification, on the· other hand,
is based completely on the nature of the expenditure. Thus grants
given under Indira Awas Yojana will be classified as investment in the
economic classification and as revenue expenditure under the budgetary
classification. This difference in classification therefore also has to be
resolved while moving from the Plan investment programmes to public
outlays.

3. The planning model generates the sectoral investment requirement for the economy as a whole without drawing any distinction between public and private investment. In earlier years, when public investment formed a dominant share of total investment in the country and industrial licensing gave government considerable control over private investment, the split between public and private investment was done by the Planning Commission on the basis of the perceived requirement for public investment, with private investment being shown as a residual. Public investment was further divided between centre and states also by the Planning Commission based partly upon requirements as given by Constitutional responsibility and partly on the basis of the ability to raise resources.

4. In the Ninth Plan, however, the procedure has had to be changed significantly. In view of the Government's serious fiscal problems, the over-all quantum of public investments has had to be determined by the ability to raise resources, both tax and non-tax, and on a realistic assessment of non-Plan expenditure. As a consequence, private investment has become dominant in meeting the Ninth Plan investment requirements of the economy. Since control over private investment by the Government has virtually ceased to exist, this Plan first tries to assess the sectoral distribution of private investment and attempts to bridge the gap between investment requirement and private investment through allocation of public investment. To this extent, the public investment pattern in the Plan is residual.

5. Even within the limited resources available for public investment, there is in fact very limited scope for substantial reorientation of the public investment pattern. It needs to be realised that a very high proportion of Plan expenditures are committed due to schemes and projects that have been started during earlier Plan periods, and which cannot be terminated without considerable disruption. Such expenditures have to be accounted for first. The residual amount can then be allocated on the basis of the gaps that have been identified and the priorities that have been set by the Government for the current Plan.

6. Even within this limited area, the degrees of freedom are restricted by the nature of the sources of funds. Since a very large portion of Plan resources is accounted for by the internal accruals of public sector enterprises, mostly in the form of depreciation reserves, their deployment is restricted to their sector of origin. Thus only about 55 per cent of the Centre's Plan resources are available initially for allocation.

7. The first level of allocation involves a decision between how much of the resources are to be distributed to states as central Plan assistance and how much is to be retained by the Centre for allocation among the ministries.

By and large, this decision is taken on a rule of thumb basis, and about 45 per cent is usually allocated to states.

8. As mentioned earlier, ministry-wise allocation within the central Plan is limited by the commitments that have been made in the past Plans which have to be provided for almost fully. After this is done, a decision is taken regarding the allocation of the remaining amount. Although the investment projections of the Plan do play an important role in this, political considerations and bargaining between ministries are important factors. However, by and large, there is a fair degree of consistency between the requirements as given by the planning model and the allocations made ministry-wise and sectorally for the five year period of the Plan.

9. The problems really start with the actual allocations that take place during the Annual Plans. It should be remembered that the Five Year Plan allocations are only indicative, and the operational allocations are made during the Annual Plans. Since Annual Plans reflect the actual resources available to the Government, they can be significantly different from the year-wise phasing that is envisaged in the Five Year Plan document. In recent years, the actual availability of resources has fallen significantly short of the Plan. In such situations, since committed expenditures on ongoing schemes and projects have to be necessarily met, the reduction in outlays falls disproportionately on new projects and schemes. An implication of this is that sectors which require special emphasis during the Plan period through a significant step-up in investment are not able to receive adequate allocations unless there are substantial reallocations from other ministries. This kind of reallocation is strongly resisted and therefore only marginal changes can be effected during the Annual Plans.

10. Efforts are being made in the Ninth Plan to protect some critical allocations through specific provisions for the Special Action Plans (SAPs) that have been directed by the Prime Minister. However, the amounts involved are not that large, and are unlikely to dramatically alter the overall structure of outlays.

* * *

In view of what he has explained, his observation – "However, by and large, there is a fair degree of consistency between the requirements as given by the planning model and the allocations made ministry-wise and sectorally for the five year period of the Plan" – would have had to be regarded as a miracle were it not explicable as a consequence of simple arithmetic: just as correlations between variables in a time series are often high simply because "time" has not been factored out, this "fair degree of consistency" is a consequence of the simple fact that the relative scale of sectors – and ministries – does not change much from year to year, even from one Plan to the next. If we set aside all analysis and explain this year's allocation to a ministry as a function just of that last year, we get correlation coefficients of 0.974, 0.987, 0.942, 0.993, 0.996, 0.980, 0.985, 0.996, 0.997 for years from 1991-92 to 1999-2000!

For reasons such as these, once the Plan document has been produced, the model plays little part in determining allocations. The model is put aside, so to say, to be aired and deployed when the next document is to be put together. This will be evident from three simple facts:

❑ In the first three years, Plan outlays are running substantially below what had been thought necessary; decision-makers have not thought it necessary to re-run the model and ascertain the consequences of this shortfall for overall growth, for sectoral demand, or for allocations between sectors;

❑ No ready-reckoner seems to exist – at least none seems to be consulted – for deducing what decisions about allocations to central ministries and states entail for sectors: yet, if the model were of concern to decision-makers, a ready reckoner would be the elementary tool every decision-maker within the Commission would keep at hand;

❑ A plethora of classifications continues: outlays *vs.* investments; Central Assistance, Special Central Assistance; Special Category States, North East Council, Border Area Development Fund, Hill Areas Development Programme...... Were decisions being taken on criteria other than administrative rules of thumb, classifications such as these would have been harmonized.

Nor is it the case that the Commission examines each scheme or project, determines the outlay on it, and the allocation to a state or ministry is arrived at as the aggregate that results from these project-specific decisions.

The Commission does not have the capacity to examine so many schemes and projects. Nor does it aim to do so.

By now it has become almost a principle that schemes or projects that fall in "the state sector" are the business of the states: accordingly, these are not scrutinized in any detail.

This immunity has been reinforced by the fact that both states and ministries can now deal directly with external lending agencies and governments. Once a project or scheme has secured external assistance, officials report, it becomes well-nigh impossible to stop or alter it and, therefore, futile to scrutinize it in any detail. With Externally Aided Projects looming large in the more attractive states today, with areas being opened up one after another for foreign direct investment, external sources of funding, officers point out, have a far greater influence in determining where funds go than the Commission. While the scale of the effect of their activities is smaller, the expansion of funds at the disposal of internal financing institutions − e.g., NABARD in regard to agriculture, HUDCO in regard to housing − has an effect in the same direction: what gets done is affected much more by what these agencies decide than by assessments, etc. of the Commission.

The same holds for packages and special schemes that get announced from time to time. In some cases the Commission has had a role. The Special Action Plan of the PM, for instance, is said to have been designed here. In just as many instances, if not more, the Commission has had to adjust to the announcements as one might to meteors: "anti-poverty" schemes have multiplied and swollen over the years, for instance, entirely independently of the Commission.

When even a substantial package arrives, it is not that the Commission reworks *inter se* priorities and allocations between the remaining ministries and sectors: it distributes the cut among the latter in some rough-and-ready manner. Roughly 80 per cent of the outlays in a Plan are said to be on projects and schemes from preceding Plans. This time round, a large chunk of the remainder was said to have been pre-empted by the Special Action Plan. This "over-riding Plan", so to say, covered five sectors and encompassed 14 ministries. The Commission imposed a 5 per cent cut on the remaining 47 ministries, and reallocated the amount to the 14 chosen ones.

Officials differ in their assessment of the impact of the Commission on projects and schemes.

Some of them report that while commenting on investment proposals takes up 60 per cent of the time of some Divisions, "the impact is not worth mentioning." Ministries take the lead, they say, we react. Our views are hardly listened to, they say, "in fact they are regarded as a nuisance." Ministries are interested only in knowing the allocation. If we persist in our objections, the ministries go to the PMO and we are seen as being, and are told we are being "difficult", "negative", that we are "standing in the way." The ministries know this, explains a Principal Adviser, they know that when the proposal goes to the Commission at the eleventh hour and the CCEA is to meet, the Commission will restate its views, but that in the end a sufficiently general formulation will be adopted which will glide over the points the Commission may have made.

The assessment of other officials is to the contrary. They say that allocation is just the end point of an extended process: the discussions and interchanges that precede it do have an impact on policies and schemes of ministries, they say. The transport sector was said to be one such sector. The Division "hardly wastes any time on allocations," it was said, "Discussions focus on policy issues, and we *have* had an impact on these."

A third set of officials reports cases of both kinds: the Bhatinda Refinery in which case, by holding on to its assessment, the Division was able to prevent authorities from endorsing an unviable project; *versus* the modernization scheme for the Rourkela steel plant in which case, the Commission, having focussed attention correctly on its deficiencies, somersaulted, and went along.

Officials differ on whether the Commission even gets enough opportunity to adequately assess investment proposals. One set maintains that the Commission neither gets sufficient time nor has the expertise to prepare an adequate evaluation: they point to the haste in which reactions have to be prepared to, say, Cabinet notes, and to the perfunctory nature of the comments – "no better than what a person with an average knowledge of the subject would think up on his own." Others report that there are enough opportunities along the way for the Commission to make a difference, but it is the Commission which does not use them: because of lack of expertise, because of the reigning compulsion to go along, because in the end ministries are going to get their way in any case, etc.

On three points, however, there seems to be agreement:

❑ Individuals apart, as an institution the Commission is not today able to bring to bear on a project or scheme expertise markedly greater than a ministry has;

❏ Projects and schemes acquire allocations when and because – on account of an array of happenings – they have ripened, and not so much because the planning process has alighted on them as being important: it is this factor which explains the striking swings in allocations for some ministries from one year to the next – neither the absorptive capacity of the ministries nor the priority of the sector in which they fall could be swinging by magnitudes of that order from one year to the next;

❏ The Commission is hampered because ministries do not furnish even the data which they have: administrative ministries have data, much of it they have put on-line, but a password is needed to access it, officials explain; they do not give the password and the Commission feels it is not befitting to go around seeking passwords; the Finance Ministry has up-to-date data on Externally Aided Projects as they ripen: even though these projects directly impinge on Plan priorities, officials report, it does not share the data with the Commission.

Annual Plan discussions with states

Visits of Chief Ministers to the Commission and their discussions with the Deputy Chairman about their Annual Plans are conspicuous events.

Moreover, an enormous amount – Rs.40,000 crores – is transferred to the states *via* the Commission.

The discussions notwithstanding, the vast transfers notwithstanding, governance in the states has continued to deteriorate or improve, the pace and quality of implementation of schemes has continued as they would have without these discussions. Whether it is the continuing decline in collections of irrigation charges; or the continuing plight of State Electricity Boards and other state enterprises; or the near collapse of Balances from Current Revenue; or the fact that as a consequence in the first three years of the current Plan, borrowing by the states has already crossed 90 per cent of what they were to have borrowed in the entire Plan – the figure for West Bengal being 121 per cent, for Maharashtra 115 per cent, for Rajasthan

106 per cent: whichever index one takes up, it indicates that, neither through its discussions with them nor through its allocations to them has the Commission been able to affect performance.

Joint Secretary, State Plans, who has experience in dealing with the Commission on behalf of a major state, has set out what the Annual Plan exercise has become in fact. He reports:

*   *   *

.....The Annual Plan discussions culminate in the meetings of the Deputy Chairman with the Chief Ministers of states. At this meeting, the Annual Plan size is finalized. The plans are supposed to be an indication of development priorities of the state.

However, in recent years, most states are suffering from mismatch between the resources available and the Plan size. At the core of it is the negative Balance of Current Revenues (BCR) of almost all states. This mismatch leads to a gap between estimated Plan size and actual Plan financing. What is a matter of concern is that this gap is both recurring and increasing every year. This is resulting in the Plan being less and less realistic, and not being able to serve as a guide to development priorities. The atmospherics of Plan preparation, particularly at the state level, contribute to this situation. During Plan preparation at the state level, internally it is known what are the likely resources which would actually be available. This should ideally be the starting point and foundation of the state's planning exercise. However, this is not the starting point of the exercise. The starting point is the end point: the outcome expected at the end of the process, i.e. the meeting between the Chief Minister and the Deputy Chairman on the Plan size. The political compulsions (with the odd exception) have traditionally been that the Plan size determined and announced for a particular year must be greater than the Plan size declared for the previous year. Chief Ministers see this as a public relations opportunity for projecting to the media and the people of the state that they have succeeded in securing more resources for their state. At the same time, the fear is also there that in case the size is not seen to increase, the opposition would derive mileage, by suggesting that a declining Plan size reflects on the ineffectiveness or lack of interest in development of the Government. There are thus pressures for the fixing of larger and larger Plan size each year, irrespective of the ground realities of available resources.

Given the above imperatives, the exercise which is done at the state level is done in all seriousness. It is not as if figures are cooked up. However, an optimistic approach is followed, with resources estimated within the bounds of possibility. Some standard examples would illustrate:

a) Returns from Public Sector Enterprises usually tend to be negative. However, in the expectation that necessary tough measures will be taken to turn them around, these are played down, or assumed to be zero.

b) Loans from outside Financial Institutions, e.g. NABARD, may be liberally estimated. NABARD loans under schemes like RIDF, are related to eligible projects that are proposed. It is always possible (though rarely feasible) that a larger number of projects would be proposed this year than before, and that these projects would find favour with the Financial Institutions.

c) Additional Central Assistance from EAPs is another area. As per the programmed disbursement schedule agreed upon with the external agency, certain amounts can be estimated to be received as Additional Central Assistance. These amounts form part of the Plan resources. Actual disbursements are typically much less than the programmed disbursements, due to implementation bottlenecks and inherent complexities of such projects.

In this manner, projections and estimates are worked out in order to facilitate fixation of a Plan size which is estimated to be more than the previous years' Plan size. At the Planning Commission level, Financial Resources Division would normally project realistic estimates of resources. However, in view of the systemic pressures mentioned above, the final estimates are closer to what the states would like to see. Scrutiny at the Commission level follows much the same approach as is done at the official level in the state, with modifications being made more in the details of the outlays – e.g. marginal variations in the figures in Additional Central Assistance from Externally Aided Projects, or borrowings from financial institutions etc. The problems are known, and there is talk of hard decisions at the highest levels. The decisions taken (in terms of Plan size fixation) are more often than not soft, which tend to go along with the *status quo*. Minutae reign, and the big picture escapes us.

The result of the exercise may be seen in the manner of Plan implementation in the states. The gap between Plan outlays and resources available creates a discretionary space. Prioritization of schemes becomes *ad hoc*; dependent on the ways and means constraints of Finance Departments. Within the Plan envelope, only such schemes are implemented for which finances are available. This undermines the sanctity of the Plan. Ideally, both Plan outlays and the budgeted amounts supporting Plan activities should be congruent. But no effective signals are sent by us indicating that these should be so. Therefore, the next year the same scenario is repeated.....

*   *   *

A mere glance at the figures shows how unreal the exercise has become in the case of most states:

Table 1

Aggregate Plan Resources: 1999-2000

	State	Approved Plan	Latest Estimates
1.	Arunachal Pradesh	665.00	497.41
2.	Assam	1750.00	1019.23
3.	Himachal Pradesh	1600.00	1356.33
4.	Jammu & Kashmir	1750.00	592.70
5.	Manipur	475.00	358.74
6.	Meghalaya	465.00	427.65
7.	Mizoram	360.00	265.45
8.	Nagaland	315.00	259.68
9.	Sikkim	250.00	201.24
10.	Tripura	475.00	431.08
	Total (10 states)	*8105.00*	*5409.51*
11.	Andhra Pradesh	5480.00	4001.61
12.	Bihar	3630.00	2318.81
13.	Goa	281.19	271.76
14.	Gujarat	6550.00	6546.13
15.	Haryana	2300.00	1379.25
16.	Karnataka	5800.00	5976.98
17.	Kerala	3250.00	2641.15
18.	Madhya Pradesh	4004.00	1638.89
19.	Maharashtra	12162.00	9955.72
20.	Orissa	3309.17	2082.30
21.	Punjab	2680.00	1627.98
22.	Rajasthan	4650.00	1507.07
23.	Tamil Nadu	5250.00	5272.10
24.	Uttar Pradesh	11400.00	4954.08
25.	West Bengal	5787.00	3696.23
25.	*Total (15 states)*	*76633.93*	*53870.06*
	Grand Total (25 states)	*84738.36*	*59279.57*

The magnitude by which the figures of Plan resources on which the Commission agreed to proceed differ from the resources which seem likely as of December 1999 is startling by itself. What is as telling is the fact that this sort of a difference between estimated resources and actuals has been recurring year after year, it seems to have been growing, and yet there seems to be little or no follow up. So much so that even the most elementary information – information which would be on an organization's finger-tips if it were chasing the matter – is not at hand:

- ❑ When one asks for a table comparing the two sets of figures, it has to be specially prepared;
- ❑ When one asks for the assurances which individual states had given over the years and what they did on those matters, the records have to be ferreted out.

The ceremony over, neither side – neither the states nor the Commission – it would seem much care about what transpired. The only point on which interest focuses is the "Plan size" the state has been able to extract from the Commission, and on that, as we have seen, both sides enter into a compact – of make-believe.

That is distressing enough. But there is an even more distressing fact. It turns out that, as the note of the Joint Secretary, State Plans, suggested, the Financial Resources Division of the Commission has consistently placed likely Plan resources of states at a much more realistic level. Its estimates have been consistently closer to what eventually transpired. But the Commission as a whole chose to adopt the unrealistic figure which the states pedaled. The consequence will be obvious from Table 2 (see page 114).

Even a cursory glance at the columns shows that the "Official Level" estimates were at least within the hockey field. But as the sizes of the respective state plans traveled towards the public occasion – the much-publicised meeting of the Deputy Chairman with the Chief Minister of the state -- the dynamics of the "photo-opportunity," so to say, took over, and the figures got larger and larger.

Several parts of the Commission – in particular, the State Plan Advisers – seem to use few independent sources of information. The data they use is preponderantly the data the states have supplied. Even the camouflaging devices – which, to common knowledge, the states are using – are not flagged: circumventing the limits on borrowing by furnishing guarantees to Corporations and then having them lend to the state governments was mentioned as a ready example; but – and this is typical – there is no data on how significant is the borrowing that is being done *via* this route.

S.No.State	1997-98 OL Est	1997-98 AP	1997-98 Actuals	1998-99 OL Est.	1998-99 AP	1998-99 Actuals	1999-00 OL Est	1999-00 AP	1999-00 Actuals
1. Arunachal Pd	539.61	600.00	448.76	467.71	625.00	449.90	451.84	665.00	497.41
2. Assam	1089.99	1510.28	1006.21	1127.57	1650.00	1260.83	1157.26	1750.00	1019.23
3. Himachal Pd	293.41	1008.00	860.92	513.40	1440.00	1010.24	716.25	1600.00	1356.33
4. Jammu & Kashmir	321.44	1551.81	728.53	699.70	1900.00	636.21	549.99	1750.00	592.70
5. Manipur	333.19	410.00	341.35	368.31	425.00	214.77	367.24	475.00	358.30
6. Meghalaya	208.72	382.00	181.76	301.55	400.00	226.86	349.47	465.00	427.65
7. Mizoram	119.97	290.00	190.50	146.53	333.00	276.31	199.36	360.00	265.45
8. Nagaland	135.68	301.00	133.71	153.01	300.00	221.60	182.49	315.00	259.68
9. Sikkim	171.34	220.00	164.63	182.78	237.00	175.80	194.52	250.00	201.68
10. Tripura	379.80	439.91	412.70	228.76	440.00	464.00	332.34	475.00	431.08
Total(10 States)	3593.15	6713.00	4469.07	4189.32	7750.00	4976.51	4500.76	8105.00	5409.51
11. Andhra Pd.	1667.78	3579.55	3899.90	3276.34	4678.95	5174.74	1672.88	5480.00	4001.61
12. Bihar	1749.08	2268.42	2412.97	2416.24	3768.74	2956.41	1877.70	3630.00	2318.81
13. Goa	195.22	230.56	197.84	203.79	291.34	223.52	235.35	281.19	271.76
14. Gujarat	4363.13	4509.62	4874.92	5005.12	5450.00	4301.90	5110.65	6550.00	6546.13
15. Haryana	1273.42	1576.04	1334.23	1826.04	2260.00	1604.92	2138.64	2300.00	1379.25
16. Karnataka	3691.23	4153.59	4944.51	4624.42	5353.00	4793.84	4004.81	5800.00	5976.98
17. Kerala	2851.10	2851.28	3367.24	3009.98	3100.00	2917.05	2193.54	3250.00	2641.15
18. Madhya Pd.	2431.45	3718.50	3656.18	2046.64	3700.00	3503.45	2717.38	4004.00	1638.89
19. Maharashtra	4751.96	8393.19	7250.60	9926.13	11600.73	9731.42	10295.54	12162.00	9955.72
20. Orissa	1986.11	2529.46	2050.31	2385.59	3084.43	2098.57	3306.25	3309.17	2082.30
21. Punjab	1074.54	2100.01	1814.20	1531.66	2500.00	1307.08	2358.25	2680.00	1627.98
22. Rajasthan	3059.32	3514.42	4055.28	3004.12	4300.00	2904.73	3566.84	4750.00	1507.07
23. Tamil Nadu	3357.76	4004.90	4010.03	4232.65	4500.00	4501.00	4978.81	5250.00	5272.10
24. Uttar Pradesh	4172.61	7246.57	4793.33	5345.90	10260.00	6124.75	7046.62	11400.00	4954.08
25. West Bengal	3232.82	3907.72	3078.49	2876.75	4594.85	3879.71	4079.67	5787.00	3696.23
Total (15 States)	39857.53	54583.83	51740.03	51711.37	69442.04	56023.09	55582.93	76633.36	53870.06
Grand Total (25 States)	43450.68	61296.83	56209.10	55900.69	77192.04	60999.60	60083.69	84738.36	59279.57

OL Est = Official Level Estimates   AP = Approved Plan   Pre-Act = Pre Actuals   LE = Latest Estimates

While notes on some states flag some issues explicitly, most notes for the Annual Plan meetings conform to a generalized format. Apart from a general paragraph on violence, the note on Assam has nothing on the disastrous effect it is having on oil production, on tea plantations, on investment in general, there is not a word on the inundation from Bangladesh and even its economic consequences; the collapse of governance, and rampant corruption are affecting every development activity in Bihar: but apart from one oblique reference in one line of one sentence, there is no reference to the first, and not even that much to the second.

Moreover, the notes do not just accept intentions of the state government as if these were commitments, they seem on occasion to adopt them as accomplished facts. Two examples will stand in for the host that can be given.

The condition which UP's finances have reached is well-known. Yet this is what the paper has to say on them:

* * *

From Fiscal Crisis to Renewed Growth

At the close of the financial year 1997-98, the Government of U.P. issued a white paper highlighting the acute fiscal stress facing the state. It was observed that over the period 1993-94 to 1997-98, while revenue receipts increased by 44%, the revenue expenditure increased by more than double these receipts. The gap between revenue receipts and revenue expenditure, as a percentage of revenue receipts had increased from 9.5% in 1993-94 to 44% in 1997-98. Also, capital expenditure which comprised 17% of the total expenditure in 1987-88, had come down to 8% in 1997-98. The Government of U.P. requested the World Bank to conduct an assessment of the key reforms needed to accelerate economic and social development and at the same time stabilize the State's finances over the medium term. The World Bank in their document, 'Uttar Pradesh: From Fiscal Crisis to Renewed Growth' have come out with a reform matrix for the State, which proposes major initiatives in (i) fiscal policy; (ii) governance; (iii) infrastructure; and (iv) Human Resources towards the state's renewed growth. Immediate steps, intermediate term measures and long-term measures have been suggested to effect the policy/institutional changes prescribed in the Report.

* * *

Not one word about the likelihood of the reforms being carried through.

The collapse over the years of investment in the industrial sector in West Bengal is very well known. But this is how the note for the Annual Plan discussions for 1999-2000 puts the position:

*   *   *

...With the commencement of New Industrial Policy of the Central Government, the state government announced in 1993, a liberal incentive scheme to catalyze growth of industries while the single window agency had been strengthened for attracting industrial investment. The state government had announced a New Industrial Policy on 23rd September, 1994. This policy was in tune with that of the liberalized environment of the country and the economic policies of the Central Government. The salient features of the policy are:
(i)   Induction of foreign technology and investment.
(ii) Allow private sector investment in power generation.
(iii) Promotion of joint assisted sectors in important economic activities.
(iv) Improvement and upgradation of industrial infrastructure through government or through private and joint sectors and
(v)   Improvement in social infrastructure facilities.
The state government has identified certain segment of industries, among others, as thrust areas. They are petro-chemical and down-stream industries, electronics, textile, leather, tourism, food and agro-processing, plantation etc. The state government has given special attention to sick State PSUs and had emphasis on programmes of rehabilitation, modernization of plant and machinery of the undertakings with a view to improve their working.
There has been a significant increase in investment in the small and large-scale industries in the state. Since the introduction of New Industrial Policy, the Industrial Entrepreneurs Memoranda (IEM) filed for the State of West Bengal were 1,138, involving investment of Rs.17,154 crore up to 31st December, 1996.

Issues

(1) With the announcement of the New Industrial Policy of the state government, a number of MOUs for setting up of industrial units in the state have been signed including foreign direct investment. Implementation of industrial projects, flow of investment and generation of employment in the state should show commensurate gains. In this connection, a research study has brought out that between 1991 and December 1996 the state received 1,406 approvals for industrial investment entailing an investment of Rs.31,256.62 crore. Moreover, the share of West Bengal in total approvals for foreign direct investment in the country between August 1991 and March 1995 was 11.69%, with only Maharashtra having a larger share. The actual

implementation of projects has also picked up. In 1996, for instance, projects involving an investment of Rs.3,458 crore were either being implemented or were in the process of being implemented. After the New Industrial Policy was announced by the state government in 1994, between November 1994 and January 31, 1997, *Shilpa Bandhu*, the 'single window' agency operating in the state, handled 909 investment proposals of which 857 were for new units and 52 for expansion of existing units, with total capital outlay for Rs.23,554 crore. How many of them have actually materialized is not known. Nevertheless, it is hearting to note that from the early 1990s there are signs of industrial revival in West Bengal. However if this revival is to be sustained capital must be convinced that a stable labour situation over the medium to long term can be ensured.

From a policy point of view it is necessary for the state government to create opportunities for the labour force to take advantage of the new openings these investments open up by providing needed skill development, information dissemination and linkages.

(2) A large number of State PSUs are sick. State government has also taken over a number of sick units in its fold. The state government has taken up programmes for reviving these units. The revival of sick industrial units in the state has not been encouraging.

(3) Recovery of outstanding dues by State Financial Corporation requires attention of the state government.

(4) One of the bottlenecks of industrial development in the state has been lack of adequate infrastructural support. The state government has invited private participation including foreign companies for infrastructural development. The progress made in this regard has not been encouraging.

(5) The setting up of Centrally Sponsored Growth Centres in 3 locations of the state has been slow. Government of India have approved setting up of 3 centres in the state and have released Rs.1.5 crore up to 31st March, 1997.

(6) In view of very large segment of unemployed persons in the state, the state government needs to take up development programmes for the service sectors – viz. banking, finance, capital market, design consultancy, software, information technology etc.

(7) Various incentives provided by the state government are becoming counter productive. These incentives are subsidies provided to entrepreneurs to set up industries. While pure techno-economic merit should decide investment flow to industries in the new policy dispensation, incentives may continue for some more time.

(8) A study undertaken in 6 areas of concentration of the informal sector in Calcutta urban area has indicated..........

*   *   *

It is only as single-line after-thoughts that some caution slips into the text in regard to official claims. "How many of them actually materialized is not known"; "The revival of sick industrial units in the state has not been encouraging"; "The progress made in this regard has not been encouraging"...... Much could have been found on such matters even from published sources!

Organization affects function

There are also several organizational features of the Commission that contribute to this state of affairs.

Foremost among these is extreme laxity. During the last two years, for instance, Advisers visited the states they are to monitor as follows:

Table 3
Visits by State Plan Advisers to States assigned to them during two years, 1998 & 1999

State	Visits by State Plan Advisers	Average days per Visit
Andhra Pradesh	1	3
Bihar	1	4
Goa	1	4
Gujarat	1	4
Haryana	0	0
Himachal Pradesh	1	2
J & K	0	0
Karnataka	1	4
Kerala	1	4
Madhya Pradesh	0	0
Maharashtra	1	3
Orissa	1	2
Punjab	0	0
Rajasthan	0	0
Tamil Nadu	0	0
Uttar Pradesh	0	0
West Bengal	1	8
Andamans etc.	1	4
Arunachal Pradesh	0	0
Assam	6	4.7
Manipur	2	1.5
Meghalaya	0	0
Mizoram	3	1.7
Nagaland	0	0
Sikkim	0	0
Tripura	2	2.5

Similarly, when the amount that they shall receive as Gross Budgetary Support cannot be indicated to the states even as late as the end of January – this is what happened this year, for instance – they naturally have to proceed on their own. And once they have committed themselves to their budgets, they get another reason to pay less attention to the Annual Plan exercise – except for extracting that notional figure, the "Annual Plan size."

The main reason, however, is the one to which officers draw attention repeatedly: the governing philosophy has become – or the perceived compulsion is – "to go along." They are allowed to mention the issues, officials say, but are then "allowed" to see the issues recede – "States have their problems," the reasoning goes.

Like central ministries, the states know this: that, after the mandatory moment of demurring, the Commission will fall in line.

Given factors such as these, the Annual Plan papers contain a hazier delineation of issues than one would secure if one parceled out the states between economic journals and papers – *Business Standard, Business India, Business Today, The Economic Times* – and asked *them* to analyse the situation in the states, to say nothing of the kind of analysis one would get if one sought it from full-fledged research institutions.

Having limped into routine, the process has lapsed into neglect. For two years the sectoral Working Groups did not meet at all: it is only this year that, at the prodding of Deputy Chairman, they have been resuscitated – to begin with for the larger states. So that Annual Plan discussions with Chief Ministers may be completed in January and February, the Commission wrote to Chief Secretaries on 1 November, 1999, and urged them to send their Annual Plan documents for 2000-01 by 15 December 1999. Not one state or Union Territory stuck to the date.

Table 4
Annual Plan Documents – 2000-01 from States

A.	States which had sent the documents by December 15, 1999 : Nil	
B.	States which had sent the documents by February 10, 2000 : 12	

No.	State	Date
1.	Mizoram	16.12.1999
2.	Punjab	31.12.1999
3.	A&N Islands	06.01.2000
4.	Lakshadweep	11.01.2000
5.	Chandigarh	12.01.2000
6.	Manipur	17.01.2000
7.	Pondicherry	17.01.2000
8.	Dadar & Nagar Haveli	18.01.2000
9.	Meghalaya	19.01.2000
10.	Assam	24.01.2000
11.	Goa	01.02.2000
12.	Himachal Pradesh	11.02.2000

On occasion, states send their Annual Plans even *after* the year is over, officials remark: Orissa sent its Annual Plan *six months after the year was over;* the Annual Plan was duly approved.

Incidentally, central ministries do not adhere to the dates much better. The Commission requested them on 28 October 1999 to forward their proposals for 2000-01 by 1 December 1999. The proposals arrived as follows:

Table 5
Annual Plan proposals for 2000-01 from Central Ministries

Received by 1 December	0
Received between 1 and 15 December	14
Received between 16 and 31 December	20
Received between 1 and 15 January	13
Received between 16 and 31 January	16
Total Departments	*68*

Note: A few departments forwarded proposals in parts; the department has been entered against the date on which its proposal was complete.

Nominalism

Plans are made to be implemented. To ensure this there is a Programme Evaluation Organization. The scale as well as the indifference to what happens as a consequence of what it does would suggest that evaluation of programmes is by now just a nominal activity.

While at any time around a thousand schemes are said to be in various stages of implementation, the PEO has the capacity to study three or four in a year.

Till mid-1997, reports of the PEO were seen as being meant for Government only. Just about 40 copies were made. Two hundred and fifty to 500 photocopies of a report are said to be made now. Most of them are sent to departments of state and central governments. Five are sent to the Parliament Library. And five to the Principal Information Officer for distribution to the press. Has the PIO ever asked for additional copies? "In 1 or 2 cases, they have," says the Adviser.

When asked what the PIO had been doing with the copies, the Adviser, Evaluation, says, "We don't know, what they do with the copies." He explains that the PEO itself "does not have the authority to give them to the press." In his written note the Adviser states:

❏ "The Planning Commission, in June 1997, took a decision to make available PEO reports to the public through the Press Information Officer. All the reports published thereafter, have been routinely sent to PIO for necessary action. PEO also took initiative to send the executive summaries of some reports to *Yojana*. This will be done for other reports also. It has come to our notice that the reports of NEE and ARWSP have received media attention."

His assessment of the action that follows in the wake of the reports is equally modest:

❏ "The past experience shows that PEO is not kept informed of the follow-up actions taken by the concerned Ministries/ Departments. However, the follow-up actions have been taken, whenever the Planning Commission has taken the initiative. For

example, the follow-up actions on the reports of MSY and NEE
were taken by the concerned Ministries immediately after they
were published."

Adviser, PEO has now asked the Principal Information Officer what
the latter has been doing with copies of the reports which are being
sent to him. The PIO says that he has not been giving any brief on
them to the press. Once or twice when they were visiting his office,
pressmen had glanced at a report or two, and that is how mention
about them had appeared in the press.

Governmental

At the root of much of the Commission's current debility are
two related factors: it has become and is perceived to be a limb of
Government; second, its culture has become entirely governmental.

The Commission is completely identified with Government.
Among Governments, with the Central Government. Among Central
Governments, with the Central Government of the moment.

This in turn entails several consequences. On the one hand,
the Commission has forgone the authority that it would have were
it perceived to be an impartial, expert body. On the other, the
Commission has become too self-conscious: it hedges what it has to
say lest a ministry get offended, lest a state Government's relations
with the current Government at the Centre get affected. Not just the
states and ministries, the Commission too is just as anxious to put the
best possible face on whatever allocations it can make – lest a ministry
or a state raise a shout.

Second, officials who man the Commission are of the same kind as
man other government departments. "As everyone is from some
governmental service, how can the Commission be anything but
governmental?," an expert outside the Commission asks.

Third, with the exception of divisions like Financial Resources and
Perspective Planning, the structure of the Commission by and large
mirrors that of the Government: most functional divisions correspond
to ministries. Even by itself this deprives the Commission of some of
its natural advantages. For instance, as we noticed earlier, with the
progressive splintering of ministries, the Commission would be the

one body which would be much more inclined to take a sectoral view of issues. But when its own divisions come to mirror ministries, its chances of doing so become that much less.

Fourth, as we have seen earlier in regard to both central ministries and states, the Commission relies overwhelmingly on official sources for information. The Adviser of the Financial Resources Division alone reported interaction with institutions that specialize in the Division's areas of work – the Reserve Bank of India, the Finance Commission, the Institute of Public Finance and Policy. Others acknowledged that the interaction ranged from the negligible to the non-existent. Most remarked that generally they interact with the central ministry, and not even with institutions under the ministry.

Fifth, the audience the Commission aims at addressing is also almost exclusively the Government: recall the disposition of reports of the Programme Evaluation Organization, of the Commission's assessments of states, etc.. What is even more debilitating is the fact that the Commission's methods of work have become entirely governmental. Within the Commission, divisions work insulated from each other: the model on which the Plan is supposedly based, for instance, is, as an Adviser put it, "a black box" for persons in other divisions. Moreover, each division functions hierarchically.

Within the Commission, as in the governmental structure in general, analysis has degenerated into administration. Administration has degenerated into notings on files. Countless examples can be given. Two will have to suffice.

A training course

Everyone agrees that skills need to be upgraded continuously: the Commission would itself have been urging this to others. We shall now see the course that had to be traversed by a proposal for a simple training course – of just one week, costing just Rs.1,40,000 – for the staff of the Programme Evaluation Organization.

The National Institute of Rural Development of Hyderabad – henceforth NIRD – sends out a circular informing all whom it may concern that it would be conducting a training course in statistical methods for evaluation of development projects during *10-14 February 1997*. This circular reaches the headquarters of the

Programme Evaluation Organization in *June 1997* – that is, about four months *after* the course concluded.

15 June 1997: The Joint Advisor, PEO, writes to NIRD asking it to send details about conducting a separate training course in evaluation techniques for different levels of officers, along with the dates on which such courses can be conducted for officers of the PEO.

25 June 1997: A Faculty Member of the NIRD replies that a separate programme can be held for Senior Research Officers and Research Officers of the PEO during February 1998. The course can be of 5 days or 10 days depending on the requirements of the PEO. If the PEO wants a field visit followed by preparation of tentative evaluation report by the participants, then a 10 day course will be more appropriate. The actual content of the course can be decided once the PEO gives its consent. If February 1998 is not convenient, NIRD may please be informed so that another time slot may be worked out. NIRD charges Rs.550 per participant per day towards course material, board and lodging, and field visits. The cost of travel from the place of work to Hyderabad and back will have to be borne by the PEO itself.

5 August 1997: The matter is discussed in detail. And it is decided that due to the heavy expenditure involved, the reply received from NIRD may be filed for the time being.

1/10 July 1997: Joint Director of the Department of Personnel and Training sends a circular about a training course that is to be conducted by the Indian Institute of Public Administration here in Delhi itself from 17 to 27 November, 1997.

14/15 July 1997: the Joint Advisor, PEO, submits the proposal of training at the IIPA to the Deputy Advisor.

1 September 1997: The Adviser (Evaluation) writes to the Joint Secretary (Training) Department of Personnel seeking information about whether the Department of Personnel and Training has any programme that covers course contents as given in the training manual of the PEO, and whether it can have the course conducted at any institution in the country or abroad, or whether the Department of Personnel and Training can organize such a course itself in evaluation techniques.

No reply is received from the DoPT.

Member (Evaluation) raises the matter of training in a discussion with the Adviser (Evaluation).

15 September 1997: Adviser (Evaluation) writes to the same NIRD seeking to know what time slots are available so that PEO officials may be deputed to attend the course at NIRD, Hyderabad.

26 November 1997: Deputy Secretary issues orders for Deputy Advisers of the Regional Evaluation Offices to attend in-service training programme at NIRD from 12 to 17 January 1998.

3 December 1997: the Joint Adviser deputes Deputy Advisers of Regional Evaluation Offices at Calcutta, Hyderabad and Lucknow to attend the course at NIRD.

9 December 1997: Suddenly a reply is received from the Joint Secretary, DoPT. He says that DoPT has not been able to identify any specific relevant course that is already being conducted in any institution. But the best course would be to involve/consider the Institute of Economic Growth, New Delhi, or the Management Development Institute, Gurgaon.

11 December 1997: the Joint Adviser who had deputed persons to attend the course at Hyderabad now directs the Career Management Section that, in view of the communication received from the DoPT, it should write to the Institute of Economic Growth and the Management Development Institute to assess the training needs of the officials of PEO.

19 December 1997: the Desk Officer of the Career Management Section issues orders directing the selected officers to attend the course at NIRD from 12 to 17 January 1998.

But, for reasons that officials are not able to recall after all this time, the training course does not take place.

23 February 1998: The Director General, NIRD replies to the letter that the Adviser (Evaluation) had sent on 15 September 1997. Two training courses/capsules have been devised, he writes: one for senior level officials of three weeks duration; the second for supervisory level officers of four weeks duration. Two slots are proposed to be allocated – in July and in October 1998 subject to the conditions that the cost of the training programmes will be borne by the PEO – as the programme has been devised specially at the request of the Planning Commission. The charges shall be Rs.3,500 per participant per week – the minimum charge, however, shall be Rs.70,000 per week for 20 participants; when the number of participants exceeds 20, extra charges will be levied at Rs.3,500 per participant per week. Could the Planning Commission send its confirmation before 15 March 1998 so that NIRD may finalise its calendar for 1998-99....

Nothing happens.

28 July 1998: Instead, the Joint Adviser (PEO) puts up a separate note for contacting different institutions to arrange training in evaluation techniques. He records that while NIRD would be more appropriate for training of PEO officials, a meeting may also be fixed with the Institute of Economic Growth to explore with it the possibility of organizing the training in that Institute.

28 October 1998: The Adviser (Evaluation) sends a reply to the letter that had come from NIRD in February 1998. He states that some modifications in the training capsules are required to suit requirements of the PEO. For instance, because of the organization's commitments and due to certain organizational constraints, it is not possible for it to send a batch of 20 officers for training for more than two weeks at a stretch. Thus the duration of each training programme needs to be restricted to two weeks or less. Second, PEO is planning to send the batch of junior officers first, and PEO wants that NIRD should cover at least modules I to V in two weeks, and that an overview of other modules may be given to the participants.

28 October 1998: The Department of Economic Affairs is pursuing the other proposal. Its Adviser requests Adviser (Evaluation) to confirm names of participants for training at the Institute of Economic Growth, Delhi from 30 November 1998 to 11 December 1998.

30 October 1998: Adviser (Evaluation) requests Adviser, Department of Economic Affairs to give specialized training in evaluation methods and techniques to the Indian Economic Service officers posted in PEO and its field units – the Regional Evaluation Offices and the PEOs.

3 December 1998: The Adviser, Department of Economic Affairs sends a letter to Director, Indian Institute of Public Administration, New Delhi stating that, IIPA, as one of the centres imparting training to Indian Economic Service officers on Project Appraisal and Evaluation Techniques, would intimate whether they can arrange such training in evaluation.

17 December 1998: Director, NIRD, Hyderabad sends its agreement to Adviser (Evaluation)'s proposal to reduce the training programme to two weeks for a batch of 20 junior officers of PEO. He states further that they would amend modules I to V to cover the topics within a period of two weeks, and that the programme can be arranged in the third week of March 1999. He reiterates the earlier condition – that the minimum charge would be Rs.70,000 per week for 20 participants.

8 November 1999: Senior Research Officer/Joint Adviser (PEO) replies to the proposal that had been sent by NIRD on 17 December *the previous year.* He sends a list of 20 participants (of Investigators' level) which has been forwarded to appropriate authorities for approval for training in evaluation methods at NIRD, Hyderabad.

11 January 1999: Adviser (Evaluation) requests Additional Adviser (Administration)/Under Secretary (General Administration) to release Rs.1.40 lakh in favour of NIRD so that the participants can be sent there for training in evaluation techniques.

21 January 1999: Under Secretary (General Administration) submits the proposal for releasing Rs.1.40 lakh from the scheme of Payment for Professional and Special Services for meeting the training needs of PEO staff, and for securing concurrence from Internal Finance Cell. He sends the file to Additional Adviser (Administration). He in turn sends the proposal to the Internal Finance Cell.

8/10 February 1999: Section Officer (Internal Finance Cell) and Director (Finance) raise a query – on such type of proposals, they record, the Internal Finance Cell had already given its observation; this may also be linked with the file, and together they may be marked to Joint Adviser (PEO).

16 February 1999: The Joint Adviser (PEO)/Adviser (Evaluation) records that the Career Management Section may link the relevant file as desired by IF Cell. He forwards the matter to the Additional Adviser (Administration). While doing so he points out that the Career Management Section had earlier written letters to Director, Institute of Economic Growth, requesting the latter to explore the possibilities of conducting training in evaluation techniques, and that this matter had remained inconclusive. Now NIRD Hyderabad is ready to impart training in evaluation, he says. He requests the Additional Adviser (Administration) to "kindly see the matter for necessary action."

16/17 February 1999: The Additional Adviser (Administration) requests the Financial Adviser to concur with the proposal of incurring an expenditure of Rs.1.40 lakh for training PEO staff from the "Payment For Professional And Special Services" Head of the Planning Commission's Budget. He marks the file to the Financial Adviser.

17 February 1999: The Financial Adviser records, "Please speak", and marks the file to the Director (Finance).

18 February 1999: The Director (Finance) marks it to the Internal Finance Cell.

18 February 1999: The Section Officer of the Internal Finance Cell marks the file to the Career Management Section, and asks it to submit the file "as referred earlier."

23 February 1999: The Director (Finance) raises a query: he points out that, in the absence of necessary instructions from the Ministry of Finance, the Internal Finance Cell has not initiated action to open a new Head of Account on Training. He therefore marks the file to the Financial Adviser.

25 February 1999: The Financial Adviser holds that there is no objection to training PEO staff. However, he adds, the question regarding appropriate Head of Account mentioned in the note of Director (Finance) as well as the reasonableness of the cost may please be looked into by Director (Administration). He marks the file to Director (Finance).

8 March 1999: Director (Finance) marks the file to Additional Adviser (Administration).

8 March 1999: The Additional Adviser records, "Please examine", and marks the file to Under Secretary (General Administration).

9 March 1999: The Under Secretary (General Administration) notes that the expenditure can be met through the Plan scheme of "Payment For Professional And Special Services", and the funds to the tune of Rs.1.40 lakh may be made available for the PEO training programme. He marks the file to Additional Adviser (Administration).

16 March 1999: The Additional Adviser (Administration) decides that the finance for training of PEO officials be made available from the Account of the "Payment for Professional and Special Services" Scheme. He marks the file to the Principal Adviser (State Plans).

16 March 1999: The Principal Adviser (State Plans) inquires "What happened to all the attempts to have training course at IIPA, New Delhi?," and marks the file back to Adviser (Evaluation).

17 March 1999: The Adviser (Evaluation) clarifies that IIPA has agreed to provide a separate course for Indian Economic Service officers only but that it is not ready to conduct a training course for Investigators of PEO. Further, "it is clarified," he records, that the Institute of Economic Growth, IIPA or any other institution will be as expensive as NIRD. Furthermore, he says, the Institute of Economic Growth and the IIPA have organized training only in Project Appraisal whereas the NIRD has credentials in conducting training programme particularly for programme evaluation techniques. Therefore, he recommends, the training proposal at NIRD be approved at the earliest. And marks the file to the Principal Adviser and Chairman, Economic Advisory Council.

18 March 1999: Recording his observations on the foregoing comments of the Adviser (Evaluation), Chairman, Economic Advisory Council, again draws attention to the advice tendered by the Financial Adviser that charges are indeed high even after the concession that NIRD has offered, and asks another Adviser to talk to NIRD for the purpose. He marks the file to the Additional Adviser (Administration).

18 March 1999: The Additional Adviser (Administration) is by now caught between opposites. He records, "May kindly see for action as considered appropriate," and marks the file to the Adviser.

1 April 1999: The Adviser (Rural Development) records that she has spoken to NIRD, and that they have agreed to charge Rs.250 for boarding and lodging plus 10% service charges, and exempt the rest. Accordingly, "PEO may kindly write to NIRD on these lines," and she marks the file to Adviser (Evaluation).

1 April 1999: Adviser (Evaluation) records, "For necessary action please," and marks the file to Joint Adviser (PEO).

5 April 1999: The Joint Adviser (PEO) states that the PEO officers have already been identified for training, and that training for 2 weeks may be held from 2.7.99. He adds that, as desired by Adviser (Rural Development), "The Career Management Section may write to NIRD and do the needful." He marks the file to Career Management Section "for necessary action."

8 April 1999: Deputy Secretary (General Administration) writes to NIRD for fixing the training charges at Rs.250 per participant for board and lodging with 10% service charges and for exemption of the rest.

11 May 1999: The Assistant Registrar (Establishment) NIRD writes back affirming that the Director General-NIRD has approved the revised charges and accordingly PEO will be required to pay only Rs.250 per participant per day for boarding and lodging charges plus 10% as service charges for the training course of PEO Investigators.

9 August 1999: The Director (Administration) informs NIRD that PEO is deputing 20 officials for the training, that the terms and conditions as stated above are acceptable. He forwards a list of 20 participants from PEO and requests that the training may now be conducted in the second/third week of September 1999. He requests NIRD to "confirm the same".

18 August 1999: NIRD writes to say that the training programme for PEO officials can now be held from 20 December 1999 to 31 December 1999 keeping in view the other training programmes of NIRD that have already been devised.

20 August 1999: Adviser/Joint Adviser (PEO) record that they have already sent the recommendations to Career Management Section for necessary action in the matter.

23 August 1999: Deputy Secretary (General Administration) writes to NIRD confirming that the time slot during 20-31 December 1999 for the PEO training is convenient, and asks NIRD to go ahead with making appropriate arrangements for the training programme.

The course, which was to have been conducted originally at NIRD, Hyderabad in February 1997, is at last conducted from 20 to 31 December 1999.

Correspondence now commences about releasing the payment of Rs.1.4 lakhs to the NIRD. NIRD writes asking that the payment may please be released at the earliest. The Adviser (Evaluation) and then the Joint Adviser (PEO) record "For necessary action please".... As I write, in early February 2000, the payment is yet to be released....

Time too is a factor of production!

Assessing a project

Consider now the obstacle course that a proposal for a buffalo and cattle breeding programme is still plodding through. Only by gleaning these steps can one fathom what has become of the Commission, a Commission that was meant to be the fount of ideas and policies.

The last year and 10 months have been spent as follows:

20 April 1998: On behalf of the Animal Husbandry and Dairying Department, the Joint Commissioner (AH&D) submits a memo to the

Expenditure Finance Committee about a National Project on Cattle and Buffalo Development. The cost of the project is estimated to be Rs.402 crore. In fact, there already are three on-going schemes, namely, Extension of Frozen Semen Technology, National Wool Production Programme and Assistance to Military Farms that together cover the major objectives of this new proposal. The new scheme clubs those three and reframes them into a Central Sector Scheme. The objective of the Scheme is to bring all the breedable cattle and buffalos under Artificial Insemination or natural service and arrange doorstep delivery of Artificial Insemination so as to produce progeny-tested bulls that have superior genetic capability."

20 May 1998: The Deputy Adviser (Project Appraisal and Management Division) conveys suggestions of the PAMD Division, and requests the Department to submit a revised proposal incorporating these so that final appraisal of the Scheme can be taken up for examination.

26 May 1998: The Deputy Commissioner concerned submits the revised proposal of the Scheme.

8 June 1998: The Joint Adviser (Agricultural Planning Studies) records that the proposal has been examined in the Agriculture Division and that the comments have been forwarded to the Project Appraisal and Management Division for appraisal.

12 June 1998: The Deputy Adviser (Project Appraisal and Management Division) circulates an Appraisal Note that has been prepared by the PAMD Division to the Departments of Animal Husbandry and Dairying, Finance, Agriculture and Cooperation. The PAMD Division has noted that Planning Commission cannot support this scheme as a Central Sector Scheme. The proposal, it says, should be considered as a Centrally *Sponsored* Scheme. The PAMD does not agree with the proposal to set up national and state autonomous bodies for monitoring the Scheme. It also records that while the memo to the Expenditure Finance Committee indicates that funds from other sources such as Integrated Rural Development Programme and external agencies will be tapped, no details have been furnished. The details of facilities that have already been created under the on-going schemes have not been mentioned in the proposal. It suggests that a representative from the Planning Commission be inducted in the project management committee. Furthermore, a mechanism needs to be evolved, it recommends, so that the functioning of the NGOs, private companies, etc. who will receive grants from this project, can be monitored.

17 July 1998: The Joint Secretary (Dairy Development) submits a reply of the appraisal note. The Animal Husbandry and Dairying Department informs that approval of the full Planning Commission is not required, and accordingly the Scheme would be placed before the Expenditure Finance Committee.

27 July 1998: The Deputy Adviser (Project Appraisal & Management Division) informs the Animal Husbandry and Dairying Department that the Scheme will be treated as a new Centrally Sponsored Scheme for the Ninth Plan. As such it *will* require approval of the full Planning Commission. He also requests the Department to send the revised proposal for consideration of the Planning Commission.

12 August 1998: The Deputy Commissioner in charge of the system of registering herds informs the Project Appraisal & Management Division that there is no need for any revised proposal. He writes that the Department has already initiated action for convening a meeting of the Expenditure Finance Committee.

28 September 1998: The Expenditure Finance Committee Meeting takes place. The EFC approves the scheme as a Centrally Sponsored Scheme for implementation in the Ninth Plan. It also decides that the Department would take approval of the full Planning Commission and Cabinet Committee on Economic Affairs.

15 October 1998: The Joint Adviser (Agricultural Planning Studies) Agriculture Division requests the Animal Husbandry and Dairying Department to send a self-contained note along with the revised Expenditure Finance Committee proposal in the light of the discussion held in the EFC meeting on 28 September 1998.

7 January 1999: The Joint Commissioner (Livestock Production) Animal Husbandry & Dairying Department informs that "as per the discussion of EFC," a note for taking approval of the full Planning Commission has been prepared, that it has been submitted for approval to the Agriculture Minister before transmission to the Planning Commission.

27 July 1999: The Principal Adviser (Agriculture) in the Planning

Commission again requests the AH&D Department to send a self-contained note for approval of the full Planning Commission.

16 August 1999: The Joint Secretary, AH&D Department submits the self-contained note on the project along with draft Expenditure Finance Committee memo, minutes of the EFC meeting held on 28 September 1998, as well as a note about the action that has been taken by the Department, and a revised memorandum considering the changes recommended by EFC, etc.

15 September 1999: The Deputy Chairman, Planning Commission, approves the draft note that has to be put up for approval to the full Planning Commission.

17 September 1999: The Senior Research Officer (Agriculture Division) sends a note to the Plan Coordination Division for approval of the full Planning Commission.

23 September 1999: The Principal Adviser (Plan Coordination and Administration) records that the Deputy Chairman, Planning Commission has indicated that approval of the full Planning Commission might be sought by circulation. Accordingly, a copy of the note on the scheme is circulated to all Members of the Planning Commission "for favour of approval and/or comments thereon, at any early date."

As I write, in early February 2000, approval from the Member (State Plans) "is awaited".

Neither in the case of that training course nor in this one about breeding cattle and buffaloes am I on the merits of the case – though the amount that was saved by the lengthy negotiations with the NIRD, as well as the change that was brought about in the content of the cattle and buffalo breeding programme will show how little was the substantive contribution of the hours and hours that were spent on the questions. The matter that concerns us at present is the organizational culture that such sequences portray. Of files going to and fro. Of the time that is spent on trifles. Of divisional and departmental "egos" swaying matters.... Here is a body that was to be the "think tank" of the governmental structure. Do such sequences – and I have chosen ones designed to cause the least embarrassment – speak to thinking?

"But you miss the point," remarks an officer well-schooled in the ways of the Commission. "Perhaps the training programme was not worth sending officers to. Perhaps that cattle and buffalo programme was not good enough in the first place. That is why the files were sent on the rounds."

That may sound the most plausible of explanations to those who know the ways and mores of government. But it also is the most cynical. Even if we take it at face value, the fact that officers feel they must deploy such round about methods suggests at the least an organization in which communication and comradeship have evaporated. After all, many of the officers who were marking notes to each other are housed in adjacent rooms. That they did not feel comfortable in just walking up to each other and, assuming the proposals to have been useless, just scotching them testifies to an organization whose work-culture is in deep disrepair, it testifies to inter-personal relations that have ossified.

Busy in meetings upon meetings

"Administration has degenerated into notings on files," I said. That perhaps should be supplemented: it has also ascended into going from meeting to meeting. The Industry & Minerals Division would be a prime example in any enumeration on this count.

The contribution of the Division to Industrial Policy would require research. When elementary information on policy is requested, information that should be on its fingertips, the Division neither has it, nor time to prepare it. But its staff is frantically busy – attending meetings. The Adviser himself is on the Boards of about 22 corporations and similar bodies. In addition to these meetings, he is busy with meetings of the Cabinet, of various Cabinet Committees, of the Committee of Secretaries, of the Public Investment Board, Expenditure Finance Committee, Standing Finance Committee. Moreover, Performance Review Meetings are scheduled for every Public Sector Undertaking. When the meeting is chaired by a Minister, the Adviser attends it. What the net contribution of the Division's staff to the proceedings and decisions of these Committees has been would take time to excavate. But one fact is apparent: the enterprises and bodies whose meetings are being attended have been continuing in ways that are very well known.

So many are the boards and committees and companies on which it is represented, that the Division had to take a few days to prepare even a list of the committees, etc. whose meetings it has to attend. Here is the list it has ultimately put together:

* * *

Boards and Committees on which I&M Division is represented

** 1. Board of National Industrial Development Corporation
\#   2. Meetings of Cabinet/various Cabinet Committees
\#   3. Committee of Secretaries
\#   4. Core Group on Disinvestment
\#   5. Steel Development Fund Management Committee
\#   6. Sugar Development Fund
*   7. PIB/EFC/SFC meetings
~   8. Study Group on Small Scale Enterprises
~   9. Expert Group on sick PSUs, Department of Heavy Industries
~ 10. Textile Committee
* 11. Science Advisory Committee of Ministry of Steel
* 12. Advisory Board of Indian Bureau of Mines
* 13. Member, Mineral Advisory Council
* 14. Committee of Textile Upgradation Fund Scheme
* 15. Review Committee of PMRY
* 16. Member, Working Group for the Fourth Quinquennial Survey on Manufacturing Enterprises of APEDA
* 17. Governing Body of APEDA
** 18. Governing Body of National Productivity Council
* 19. Governing Body of Central Manufacturing Technology Institute
   20. Governing Bodies of Research Advisory Councils of various Textiles Research Associations like ATIRA, BTRA, SITRA, NITRA, SASMIRA, IJRA, WRA, etc.
   21. Various Development Councils: e.g. on Automobiles, Paper, Pulp, Cement, Sugar, Tyres and Tubes, Soaps & Detergents etc.
* 22. All India Handloom Board
** 23. All India Small Scale Industries Board
   24. Quarterly Performance Review Meetings in various Ministries/Departments
   25. MOU (including Ad-hoc Task Force) Committee Meetings
   26. Central and State Geological Programming Boards
* 27. National Centre for Upgradation of Textile Education
* 28. UNDP assisted Jute Development Programme: Steering Committee
* 29. Management Board of UNDP assisted Khadi and Village Industries Project

* 30. UNDP assisted National Leather Development Programme
    31. Some Committees of the Bureau of Indian Standards
    32. Various Review Committees: e.g. for Growth Centres, Crucial Infra-
         structure Balancing Scheme, EPIP, IIDCs, etc.
* 33. All India Power looms Board
~ 34. Committee to suggest modalities for implementation of recommenda-
        tions of the Hanumantha Rao Committee on Fertilizers
@ 35. Committee to review the progress made in installation and operation
        of Polymetallic Nodules Pilot Plant at Hindustan Zinc Limited
@ 36. Multi-Disciplinary Committee on Taxation Regime for the Mineral
        Sector
@ 37. Project Review & Steering Group on Technologies for E-Commerce at
        CMC, Hyderabad
@ 38. Inter-Ministerial Group to analyse and work out the specifics for the
        possible take over of Sindri and Namrup units of Fertilizer Corporation
        of India Ltd. and Hindustan Fertilizer Corporation Ltd.

**   Only Adviser (I&M) can attend as the membership is by name.

*   Meetings are normally attended by Adviser (I&M) and failing that by next senior-
     most officer concerned.

Secretary, Planning Commission is a member, but meetings are normally
     attended by Adviser (I&M).

     Not a Standing Committee.

@   Meetings are normally attended by Additional Adviser (I&M) and failing that by
     the next senior-most officer concerned.

     Where there is no *, the meetings are generally attended by the concerned Joint/
     Deputy Adviser.

     MOU meetings are held for most of the PSUs, numbering about 200 in the I&M's
     sector.

     Performance Review Meetings are also expected to be held for every PSU. Some
     of the Ministries like Steel/Mines/Fertilizers/Surface Transport/Petroleum &
     Natural Gas/Atomic Energy hold them regularly; but some others like Heavy
     Industries, Chemicals & Petro-chemicals do not generally hold them. The
     Adviser generally attends only if the meeting is chaired by the Minister – this is
     often the case in regard to meetings of PSUs of the Steel Ministry.

*   *   *

In the case of several of the committees listed above, while only one
entry is made, the group handles a host of issues, and so it has several
meetings every month.

With all these meetings to attend, to, one must presume, prepare
for, and follow up, where would one find time for reflection and

research on industrial policy? The designation – the Industry and Minerals Division – just becomes the *ex officio* name-board that gets one on to the Boards and committees connected with industries or minerals.

The changes we need

1. From an organization that sees its role to be mainly that of an investment planner, the Commission should be transformed into a body the principal functions of which are:

❏ To frame policy options for Government on the specific issues which it has to confront;

> Some examples that came up during the meetings are: Financial sector reforms; disinvestment strategies; POL pricing; policies for the sugar sector; the Public Distribution System; finances of the Railways; winnowing and convergence of anti-poverty schemes; a review of the BIFR, of "financial packages", of "restructuring packages"; activities that Government can leverage – a private industrial house is eager to set up a world-class Science and Technology University: what can the Government do to facilitate this?; management of the rapidly-burgeoning pension funds of the Government; in the coming years TB, water-borne diseases, AIDS will dominate: what technologies can be deployed or developed to contain these?; strategies that foreign companies are likely adopt *vis a vis* Indian competitors and partners; steps which can be taken to boost low-tech. exports like toys, sports goods, etc.; the rate of use of non-renewable resources, and technologies that need to be devised to provide substitutes.

❏ To be a think-tank not just for Government but for our country and society at large;

> For instance: interests insist that Government continue to subsidize the use of chemical fertilizers; when the discussion shifts to the deteriorating condition of our soils, we blame these very fertilizers, and demand allocations for rehabilitating the soil; and when discussion shifts to health, we point to the growing incidence of cancer, blame it in part on the excessive use of chemical fertilizers and pesticides, and demand higher allocations for cancer wards. What is the way out of this vicious circle?

❏ To anticipate trends – in technology, in international economic relations, etc. – and advise Government about the measures which can be taken to put the trends to work;

For instance, by 2005 WTO agreements on government procurement and trade in services may come into effect; these are bound to have far-reaching consequences for an industry such as Construction which today employs 31 million Indians; what steps should be taken forthwith to prepare this industry for the coming regimen? Or, what are the consequences going to be of the agreements that some countries are advocating in regard to emission standards, child labour, etc.? Similarly, when China joins WTO, it will acquire progressive access to Indian markets; even US department stores are today flooded with Chinese consumer goods; what will this access for Chinese goods entail for the policy of reserving items for small industries; which of our industries will be affected; what should be done to prepare them for that day? Similarly, what technologies are going to dominate economies 10, 20 years from now? Biotechnology? Nanotechnology? Robotics? Designer materials? Launching payloads into space? Non-conventional energy? How will each of these impact India? In which of them should India aim to be a leader?

❑ To awaken our people to the steps which have to be taken, and thereby prepare them for hard decisions – that is, the public advocacy of decisions which the country needs;

For instance, the perilous condition of state finances, and the urgent need to raise user charges; similarly, the extent to which subsidies are actually helping the poor.

❑ To present to the Prime Minister and Government an independent assessment of policies proposed by, and claims made by ministries and states;

The recent presentation on drinking water, for instance; or devices being used by the states to divert Plan funds to non-Plan uses, devices being used by them to get around borrowing limits, etc.

❑ To monitor projects and schemes so as to minimize cost and time over-runs, and make outlays more productive;

Recall, for instance, the exercise done recently to identify irrigation schemes that can be brought to completion swiftly by the injection of marginal funds; the rationale or otherwise for shifting resources from building new schools to repairing existing ones.

❑ To evaluate the impact of projects and schemes, and thereby delineate changes that need to be made in them;

Anti-poverty schemes, for instance; similarly, the contrast between the working of the mid-day meal scheme in Tamil Nadu, Gujarat, etc., and in the North Indian states; what has been the experience with short-haul private airlines – like Vayudoot, Damania, Modiluft, NEPC, East-West – and what lessons does it hold for the future?

2. On some matters the PM and Government would want the advice of the Commission in confidence; on matters other than these, the Commission should make its findings public. Apart from other advantages that this will secure, it will goad the Commission to improve its output. In particular, the Commission should publish every year

❑ A mid-year review of the economy, with particular reference to the way assumptions made in the Budget and the policies set out in it are faring in practice; this should be prepared around October so that there is enough time to take corrective measures;
❑ Its assessment of states.

3. A mechanism must be devised for the Commission to make presentations on policy issues periodically – I would say, monthly – to

❑ The PM personally,
❑ The Cabinet Committee on Economic Affairs.

It should also become a practice for the Commission – perhaps one or two members, the Secretary and the concerned Adviser – to visit the states that are particularly affected by a policy or a problem, and make presentations on that matter to the Chief Ministers there.

On issues that transcend individual states – the condition of state finances, the formulae for allocation of funds between states are ready examples – the Commission should have occasion to make presentations at the meetings of the National Development Council.

4. The structure and staffing of the Commission have to be drastically altered. In particular,

❑ The Commission must not be used as a parking-lot;
❑ A committee of three or four officers should be set up under the Secretary of the Commission to sift officers: with the specific mandate that every officer – irrespective of service – who does not have expertise for the work of the Commission must be redeployed outside the Commission;

❏ To break the bureaucratic culture into which the Commission has lapsed, as well as to improve its output, the staff of the Commission should be constituted in twos and threes to work on specific issues; they should form just the core of the team, their first charge being to induct the very best experts on that issue for preparing the policy paper; the moment work on that issue is complete, the group should disband, the staff being apportioned or re-grouped for work on the next issue.

5. In regard to Annual Plan discussions with states the Commission should, at the least

❏ Develop and use independent sources of information about developments in states;
❏ Associate research organizations with preparing the assessments;
❏ Publish the assessments;
❏ Make the Annual Plan discussions low-visibility occasions: perhaps by confining them to officials;
❏ Ensure that Plan outlays, etc. are confined to realistic, professionally assessed levels;
❏ Move toward linking allocations to performance – in regard to the pace at which projects and schemes are being executed, and to accomplishment of macro-targets for resource mobilization, turnaround of state enterprises, etc.

6. A staggering quantum of resources – around Rs.85,000 crore – are routed to the states through the Planning Commission and the Finance Commission every year. Yet performance remains what it would be in any case. Neither do the outlays which are routed to central ministries through the Finance Ministry and the Planning Commission have any discernable effect on the pace and quality of execution of projects and schemes. Often, devolutions by one agency strike the other as bolts from the blue: recall the sudden decision of the Finance Commission in January to assign Rs.15,000 crore to the states, and the uncertainty this created because of the impact it was liable to have on Gross Budgetary Support available for the Plan this year. The formulae by which funds are distributed between states, the conditions that are or can be attached, the relationship that should

subsist between the Finance Commission, the Planning Commission and the Finance Ministry all require a thorough re-examination.

❏ Should the amount be placed with say, the Planning Commission, in an escrow account to be released as the project is executed, or the improvements affected?

❏ How may the allocations be linked to better execution of projects and schemes, and to better attainment of macro-economic objectives? How can a substantial part of the funds routed through the Commission be made into an "Incentive Fund" – the state or the ministry getting allocations from it as and when it takes specific policy steps? Especially so as the Centre's finances are also hard-pressed now. Especially because allocations are being tilted in favour of the "poorer" states, and it is all the more imperative that the system ensure that the funds are spent wisely – for these states are not poorer so much in per capita income as in governance.

❏ *All* Plan resources are in a sense borrowed funds. But at present the entity that spends the funds – for instance, the individual state – is so far removed from the borrowing that for it the funds are a costless resource. The Centre becomes in effect the largest financial intermediary – with the distinction that it has next to no effect on the utilization of the funds it has helped garner. Why not "disintermediate"? Why not have the states be rated for their creditworthiness directly and independently?

7. The changeover to being a Policy Planning Staff can only be brought about after some of the functions which now take up much time of the Commission staff are jettisoned. In the discussions, three examples of such functions were urged:

❏ The Commission should hold State Plan discussions with fewer states; for these states, the analysis and discussions should be thorough;

❏ In regard to central ministries, the Commission should examine only policy issues; its comments on proposals for individual schemes or projects should not be sought, neither should they be given; on the ministries about which it has little expertise, the Commission should not attempt to give any advice;

❑ Advisers and others who are members of Boards, etc., by virtue of the office they hold in the Commission, should be withdrawn from these Boards.

Next steps

1) The Prime Minister to mandate a new role for the Commission;
2) A Committee consisting of 3 or 4 officers headed by the present Secretary of the Commission to winnow the officers – with the specific direction that only those who have expertise in regard to the functions are to be retained.
3) The Commission must be run on a tighter leash: a glance at Table 3 above is enough to show how lax its functioning has become: in *two years* State Plan Advisers did not visit 11 states even once, 11 states were visited just once; on the average the officer was in the state for just about three days.
4) The Commission should draw up a list of policy issues which it will examine, set up mission-groups for each – including in each instance experts on the subject outside the Commission.
5) Between them the Finance Ministry, the Planning Commission and the Finance Commission route an astronomical quantum of resources. Their impact on policies and performance is far short of what it should be. A group should be set up to examine how the transfers may be dovetailed to ensure improved policies and performance – both by central ministries and the states.
6) A paper should be prepared for the National Development Council on the present system of allocations and devolution of funds, and alternatives under which these allocations and devolution are linked directly to performance. A meeting of the National Development Council should be set apart to consider these alternatives. Discussion of this paper should be preceded by discussion of the perilous condition that state finances have reached, and the unconscionable wastage that is implicit in the present arrangements.

Three final words

As for the Commission, such authority as it seeks, it must secure by the force of ideas, by the fact that the solutions it is proposing are useful to Government and to society, by the fact that it is speaking the whole truth, often the inconvenient truth – it should secure credibility by being perceived to be an impartial tribune, and by the fact that, whenever its warnings have been ignored, a heavy cost has had to be paid.

Second, this note is about the Planning Commission. Therefore, only those infirmities are listed here, and only those changes which relate directly to the functioning of the Commission. Agencies other than the Commission have contributed a good deal to bringing affairs to the pass described in this note. After all, the shortcomings which mar programmes executed by, say, the Rural Development Department should have been rectified by that Department itself. That they have persisted and grown is primarily the responsibility of that Department. Similarly, when suggestions for rectifying the schemes have been advanced by the Commission, the Departments have often persisted in their ways – at times securing from higher authorities a reversal of decisions which would have ensured better implementation. In a word, to be effective, reform of the Planning Commission has to be accompanied by reform of other Ministries.

A sector

6

Environment: the vital lesson

"Thousands of tonnes of toxic waste are being illegally shipped to India for recycling or dumping, despite a New Delhi court order banning import of toxic materials. Every Indian port is a floodgate standing open for hazardous waste" – that is from *State of the Environment, India, 2001,* a report jointly produced by the Ministry of Environment, Government of India, TERI, and the United Nations Environment Programme. "Of course," it adds, not quite sensing the irony, "Indian Government is keeping a tight rein on hazardous waste imports by licensing only five companies to accept metallic waste and letting only three companies export such waste to India for recycling." Only to add in the very next sentence, "In fact, 151 different importing companies have imported nearly 73,000 tonnes of toxic zinc and lead residues from 43 countries. In 1995, Australia exported 1,450 tonnes of hazardous waste like scrap lead batteries, zinc and copper ash to India. Huge quantities of PVC waste are still exported to Asia despite an international agreement.... A Greenpeace analysis of India's foreign trade found that at least 1,127 tonnes of zinc ash were imported mainly from the United States since May 1996. Some 569 tonnes of lead battery waste were brought in through the main seaport of Bombay between October 1996 and January 1997. About 40,000 tonnes of broken lead batteries were imported during 1996. While lead acid batteries were in the Basel Ban List, India's Directorate General of Foreign Trade last year allowed free imports of battery plates and terminals. Some 150 companies are importing toxic waste into India though only seven are licensed to do so."

"Indian Government is keeping a tight rein"?

Giving details of water pollution, the same study narrates,

"The water quality monitoring results obtained during 1998 indicate that organic and bacterial contamination still continue to be critical sources of pollution in Indian aquatic resources.... The Yamuna river is the most polluted in the country having high BOD [Bio-chemical Oxygen Demand] and coliform in the stretch between Delhi and Etawah. Other severely polluted rivers are the Sabarmati at Ahmedabad, Gomti at Lucknow, Kali, Adyar, Cooum (entire stretches), Veghai at Madurai, and Musi d/s of Hyderabad....

"CPCB [Central Pollution Control Board] has also carried out limited water quality monitoring of the wells of different states and calculated per cent violations over the distressed levels of water quality in terms of pH, dissolved oxygen, BOD and total coliform. Certain locations in these states reported 100% violation over the desired level for dissolved oxygen and total coliform.... CWC's [Central Water Commission's] studies on chemical composition of groundwater in phreatic zones have revealed that in many cases anomalously high concentrations of nitrates, potassium and even phosphates are present in contrast to their virtual absence or low concentration (nitrate and potassium < 10 mg/1) in semi-confined and confined aquifers. The unsystematic use of synthetic fertilizers coupled with improper water management has affected the groundwater quality in many parts of the country. The statewise brief account of the incidence of groundwater pollution also reflects the occurrence of high concentrations of heavy/toxic metals, fluoride and nitrates at different locations around the country. The presence of zinc in shallow aquifers of Delhi is reported at places located close to areas of intensive agricultural practices coupled with extensive use of chemical fertilizers.... Even with strong legislative provisions such as the Water (Prevention and Control of Pollution) Act and the Environment Protection Act, since 1974 and 1986 respectively, 851 defaulting industries were located along the rivers and lakes in 1997. The Water Cess Act, 1977 has also failed to act as a market-based instrument in reducing the quantity of polluted discharges."

I request TERI for information about rivers. Quoting official studies, its experts report that, as against the standard of 3 mg/1 of Biochemical Oxygen Demand,

"Out of the total riverine length in India of around 45,000 km, 14 per cent show high pollution with a BOD in excess of 6 mg/1, 19 per cent show moderate pollution – BOD between 3 and 6 mg/1. More than 80 per cent of the domestic wastewater generated in Class 1 cities and Class 2 towns together is disposed untreated thereby resulting in surface water pollution. Maharashtra followed by Uttar Pradesh have the maximum river stretches showing BOD > 6 mg/1. River Ganga basin (comprising Yamuna basin too) followed by Godavari and Krishna basin show more than 25 per cent of their riverine lengths having BOD greater than the standard 3 mg/1."

And lakes?

"Lakes also show similar signs of presence of high BOD levels. For instance, Hussain Sagar lake in Hyderabad-Secunderabad shows BOD levels of 8-19 mg/1 as against the standard of 3 mg/1. The case is the same with Renuka lake (BOD 8 mg/1) in Himachal Pradesh, Ulsoor lake in Karnataka (BOD 6-18 mg/1), Lower and Upper lake in Bhopal (BOD 6-8 mg/1), Ward lake in Shillong (BOD 9-12 mg/1), Umiam lake in Meghalaya (7-13 mg/1) etc."

And, as we shall see in a moment, there are laws galore and rules under them, and Boards and appellate authorities dedicated specially to enforcement of those laws and rules.

Not just that, successive governments – both central and state – have time and again resolved to "tackle the problem on a war footing". The Drinking Water and Sanitation Decade had the provision of safe drinking water to all and the provision of good sanitary services to all as its main objectives. That Decade was launched in 1980.

"More than a decade after the list for network of air quality monitoring stations across the country was approved," reports *The Hindu* (20 April 2004), the Central Pollution Control Board has suddenly realized that "while the countrywide approved list of air quality monitoring stations has 295 stations on paper, at present only around 200 stations are operational.... Many State Pollution Boards have not operated some of the monitoring stations located in their area ever since the network of 295 stations was approved in 1992." Reason? "Lack of manpower"! And what is the solution that the authorities have hit upon after a decade of things having remained in this condition? The Board has now decided that the state authorities can hire people on a contract basis for monitoring work. Not so revolutionary a concept that it required a decade to burst forth.

A solid waste?

Similarly, there has been a shelf-full of legislation about the way solid wastes are to be disposed, in particular about the disposal of hazardous wastes.

In the beginning there was – as there always is – a "High-Powered Committee" on urban waste. That was in 1975.

By 1986, the umbrella law was in place: the Environment (Protection) Act of 1986.

In 1989, under this Act, Government mandated the Hazardous Wastes (Management and Handling) Rules.

It also mandated the Manufacture, Storage and Import of Hazardous Chemicals Rules.

And then the Rules for the Manufacture, Use, Import and Storage of Hazardous Micro-organisms, Genetically Engineered Organisms or Cells. All in 1989.

Next year, in 1990, the National Waste Management Council was constituted.

In 1991, the Ministry of Environment and Forests issued Guidelines for Management and Handling of Hazardous Wastes.

In 1993, the National Waste Management Council constituted the National Plastic Waste Management Task Force.

The relevant Rules for Management and Handling of Hazardous Chemicals – as distinct from Rules for Management and Handling of Hazardous Wastes – having been issued in 1989, the Guidelines for Management and Handling of Hazardous Wastes having been issued in 1991, in 1996 Government published Guidelines for Safe Road Transport of Hazardous Chemicals. These set out the basic rules, and also provided for the establishment of a Transport Emergency Plan and for provisions for the Identification and Assessment of Hazards.

That same year, in 1995, another High-Powered Committee was set up on urban waste. It elaborated on and added to the recommendations of the 1975 High-Powered Committee.

In 1998, the Bio-medical Waste (Management and Handling) Rules were issued.

And the Hazardous Wastes (Management and Handling) Rules were tightened.

And draft Municipal Solid Wastes (Management and Handling) Rules were issued.

In 1998 also, the recommendations of the National Plastic Waste Management Task Force, which had been set up by the National Waste Management Council, resulted in the draft Recycled Plastic Usage Rules – they mandated a ban on storing, carrying, and packing of food items in bags made of recycled plastic.

Next year, 1999, this resulted in the final Recycled Plastic Manufacture and Usage Rules.

In 2000, the Hazardous Wastes (Management and Handling) Rules were further tightened.

The same year, the draft Rules for Management and Handling of Solid Municipal Wastes that had been issued in 1998, led to the final Municipal Solid Wastes (Management and Handling) Rules.

Along the way, the Ministry of Urban Affairs and Employment has engaged the National Environmental Engineering Institute to formulate a "Strategy Paper" on managing municipal waste, and to prepare a Manual on managing solid waste.

The same ministry's Central Public Health Environmental Engineering Organization has prepared a "Policy Paper" for promoting the integrated provision of water, sanitation, solid waste management facilities and drainage utilities.

The Ministry of Environment and Forests has prepared a "Master Plan" for managing solid municipal waste.

The Central Pollution Control Board has prepared Guidelines for the safe disposal of hospital wastes....

And in reality? To take just one instance, *The Hindu* (21 April 2004) carries a report, "Hospital incinerators the biggest polluters." The news story is about the findings of a study conducted by Toxic Links. True, guidelines have been issued that discourage on-site incinerators and permit new incinerators to be set up only in certain unavoidable circumstances. "But all this seems to be happening only on paper," the paper quotes the expert of Toxic Links as saying. The reason is simple as can be! "In practice hospitals have not been notified (through an amendment in the rules) about the limits of incineration and they continue to incinerate all categories of waste proposed in the rules. State Pollution Control Boards continue giving statements instigating hospitals to go in for on-site incineration and some State Governments are also looking for installing unapproved technologies like Plasma Pyrolysis." The fact that follows is as telling:

"Delhi had around 59 medical waste incinerators in 2000, but because of the complexities involved in meeting the emission standards, most private hospitals decided to shut them down. Private hospitals have acknowledged the economic and environmental ramifications of these machines, but government hospitals have turned a blind eye to this menace. Even today most incinerators in Delhi do not have pollution control equipments...."

One thing we can be certain about: more rules, followed by more amendments and further elaborations of those rules and amendments are on their way – for, when it talks about the latest set of final Rules, the report, *State of the Environment, 2001,* issued by the Ministry of Environment along with TERI, etc. states, "These Rules along with Rules for biomedical waste management do not clearly identify the role and responsibilities to be undertaken by the CPCB [the Central Pollution Control Board] and the SPCBs [the State Pollution Control Boards]." So many editions of Rules, so many committees and task forces, and even that elementary thing is not yet clear? In any case, can the state of affairs in regard to incinerators that the report in *The Hindu* sets out possibly be attributed to the functions of the authorities not having been clarified as yet?

And again, "The rules promulgated by the MoEF [the Ministry of Environment and Forests] in the year 2000 dealing with hazardous waste management fail to provide any incentive for waste reduction/ minimization efforts. Industries are therefore reluctant to adopt such measures."

And yet again, "In the absence of standards for clean up of contaminated sites and limits for disposal of wastes on land, those industries which are causing contamination of land and water bodies through inappropriate waste disposal are not legally bound to clean the site unless ordered by judicial intervention to do so...." So many editions of rules, and even this basic element – the standard against which conduct is to be judged – missing? So many laws and enforcement authorities and still the offenders can pollute as they please because they "are not legally bound to clean the site unless ordered by judicial intervention to do so"?

A disconnect

There is a glaring disconnect in this field. When I read the literature about the condition of our environment, including, as will be evident from the passages that have been reproduced above, reports of governmental agencies, when I travel through our cities, or cross bridges over our rivers, I get quite a horrifying picture. On the other hand, when I ask for figures from official quarters, I get a picture of much activity and substantial achievement.

As a result of directions issued by the Central and State Pollution Control Boards, I am told,

❏ Out of the 1,551 highly polluting industries that had been identified in 1991 for priority action, 1,351 have installed pollution control facilities, 178 have been closed, and action has been initiated against the remaining 22 defaulters.

❏ Out of 604 industries in the 17 marked categories that were established after 11 January 1992, 527 have provided the pollution control equipment that was required, 46 have been closed, and action has been initiated against the remaining 31 defaulting units.

❏ Out of the 851 units that were identified as ones that were discharging effluents into lakes and rivers, 608 have provided effluent treatment plants, 238 have been closed, and action has been taken against 5.

❏ Up to March 2003, the latest period for which figures could be excavated, 7,357 cases had been filed under the Water and Air Acts. Of these, 4,170 had been decided. Decisions in 2,319 cases had gone in favour of the Board – that is, against the polluting units – and 1,851 had gone against it.

Directions have been issued, 3,000 surprise inspections have been conducted.... Since April 1994 a new procedure is in place under which public hearings are mandatory before a project can be considered from the environmental angle.... As a result of such steps, the authorities maintain,

❏ Had treatment plants not been installed, given the level and composition of industries, industrial water pollution load in terms of Bio-chemical Oxygen Demand (BOD) would today be 9,500 tonnes a day; because they have been installed, it is 1,700 tonnes a day.

❏ Similarly, had courts and governments not ensured that Electrostatic Precipitators and back filters are put in place, industrial air pollution load in terms of Particulate Matter would have been 3 lakh tonnes a day; because they are in place, it is 5,400 tonnes a day.

I ask the Center for Science and Environment for their assessment of these claims. They write back:

> The note is clearly flawed and we can analyse it further for you. But from the comments below, you will understand why it misrepresents key facts.
> 1. The list of polluting industries is clearly poor. The data is for just 2155 medium and large industries. But if we just consider the total number of medium and large factories in the country *(Annual Survey of Industries, 2002)*, which is 1,28,549, then the Boards are not monitoring even 2% of the total factories in the country (actual monitoring is 1.67% of total factories). This also leaves out an estimated 3.37 million Small Scale Industries.
> Worse still, of the less than 2% factories it monitors, the list does not include polluting industries like battery, automobile, paints, food processing, mining, electroplating etc.
> 2. It is a known fact that the major organic pollution load (BOD load) is from the food processing industry. Therefore, when the Board uses BOD as a performance measurement tool, it will obviously be misleading because it does not include the major BOD load generator in its list of polluting industries. In fact, the only way to measure the pollution impact, from this group of industries, would be to use the indicator Chemical Oxygen Demand (COD), which it has not mentioned.
> 3. Take the data they have supplied for BOD ("BOD reduced from 9500 tonnes per day to 1700 tonnes per day"). The distillery, sugar and paper sectors are key industries, which have a high BOD load monitored by the Board under its list of polluting industries. The Board has set a norm for BOD load in the distillery effluent (in waterways) as 30 mg/l. But all information available indicates that the sector is definitely not meeting this effluent standard. In fact, there is enough evidence to suggest that it is technically unfeasible to meet this standard. We know that there are 177 distillery plants in the CPCB list. Therefore, if we take their defaulter status, it would mean that only 22 are defaulters (assuming that all defaulting units are distilleries). Knowing the state of the distillery sector, we can clearly state that they are not meeting the standard that is set for them and therefore, would be a defaulting unit. The issue always is whether the Pollution Control Boards monitor the status of the pollution control equipment and the effluent discharge. This is an important issue because the capacities and budget of the Pollution Control Boards are quite pathetic and enforcement would be practically impossible.
> 4. We further analysed BOD to see what reductions are possible. We know the annual wastewater discharge from the original 1551 industries (2003 data). We also know the BOD limit set by the Board for the different sectors. When we calculate, as we did, we find that, according to the

information given by the Ministry, the BOD concentration has reduced from 118 mg/l to 21 mg/l. Distillery and sugar constitute more than one-third of the total plants (569 plants) under the CPCB list. If we assume that distilleries are meeting 100 mg/l standard and sugar plants are meeting 30 mg/l standard (a highly optimistic scenario), the rest of the 982 industries will have on an average a BOD load of just 3.5 mg/l. And if this is indeed the case, the Ministry should reduce its BOD standard immediately from 30 mg/l to 5 mg/l for all other industries other than sugar and distilleries.

5. Caustic-chlorine industry is included in the list of polluting industries. The pollution from this industry is not biological in nature. When we rated this industry we found to our horror that almost 90 per cent of the mercury consumed by this industry is not accounted for and that the pollution boards monitor just 2 per cent of the total mercury inventory of the industry. Therefore, to say that this industry is meeting standards is ridiculous. The standards are poor and do not even represent the problem of the industry. We know that mercury is a neurotoxin and that it leads to major mental problems and can even penetrate the placenta.

6. You will need to ask for details of the so-called defaulter list of 22 industries. For instance, the CPCB 2002 *Annual Report* (p.53) says that out of the 83 coal power plants that are classified under the polluting industries, only 48 plants comply with emission standards (therefore 35 do not and are defaulters). Furthermore, 52 out of 83 meet the effluent standards (again 31 defaulters). Much more than the total 22 defaulters claimed in the note....

Circumstantial evidence from the courts

In addition there is circumstantial evidence – of what the courts have had to say on the state of affairs, and what they have felt compelled to do.

Several facts about environmental litigation suggest that the Executive has to be much more active:

❑ Concerned citizens have had to repeatedly request the courts to step in and enforce the laws.

❑ Often, they have had to approach the courts to arrest the most blatant violations – of the directions of the courts themselves as much as of the laws and rules.

❑ Just as often, as even persistent efforts to get relief had got nowhere, concerned citizens have had to approach the courts for the most trivial of matters – about the condition of the garbage bins in their colony....

❏ The courts have ever so often had to direct governmental bodies –
central ministries, state governments, municipal bodies – to abide
by the laws relating to the environment.

❏ Ever so often, quasi-official bodies – the Central Pollution Control
Board, to take a patent example – has in its submissions had to
request the courts to direct official bodies to comply with the
directions. The tortuous course of litigation in regard to cleaning
the Ganga is an apt illustration. The Supreme Court, as we shall
just see, has had the Central Pollution Control Board submit
periodic reports. The Board in turn has requested the Court to
issue directions to Municipalities, Nagar Palikas, and other local
bodies in Uttar Pradesh, Bihar and West Bengal to maintain the
sewage treatment plants and systems, the sewage pumping
stations, crematoria, low cost toilets and other structures that had
been constructed under the Ganga Action Plan. The Court in turn
felt compelled to issue notices to all the 122 Municipal Councils
as well as the 7 state governments along the way of the Ganga....
[See as an instance, proceedings relating to *MC Mehta vs. Union of
India & others,* Writ Petition (Civil) No.3727/1985.]

❏ Ever so often, the courts have had to stress that the technologies
required to clean up the aspect of the environment that was
before them are readily available, and that installing them will not
cost much.

❏ Ever so often, the courts have felt it prudent to keep the cases on
board – as the record showed that, unless the official agencies
know that the matter will keep coming up periodically, they
would disregard the directions. The Courts have had to demand
that reports be submitted to them – by experts outside
governments – every four months, every two months, some times
even every month....

And ever so often, the reports sought by the courts have themselves
documented how tardy has been the compliance with their
directions. In March 1996, and again in April 1999, as we shall soon
see in greater detail, the Supreme Court felt compelled to direct the
Central Pollution Control Board to inspect the treatment of municipal
solid waste in Delhi – and to report every 2 months, later every
4 months. For 2002/03, the Board reported *inter alia,*

❑ An average of only 30 per cent of waste receptacles (*dhalaos*, dustbins) in the areas coming under the Municipal Corporation of Delhi are found to be properly maintained. The figures for the NDMC and the Cantonment areas are far better – 90 per cent and 40 per cent.

❑ There has been "steep deterioration in maintenance of waste receptacles" in 5 of the MCD zones.

❑ Lifting and transportation of garbage from waste receptacles in the MCD areas "suffers from an inadequate number of vehicles, thus causing a major obstacle in improvement of MSW management in Delhi."

❑ "All the three landfill sites of the NCT [National Capital Territory] of Delhi (Bhalswa, Ghazipur and Okhla) have exhausted their capacity. Efforts to identify and develop new landfill sites are yet to gain required priority and momentum from the concerned authorities. Pending this development, more than 1.5 million MT of MSW is being dumped in these exhausted sites without proper care and precautions to avoid public health and environmental impacts."

❑ "The MSW compost plants operated by MCD and NDMC are dilapidated and operating at less than 15% of the installed capacities. The privately operated new compost plant at Bhalswa is also in a state of redundancy due to various operational and management issues."

If this is the state of affairs in Delhi itself, if this is the state of affairs in regard to such a simple thing as municipal solid waste, if this is the state of the plants that the authorities' radar shows as having been installed and working, if this is the state of affairs on a matter – the treatment of municipal solid waste – that the Supreme Court and the Delhi High Court have themselves been monitoring since 1996, what are we to infer about the claims in general?

Proceedings relating to water pollution turn out to hold little that can provide more cheer. As other avenues had failed to trigger any action, the matter was taken to the Supreme Court in 1994. After a series of hearings and directions, and after receiving several assurances, the Court expressed the hope that steps will be taken so that by 31 March 2003 Yamuna's water reaches at least the minimum

desired quality level – Class C. The report submitted by the Delhi Jal
Board itself to the Central Pollution Control Board in November 2002,
indicated that "at present, about 3,300 MLD of wastewater is
generated in Delhi and about 55% of the volume is disposed of
untreated. There is a wide gap between wastewater generation and
actual treatment of wastewater...." [See the proceedings on Writ
Petition (Civil) No.725/1994.]

The sequence turns out to be no different when we follow the
course of litigation in regard to pollution of Gomti. Other remedies
having got nowhere, concerned citizens approach the Supreme Court
in 1990 for steps to clean the river by putting checks on industries
located in Lucknow, Sitapur and Lakhimpur Kheri. The Central
Pollution Board is directed to inspect the sites. It files a series of
inspection reports – each details the same sorry condition. It seems
that the Nagarpalikas and Municipalities are themselves and directly
discharging into the Gomti the polluted water without treating it in
any way, observes the Court. More inspections, more reports.... The
Court then directs the Central Pollution Board to furnish particulars
of technologies that the Municipalities, etc. can adopt to process
the pollutants – as if it is the difficulty of obtaining the relevant
information that is coming in the way of their doing the right thing.
Those details are at last furnished. By now it is 2002 – the case, recall,
was filed in 1990. Having deliberated on the details, the Court directs
the UP Government to acquire land in all the cities under reference
within three months for oxidation ponds. The state comes back to
the Court. A high level meeting has taken place of the National River
Conservation Authority, it informs the Court. This body is considering
conservation of rivers in all respects. Unless this Authority includes
the towns in its list for providing sewage treatment through oxidation
ponds, the state maintains, it may not be necessary to acquire the
land. Accordingly, would the Court please modify its order? "This
stand of the state is wholly unreasonable," the Court is compelled to
say. "Whether the said authority (NRCA) includes the town or not,
since these towns have been identified to be the chief source of
pollution for River Gomti, we consider it to be the state's obligation to
provide necessary land required to have oxidation ponds." "In the
aforesaid town," the Court continues, "the state cannot be absolved
of its liability on the pretext that no decision has been taken by the

said National River Conservation Authority. We, therefore, direct the state of Uttar Pradesh to acquire the necessary land required for having oxidation ponds, and complete the process within three months from today." The Court rejects the petition, and directs the state to report compliance through an affidavit.

You would think that nothing could be more final and binding. But the state comes back to the Court with yet another trifling plea to modify the order. "It is unfortunate," observes the Court, "that the Executive Government having failed to discharge its obligation, the Court is called upon to pass such orders; and such orders when passed after hearing the state as well as the other authorities, such frivolous applications are filed on one plea or another [*sic.*]. We direct that the state Government must comply with the order as expeditiously as possible." A dangerous phrasing – given the attitude that the Executive had exhibited! "Three months from today" modified to "as expeditiously as possible"!.... [See proceedings in regard to *Vineet Kumar Mathur vs. Union of India & others,* Writ petition (Civil) No.327/1990.]

And then some of the orders of the courts themselves give a glimpse of collusion between those in the Executive who are to enforce laws and those who are violating them. The Gomti river case itself provides a sorry illustration. After units have repeatedly failed to clean up their processes, the Supreme Court at last directs that units that have not installed the effluent treatment facilities by 21 March 1993 shall be closed from 31 March 1993. Mohan Meakins fails to do so. Nonetheless, the State Pollution Control Board gives its plant permission to continue operations. The Supreme Court directs the Secretary and the Chairman of the Board to show cause why they should not be punished for contempt of Court.

The officials file patently untenable, indeed laughable affidavits. The Secretary of the state Pollution Control Board swears on oath that the Chairman of the Board "directed [him] not to raise any objection in granting consent" to the Mohan Meakins, and that "in view of the said direction he had to and did give the consent."

The Chairman advances patently specious arguments to justify the direction. It is the Secretary of the Board who moved the proposal for reviewing the orders that had been given asking the unit to shut operations, he swears on oath. It is his proposal that I approved, he says, and adds, "But such approval of the deponent [that is, the Chairman] for reviewing consent does not mean that M/s Mohan Meakins was allowed to operate its industrial plant after 31.3.93 in defiance of the order.... of this Hon'ble Court." What else was it meant to do?

The Special Secretary of the Government of Uttar Pradesh swears an affidavit too: yes, Government gave the direction to the state Pollution Control Board, he says, "but stating at the same time," as the Supreme Court put it in its ruling, "that they were general instructions and were not meant for a particular industry. It was further stated in this affidavit that any such general instructions were not supposed to be relied upon by the Pollution Control Board to act in contravention of this Court's order"!

The officials insinuate that the pollution levels emanating from the plant were just marginally higher, that the unit had in fact installed the required equipment. The Court shows that the orders they had themselves issued directing the company to cease operations prove the contrary.

Soon, both the Chairman and Secretary are offering an "unconditional apology".

The Supreme Court finds the permission that has been given to the company to be a direct violation of its order. It finds the affidavits to be riddled with evasions, contradictions and worse. "It looks as if for both of them," the Court fumes, "the orders of the Uttar Pradesh Government issued on April 20, 1993 were sacrosanct and superseded the orders of this Court as well. It is a matter of regret that even responsible and senior officers of Government have acted in this manner. It is clear enough that the officials were anxious to somehow make out a case for enabling Mohan Meakins to operate its plant and machinery regardless of the orders of this Court...." [*Vineet Kumar Mathur vs. Union of India and ors.*, Judgment of 08/11/1995.]

Having come to such conclusions, the Court decides to accept the apologies of the officers, and everyone gets back to business as usual.

At the least, such facts and incidents – and they can be multiplied many times over – do not suggest that legislatures are following up the fate of the laws that they have passed, and they *do* seem to suggest that the Executive has to be dragged to do its duty.

But are courts doing all they can?

7

Demand, and file

Solid waste had become a major health hazard for residents of Delhi by the mid-1990s. B.L. Wadehra, a senior advocate and activist requested the courts to direct the municipal authorities to improve the methods of collecting, transporting and disposing garbage. The Supreme Court gave two far-reaching orders – on 1 March 1996 and on 23 January 1998. To ensure that improvements actually take place, it directed the Central Pollution Control Board to organize a comprehensive inspection of what follow-up steps were being taken every two months, and to report the results to the Supreme Court.

In its first report itself, the Board recorded the most distressing condition of waste collection, transportation and treatment in the Delhi area. It set out an Action Plan – a detailed, step-by-step road map of what the municipal authorities should do.

The hearing came and went. It was time to file the second report. The Board narrated how it had found that "both the authorities, i.e. Municipal Corporation of Delhi (MCD) and the New Delhi Municipal Council (NDMC), are continuing with routine operations for management of municipal solid wastes without showing any marked improved practices adopted for collection and transportation of garbage."

It went on to remark that "the NDMC has been continuing collection and storage of garbage by using combination of trolleys and dustbins," and that "Problems associated with this system as stated in the first report, are still continuing." It informed the Court that "the MCD has also not taken initiatives to show significant improvement in collection, storage, and transportation of garbage," but that at least it "has set up a good number of bins which are placed at short distances in a number of zones." The Board did add even at this stage, "MCD is required to create awareness amongst public for its [*sic*] usage."

The CPCB recounted that it had submitted with its first report a detailed Action Plan, and that "It is to submit before the Hon'ble Court that unless such an action plan is implemented, significant improvement in management of municipal solid waste cannot be expected. Therefore, an Action Plan as suggested by CPCB for implementation by the MCD and NDMC.... may be considered by this Hon'ble Court."

The concluding passage of its affidavit too is worth noting. The case had been the subject of active hearings now for several years. The Board had been conducting its bi-monthly inspections as directed. Observing what was happening in the field, the Board felt constrained to point out, "Bimonthly on-going inspections being carried out by CPCB may not help much. Instead, CPCB may be directed to monitor the progress of implementation of action plan on quarterly basis and submit reports to the Hon'ble Court."

The hearing came and went. The Board's report was received and presumably filed. The order that it carry out inspections every two months continued to hold.

By now 13 reports had been submitted to the High Court of Delhi. It was time to submit the third report to the Supreme Court. The very sentences of the second report figured again. "It has been observed that both the authorities, i.e., Municipal Corporation of Delhi (MCD) and the New Delhi Municipal Council (NDMC) are continuing with routine operations for management of municipal solid wastes.... The NDMC has been continuing collection and storage of garbage by using combination of trolleys and dustbins. Problems associated with this system as stated in the first report, are still continuing...."

The Board once again recalled that it had submitted a detailed "time-bound Action Plan" with its first report, that "It is to submit before the Hon'ble Court that unless, such an Action Plan is considered for implementation, significant improvement in management of municipal solid waste cannot be expected. The same was submitted along with the second report and it was prayed before the Court for consideration. Therefore, the Action Plan as suggested by CPCB for implementation by the MCD and NDMC.... may be considered by this Hon'ble Court."

It repeated that the bimonthly inspections were having little effect, that the *thirteen* reports which it had submitted by now had little effect, that, therefore, could the Court please direct that the inspections be conducted on a quarterly basis.

Time for the next round! The 14th inspection report since the orders of the Supreme Court. The CPCB has inspected 700 waste receptacles in the MCD area and over 375 in the NDMC area, the Board reports. The result? The two municipal bodies "are continuing with routine nature of operations for management of municipal solid wastes, without any sign of improvement.... As reported in the earlier reports, the problems with the system [of using a combination of trolleys and dustbins by the NDMC] remain unresolved." Furthermore, "during the present round of inspection it was observed that no progress has been made by MCD with respect to maintenance of waste receptacles, collection, storage, transportation and disposal of garbage and the implementation of the Action Plan from the last inspection report."

The Board reiterated what it had been trying to get the Court to appreciate: "CPCB still gives emphasis on the implementation of the Action Plan submitted to this Hon'ble Court.... for improvement in overall management of municipal solid waste in Delhi." And that once again, "It is to submit before the Hon'ble Court that unless, such an Action Plan is considered for implementation, no significant improvement in management of municipal solid waste can be expected. The same was submitted along with the two subsequent reports and it was prayed before the Court for consideration for implementation by MCD and NDMC...."

It once again reiterated its conclusion and its recommendation: "Bi-monthly inspections being carried out by CPCB in compliance of the orders of the Hon'ble Supreme Court, dated 1-3-1996 and 23-1-1998, and the fourteen reports submitted so far, have shown no improvement in maintenance of waste receptacles and sanitation with respect to handling of municipal solid waste in the absence of any time-targeted Action Plan." And it tried again to slip in its plaintive plea – of being spared the bimonthly exercise in futility – by offering to do more: "If the afore-mentioned Action Plan is accepted by the Hon'ble Court for implementation, CPCB will assist in monitoring the progress of implementation of the Action Plan on quarterly basis and submit reports to the Court."

Did that move the Court? To any course – to pull up the municipal authorities, to enforce the Action Plan, or to reduce the frequency of the inspections? None of the above.

The 15th report, 5th since the orders of the Supreme Court. 66% of the waste receptacles in the MCD area "are without doors or with broken doors or without covers or with broken covers or dilapidated, and 56% are in insanitary conditions...." In the NDMC area, 28% and 41%.... Passages, the very words remain distressingly the same.... Hence, concerted action by the numerous agencies involved is the need of the hour, as is the time targeted Action Plan, bimonthly inspections and reports yield no improvement....

The 16th report, the 6th since the orders of the Supreme Court itself. "Based on the joint inspection carried out during December 2-8, 1998," the CPCB informed the Court, "when 560 waste receptacles in the MCD area and 58 in NDMC area were inspected, it has been observed that 305 waste receptacles (i.e. 55% of 560) are in dilapidated condition, without doors or with broken doors or without covers or with broken covers, and 125 waste receptacles (i.e. 22% of 560) are in insanitary condition in the MCD area, while 40 waste receptacles (i.e. 69% of 58) are without doors or with broken doors or without covers or with broken covers and 19 waste receptacles (i.e. 33% of 58) are in insanitary condition in the NDMC area. Only 223 waste receptacles (40% of 560) in MCD area and 18 waste receptacles (31% of 58) in NDMC area are maintained satisfactorily."

Waste was being lifted from most of the collection centres, said the Board, adding, "However, the maintenance with respect to structure has not shown any improvement since a long time." It added a new element, one about which we are to hear more and more as report succeeds report: "Depositing of garbage in open spaces, parks, on the banks of drains, etc. are [*sic*] observed to be continuing during inspection." And, "Open sites, designated as waste receptacles, are still continued even after CPCB's constant persuasion to stop them."

What is to become the standard sequence of paragraphs follows:

"Stray animals are seen in the waste receptacles located at JJ Colonies, squatters, etc.... Rag pickers are also without exception seen working barehanded within the waste receptacles.... Insanitary conditions are observed in the areas of MCD and NDMC, particularly in slums, JJ Clusters and squatters, near food & fruit vendors and near motor repair shops...." The observation that we will by now surely know by heart: "The NDMC has been using trolleys and dustbins for collection and storage of garbage. The problems with the system remain unresolved as reported earlier...." Unfortunately, in spite of repeated exhortations, "The mass awareness programme has not been taken up in areas of MCD and NDMC especially in slums, squatters, etc...."

And hence the recommendation to go on repeating which, in view of the Court's demonstrated disinclination, must have required some courage: "CPCB is still of the opinion that there should be a time targeted Action Plan for implementation by MCD/NDMC, like the one submitted to this Hon'ble Court.... for improvement in overall management of municipal solid waste in Delhi...."

Another two months pass. Time to conduct yet another round of inspections. Time to submit yet another report – the 17th before the High Court and the Supreme Court, the 7th since the orders of the latter. The same state of affairs: 48% waste receptacles in the MCD area, 22% in the NDMC area "are maintained improperly, which indicates that the overall management of municipal solid waste has not shown any sign of improvement." "....Depositing of garbage in open spaces, parks, on the banks of drains etc. are observed to be continuing during inspection.... Open sites, designated as waste receptacles, are still continued even after CPCB's constant persuasion to stop them.... Stray animals are seen in 31% of the waste receptacles inspected, while rag pickers working barehanded are observed in 18% of the waste receptacles inspected.... Burning of garbage inside and in the vicinity of waste receptacles is quite common observation during this round of inspection." One improvement was noticed, namely, "MCD has installed a quite number of small dustbins on the road side, near bus stops, near shopping complexes and housing colonies." "However," the inspectors found, "lifting of garbage from these waste receptacles are [sic.] not regularised. Therefore, most of them are overflowing or the waste was dumped around the waste receptacles."

The next finding held greater peril: "Hospital and slaughter house wastes were observed mixed with domestic waste in the waste receptacles located nearby hospitals and slaughter houses; and also in the areas of unauthorised slaughter houses." And nothing had been done on the *sine qua non:* "The mass awareness programme is yet to be initiated by MCD and NDMC."

As little had happened, the old recommendation was still relevant: "CPCB is still of the opinion that there should be a time targeted Action Plan for implementation by MCD/NDMC, like the one submitted to this Hon'ble Court.... for improvement in overall management of municipal solid waste in Delhi."

The same fact, the same conclusion, and the same offer: the bi-monthly inspections and reports being given to the Supreme Court "have not shown any improvement in maintenance of waste receptacles and sanitation with respect to handling of municipal solid waste in the absence of any time-targeted Action Plan. Until the aforesaid Action Plan is accepted and implemented, regular monitoring of the routine programme on solid waste management in Delhi is proving to be futile. In the event of acceptance of the time bound Action Plan, CPCB will assist in monitoring the progress of implementation of the time targeted Action Plan on quarterly basis and submit reports to the Court."

19th report.... 20th report. 651 waste receptacles inspected in the MCD area, 150 in the NDMC area. 48 per cent in the former, 18 per cent in the latter "maintained improperly, which indicates that the overall management of municipal solid waste at the root level has not shown any sign of improvement." "....Heaps of garbage in open spaces, parks, on the banks of drains etc. were observed during inspection.... Open sites, designated as waste receptacles, are still continued even after CPCB's three years of constant persuasion to stop them.... Stray animals and rag pickers invade the waste receptacles.... Burning of garbage inside and in the vicinity of waste receptacles is quite common observation during this round of in-spection. The problems of waste disposal are further compounded by indiscriminate burning of leaves, twigs etc. in the street sweepings...."

The old fact, and the old grammatical mistake to go with it: "MCD has installed a number of small dustbins on the roadside, near bus stops, near shopping complexes and housing colonies. However, it was observed that lifting of garbage from these waste receptacles are not regularised. Therefore, most of them are overflowing or the waste was dumped around the waste receptacles." The continuing peril: "....Hospital and slaughter house wastes were observed mixed with domestic waste in the waste receptacles located nearby hospitals and slaughter houses; and also in the areas of unauthorised slaughter houses." The continuing neglect of the most elementary requirement: "The mass awareness programme to the common people as well as training to road sweepers and *Safai Karamcharis* is yet to be initiated by MCD and NDMC."

The same faith in the Action Plan. The emphasis once again on getting agencies to act in concert: "Since a large number of agencies are involved in solid waste management in their respective areas, a concerted approach for coordination among themselves may be evolved to tackle the problem in a holistic way."

The same lament – that the inspections and reports "have not shown significant improvement in maintenance of waste receptacles and sanitation with respect to handling of municipal solid waste in the absence of any time-targeted Action Plan." The same remedy: "Until aforesaid Action Plan is accepted and implemented, regular monitoring of the routine programme on solid waste management in Delhi is proving to be futile." The same plea: "Therefore it is prayed before the Hon'ble Court that CPCB will assist in monitoring the progress of implementation of the time targeted Action Plan on half yearly basis and submit reports to the Court."

Board hears nothing of what the Court has concluded as a result of its findings. 21st report....

22nd report, 12th since the orders of the Supreme Court. By now a high-powered committee that was constituted by the Supreme Court in another case [*Almitra H Patel vs. Union of India*] has submitted its report – on "Solid Waste Management in Class-I Cities." The Central Pollution Control Board sees some hope of getting itself off what is turning out to be a futile exercise: all Class-I cities are to mandatorily required to implement recommendations of the Committee – hence Delhi municipal bodies too have to do so. The Board recalls that it has been carrying out inspections every two months for 3 years, that it too has made a series of recommendations, that in addition the MCD has engaged the services of the National Environmental Engineering Research Institute for executing various works relating to management of municipal solid waste.

Advice has been requested from this specialized body, yet elementary things remain to be done: "It has been observed that both the authorities could not make any significant impact in the capital except making some efforts in improving methods adopted for storage and transportation of waste and disposal. The methods of storage, transportation and disposal have not been upgraded as per the recommendations of CPCB. The important observations reveal that old practices of waste storage in open sites and transporting the garbage in open truck is still continued [*sic*]."

The per cent of waste receptacles that are improperly maintained has climbed to 64% in the MCD area, it has improved to 15% in the NDMC area, "which" as always "indicates that the overall management of municipal solid waste at the collection storage and transportation [*sic*] have not shown any sign of improvement." "....Dumping of garbage in open spaces, parks on the banks of drains etc., which were not collected, were observed during inspection.... Open sites, designated as waste receptacles, are still continued even after CPCB's more than three years of constant persuasion to stop them.... Instead MCD continued to designate new open sites as waste receptacles.... Stray animals and rag pickers still continued to invade the waste receptacles...."

The old problems continue, the improvements that have been instituted have given rise to new problems: "MCD has installed a number of small dustbins on the road side, near bus stops, near shopping complexes and housing colonies. However, it was observed that most of them are overflowing or the waste was dumped around the waste receptacles, besides being either broken or rusted or out of proper use or even disappeared from the locations [*sic*]. This has compounded the problem of new open sites in many areas. Further, some of the newly constructed *dhalaos* are not open to public, but are used as office and stores."

At least these new developments – dustbins disappearing, *dhalaos* being used as offices! – should have caught someone's eye. Whether they did or not is evident from subsequent reports.

The oft-repeated fact: "Hospital and slaughter house waste were observed mixed with domestic waste in the waste receptacles located nearby hospitals and slaughter houses; and also in the areas of unauthorised slaughter houses." A new element: "Open defecation is also observed in the surroundings of waste receptacles especially where JJ Clusters and slums exist." A new observation: That, "during this round of inspection special attention was given on the transporting vehicles, which has shown that 16% of the vehicles observed on the roads are not covered, while the remaining are covered temporarily with tarpaulin, plastic or with jute material which are either torn or half covered, which is not a permanent solution."

Mass awareness programme is yet to begin.... Time targeted Action Plan as proposed in our 1 report is what is needed.... And "a concerted approach for coordination among themselves may be evolved to tackle the problem in a holistic way."

An even more ominous conclusion: neither the 20 inspections that have been carried out nor the reports that have been submitted to the Delhi High Court and the Supreme Court have resulted in any improvement. Indeed, "During this inspection it was observed that the situation has degraded from [*sic.*] the last observations."

As drawing attention to the Action Plan that the Board had prepared and submitted has not yielded any result, the Board now proposes that the two bodies involved – the MCD and NDMC – may be directed to prepare an Action Plan of their own....

23rd report, 13th since the orders of the Supreme Court. By now the typists just repeat the same text. All they have to do is to fill a new figure here and there. So, 68% of waste receptacles in the MCD area, 18% in NDMC area inadequately maintained.... "Overall management of municipal solid waste at the collection, storage and transportation stages has not shown any sign of improvement. It is high time that both the authorities should go for dumper placer in the place of masonry waste receptacles." "Dumping of garbage in open spaces, parks, on the banks of drains, etc., which were not collected, were [*sic.*] observed during inspection...." The cause identified: "Further, this can be correlated with the collection and transportation of garbage in the city. For example, only 80-85% of the waste generated is collected and transported daily; i.e. every day 15-20% of garbage remains uncollected."

"Open sites, designated as waste receptacles, are still continued even after CPCB's four [the number of years is all that has to be altered in the type-script] years of constant persuasion to stop them. Instead of providing permanent waste collection receptacles, MCD continues to designate new open sties...." Stray animals and rag pickers are still.... The figures have gone up to 34% and 29% in the two areas....

Indiscriminate burning.... "Most of them [the new dustbins that were installed] have disappeared and these spots have become the open dumping sites of garbage and are not attended by the *Safai Karamcharis*." "Hospital and slaughter house wastes were mixed with domestic waste...." Open defecation.... The percentage of uncovered vehicles has gone up to 33%, the condition of the ones that are covered remains woeful: "the remaining are covered temporarily with tarpaulin or plastic or jute material, which are either torn or half covered, which result in spill over of the garbage on the roads, is a common scene." House to house collections have indeed begun in some areas, but inspections of these areas reveal that "even though door to door collections were practiced in the identified areas, cleanliness was not observed in most of the areas. Heaps of garbage was [*sic*] observed in the back lane of houses and market areas."

The CPCB now draws attention to another problem – one that is going to go on swelling, one that screams for urgent action: "The life span of Bhalswa landfill site is almost completed and it cannot accept no more garbage [*sic*]. In such case [*sic*] the pressure on the other two land fill sites will increase and as a result their life span will get reduced. At present only 24.6 acres of land at Jetpur was available for landfill site. More land is required for landfill sites for the future."

Recommendations made for four years. Inspections carried out. Reports submitted. A high-powered committee's report now available. Mandatory to implement those recommendations. NEERI now in the loop. Yet, "it is prayed before the Hon'ble Court that system of solid waste management in Delhi has not improved." Therefore, "due attention should be given to improve the situation as per the recommendations given by CPCB in the past.... as well as taking a note of recommendations contained in the Burman Committee Report submitted to the Hon'ble Supreme Court. The concerned authorities should prepare an action plan along with the time schedule."

.... 17 May 2001: 25th report, 15th in the series after the orders of the Supreme Court.

All the old observations, and another lot of alarming developments. By now the percentage of "very badly maintained" waste receptacles in MCD has risen to 79%, in NDMC it has fallen to 18%, but in the cantonment it has risen to 40%. Unauthorized dumping of garbage in open spaces, parks, on the banks of drains, etc.... In part because every day "about 16% to 25% of garbage remains uncollected." "Open sites, designated as waste receptacles, are still continued even after more than [the number is all that has to be typed afresh] five years of constant persuasion by CPCB to stop them." "Stray animals and rag pickers still invade the waste receptacles...." Indiscriminate burning of leaves, twigs, rubber, papers, plastics etc. in the street, in and around most of the waste receptacles.... Additional dustbins installed at places, "However, most of them have disappeared and these spots have become the open dumping sites of garbage and are not attended by the *Safai Karamcharis*.... Hospital and slaughter house wastes were mixed with domestic waste in the waste receptacles located nearby hospitals and slaughter houses and also in the areas of unauthorized slaughterings.... Open defacation was also observed in the surroundings of waste receptacles.... A third of the vehicles are uncovered, while the remaining "were covered temporarily with tarpaulin or plastic or jute sheets, which were torn or half covered, which results in spill over of the garbage on the roads which is a common sight."

"A concerted approach for coordination" urgently needed among the large number of agencies involved....

Attention is again drawn to that ominous development: "The life span of Bhalswa landfill site is almost expired [*sic.*] and it cannot accept any more garbage. In such case [*sic.*] the pressure on the other two landfill sites will increase. As a result their life span get reduced [*sic.*]." By now there is yet another lapse: "The land for alternative sanitary landfill sites allotted by DDA has not been developed by MCD, so far." Furthermore, "For various reasons like high content of inorganic matter in the garbage, intermittent supply of electricity and water scarcity, the Bhalswa compost plant is under utilized. Therefore the Government may provide continuous power supply and water supply to run the plant to full capacity...."

The position in regard to that new drive – door-to-door collection – remains so unchanged that there is no need to alter the words: "The inspection of the locations, where door-to-door collection was initiated, was carried out. It was observed that even though door-to-door collections are practiced in the identified areas, still cleanliness was not observed in most of the areas. Heaps of garbage were observed in the back lane of houses and market areas. Further, most of the waste receptacles are found to be full with garbage in certain areas."

By now the CPCB is able to point to *five years* of inspections, and to as many years over which it has been making recommendations – on the orders of the highest Court of the country. It is able to point once again to the findings and recommendations of the Committee appointed on orders of the Court itself, and to the fact that MCD, NDMC etc. are bound by law to implement those recommendations. Not just that, by now the Government has also notified Municipal Solid Waste (Management and Handling) Rules. These too have mandatory status.... And yet, "the system of solid waste management in Delhi has not improved. Thus the health of a large population of Delhi is at risk. Therefore, due attention should be given to improve the situation as per the recommendations given by CPCB in the past.... and taking a note of recommendations contained in the Burman Committee Report submitted to the Hon'ble Supreme Court and the notification on Municipal Solid Waste (Management and Handling) Rules, 1999. The concerned authorities should prepare an action plan along with the time schedule to implement it with immediate effect...."

And, as usual, in the end the plea that this recurring futile burden may please be made less frequent: "Since there is no improvement in municipal solid waste management in the city, the purpose of frequent monitoring is defeated." Moreover, time has come for action against those who are just not acting on the directions of the Supreme Court: "It is also prayed that stringent action is required to be taken for repeated violation of the Hon'ble Supreme Court's orders in this regard...."

May 2002: 27th report, 17th in the series. General conclusion: "Compared to the enormity of the task of improvement of management of MSW in Delhi, the scale of efforts being undertaken by Municipal Corporation of Delhi (MCD) and New Delhi Municipal Council (NDMC) authorities has consistently fallen short of the need. Consequently, the status of MSW management in Delhi is not showing much improvement despite their efforts." The numerous reports. The High Powered Committee. The Rules. The mandatory duties imposed by these on the municipal bodies. And yet, "none of the three civic authorities (MCD, NDMC and DCB) is complying with the provisions of the Municipal Solid Waste (Management and Handling) Rules, 2000 notified under the Environment (Protection) Rules, 1986."

Once again, the absolutely choked condition of the Bhalswa landfill site, the need to acquire and develop new sites, the pitiable condition of the Bhalswa compost plant – "launched as a pioneering project for recovery of resources from municipal solid waste [and which] is now lying defunct"; the other plant of MCD – at Okhla – also "needs complete overhaul or replacement"; the NDMC composting plant at Okhla also "is operating at low efficiency and has almost completed its design life".... The long period for which all this has been known, and yet, "Only NDMC has applied for grant of authorization from the Delhi Pollution Control Committee for operating their compost plant at Okhla as required by the MSW (Management and Handling) Rules, 2000. MCD has not applied for grant of authorization for setting up and operation of compost plants at Okhla and Bhalswa and for waste disposal facilities at Bhalswa, Ghazipur and Okhla. Similarly, DCB is not maintaining its abandoned landfill site according to the provisions of the MSW (Management and Handling) Rules, 2000."

The urgent need – now put in bold type – for a "Master Plan for Management of Municipal Solid Wastes", a plan "to be implemented in a phased manner with measurable improvement indicators and to make organized attempts to achieve results in a time-bound manner...."

The absence of any improvement as a consequence of these inspections.... Could the Court please ask the Delhi Pollution Control Committee to monitor the matter.... Could these inspections not be mandated for once in six months....

The specifics as before – some improvement in the condition of waste receptacles but...., the unauthorized dumping in open spaces, the continuing disregard of the Rules as well as of five years of "constant persuasion" – "Open sites continue to be designated as waste receptacles...." The same grabbing of *dhalaos* – "Many *dhalaos*/dustbins are being used as office space in some MCD localities".... Indiscriminate burning.... Hospital wastes mixed with.... In the garbage stations operationalized with private participation the garbage is indeed segregated, but "they are mixed again at the time of collection by trucks for disposal...."

September 2002: 27th report. Improvement in some areas in the condition of receptacles, worsening in others.... Other features continue in the same sorry state. Alarming deterioration in many respects.... "All the 3 composting plants (2 plants of MCD and 1 plant of NDMC) in Delhi are running at very low capacities due to garbage quality, lack of repairs and maintenance and difficulties in marketing the compost product. The municipal authorities need to attend to the problems faced by these plants urgently.... There is an urgent need to develop and operationalize new landfill sites, as all the three existing landfill sites (Bhalswa, Ghazipur and Okhla) have exhausted their life span about 5 years ago and are overflowing with garbage dumped without proper care...." And yet, even now, "only NDMC has applied for grant of authorization from the Delhi Pollution Control Committee for operating their compost plant at Okhla as required by the MSW (Management and Handling) Rules, 2000. MCD has not applied for grant of authorization for setting up and operation of compost plants at Okhla and Bhalswa and for waste disposal facilities at Bhalswa, Ghazipur and Okhla. Similarly, DCB is not maintaining its abandoned landfill site according to the provisions of the MSW (Management and Handling) Rules, 2000."

The physical and hygienic condition of *dhalaos* "is consistently deteriorating" in .... areas that are thickly populated – all put in bold type. "The physical and hygienic conditions of waste receptacles in the Delhi Cantonment Area are consistently deteriorating...." 'The poor coordination between the Engineering Maintenance Wing and the Sanitation Wing of the MCD is resulting in inadequate provision and maintenance of waste receptacles...." "An acute shortage of collection trucks to transport garbage...." In three overcrowded zones garbage is found to be "overflowing and occupying the road space for more than four days leading to serious public health risks and traffic hazards".... Need for "urgent action", for dealing with the hazard "on a war footing".... The *dhalaos* still being used as offices.... The unauthorised dumping in open spaces....

The numerous reports, the committee, the Rules that have been notified, the mandatory duties, the inspections to no avail. Pray ask the Delhi Pollution Control Committee to monitor. Pray let these inspections be done once every six months....

28th report, 18th in the series. Several things that we would know by heart by now: "The physical and hygienic status of *dhalaos* is consistently deteriorating in.... Improvements.... need to be carried out on war-footing...." "The poor coordination between.... Almost all the waste receptacles in.... are in dire need of repairs or reconstruction." "The privately maintained *dhalaos,* in general, are well maintained and garbage is lifted on a daily basis" but some of them do not have roof covers and proper arrangements have not been made for draining out run-off during rains...." Stray cattle feeding in 45% of receptacles in the MCD area, rag pickers seen in 30%.... "Black and yellow bags containing biomedical wastes were observed in almost all receptacles located near major (public and private) hospitals. These waste [bags] of these colour categories are to be either securely landfilled or incinerated." For the first time, all garbage collection trucks were observed to have been covered fully with jute cloth cover....

In the MCD area, two-thirds of the waste receptacles turn out to be inadequately maintained, in the NDMC the figure has fallen to 9%, but in the Cantonment area it is still 58%. "Open sites are continuing to be designated as waste receptacles...." Some of the structures constructed to contain garbage continue to be used as offices in the MCD area....

The CPCB is driven by now to put its pleas – have the Delhi Pollution Control Committee monitor, reduce the frequency of these inspections to once in six months – not just in bold type, but in bold italics!

The problem of landfill sites and compost plants – a problem that has been before everyone's eyes for years – continues to swell. Even though the matter has been brought to the attention of all concerned including the highest Court for years, only NDMC has as yet applied for grant of authorization to operate their compost plant at Okhla as required by the Rules. MCD "has not applied for grant of authorization for setting up and operation of compost plants at Okhla and Bhalswa and for waste disposal facilities at Bhalswa, Ghazipur and Okhla. Similarly, DCB is not maintaining its abandoned landfill site." Furthermore, the CPCB informs the Court, "both the 2 composting plants run by MCD (one at Okhla – MCD managed, and the other at Bhalswa – managed by a private contractor) were found not operating during the inspection and no fresh garbage has been processed by these plants for the last more than 3 months [*sic*]. Poor quality of garbage, lack of repairs and maintenance and difficulties in marketing the compost product are some of the major reasons for their current state of affairs. MCD needs to attend the problems faced by these compost plants urgently." Although it is functioning at "low operational efficiency", the compost plant at Okhla maintained by NDMC is producing good quality compost. But its condition has deteriorated so much that even this plant "needs complete revamping."

And of course there remains the problem of landfill sites. Once again the Supreme Court is informed, "There is an urgent need to develop and operationalize new landfill sites, as all the three existing landfill sites (Bhalswa, Ghazipur and Okhla) have exhausted their life span about 5 years ago and are overflowing with garbage dumped without proper care."

June 2003. Time to submit the 20th report in the series after the Supreme Court's orders. The report is based on inspections conducted during April-May 2003. It documents deterioration all round – even in the one or two matters in which we had seen some marginal improvement.

"There is a clear trend of declining status of MSW management in Municipal Corporation of Delhi (MCD) maintained areas," the CPCB points out. "MCD is yet to be seized of the enormity of the task of improving management of MSW in Delhi and the efforts being undertaken by Municipal Corporation of Delhi (MCD) are not commensurate with the level and urgency demanded by the situation."

In fact, the very fact that land tracts are owned by Government makes them ready sites for dumping garbage. The Board states, "The Delhi Development Authority (DDA) is in possession of small pieces of undeveloped and unprotected land all over the city. It has been observed, wherever there is such land, it is converted into open dumpsites for garbage and all other sorts of wastes, thus creating unhygienic conditions to the surrounding localities [*sic*.]. DDA should take immediate steps to protect their undeveloped vacant land plots from becoming open garbage dumpsites."

None of the three municipal authorities is abiding by all the Rules that have been notified.... Physical and hygienic status consistently deteriorating in.... Improvements need to be carried out on a war-footing.... All the old problems.... The "garbage structures as offices" phenomenon is made specific: "While there is an apparent shortage of waste receptacles to properly store the garbage, a number of *dhalaos* – many of them newly constructed – are being used as office space/ store room. Following is an indicative list of such locations...."

An activity that was just about coping has crashed. We now read – in bold type, "The garbage transportation system of MCD is in complete disorder. Perhaps, the non-availability of sufficient number of loaders and collection trucks can be singled out as the main reason for the poor state of MSW management by MCD. Due to non-availability of lifting vehicles, majority of waste receptacles are found to be overflowing with rotting garbage thereby becoming breeding grounds of vectors, rodents, mosquitoes, flies and pathogenic microorganisms posing severe health hazards to the population living around. Shortage of collection vehicles and loaders has been reported by almost all of the Sanitary Inspectors met during inspection. After taking into account vehicles that may not be in operation at any time, MCD will require roughly twice the number of vehicles that are in its current fleet so that garbage is transported from receptacles on a daily basis. Along with this, the number of loaders also has to be doubled...."

Remember the jute covers over trucks? That little improvement too has frayed. We now learn, "All the garbage collection trucks use jute or polyethylene cloth as a temporary measure to cover the garbage during transport. It has been observed during the current monitoring period that most of such covering cloths were inadequate in size and shape to properly cover the garbage. As a result, garbage trucks spilling and spreading garbage all along their route to landfill site has been observed on a number of occasions."

The problem of those compost plants and landfill sites has become even worse. The CPCB informs the Supreme Court,

❑ "MCD is yet to take any recognizable step to increase the MSW processing capacity by way of installing new plants for the same. The existing composting plant operated by MCD at Okhla is not working any more. Similarly, the other plant at Bhalswa – managed by private contractor – was also operating at less than 1/5ᵗʰ of installed capacity. Poor quality of garbage, lack of repairs and maintenance and difficulties in marketing the compost product are some of the major reasons for their current state of affairs. MCD needs to attend to the problems faced by these compost plants urgently.

❑ "The NDMC managed compost plant at Okhla also is becoming defunct and there is no attempt on the part of NDMC to renovate the old plant or to install a new plant.

❑ "There is an urgent need to develop and operationalize new landfill sites, as all the three existing landfill sites (Bhalswa, Ghazipur and Okhla) have exhausted their life span since about last 5 years [*sic.*] and are overflowing with garbage dumped without proper care...."

We are already in June 2003. The Board politely reiterates what it has been emphasizing for the previous two and a half years, that is since the Rules were notified. "According to the MSW (Management and Handling) Rules, 2000," it repeats, "new landfill sites for future use need to be identified and developed by 31.12.2002."

All the other recommendations and pleas too are there – in bold type.

September 2003. 21ˢᵗ report since the Supreme Court's orders. The words are the same: "There is a clear trend of declining status of MSW management in MCD managed areas.... MCD is yet to be seized of the enormity of the task of improving management of MSW in Delhi, and the efforts being undertaken by Municipal Corporation of Delhi (MCD) are not commensurate with the level and urgency demanded by the situation.... The Delhi Development Authority (DDA) is in possession of small pieces of undeveloped and unprotected land all over the city. It has been observed, wherever there is such land, it is converted into open dumpsites for garbage and all other sorts of wastes, thus creating unhygienic conditions to the surrounding localities.... The physical and sanitary status of *dhalaos* is consistently deteriorating in.... The garbage transportation system is in complete disorder...." The cloth covering the trucks is inadequate in size and shape and "as a result, garbage trucks spilling and spreading garbage all along their route to landfill site has [*sic.*] been observed on a number of occasions...."

At last MCD has also applied for authorization to operate its composting plant. The applications are now pending with the Delhi Pollution Control Committee. But for the rest, things are as they were:

❑ "MCD is yet to take any recognizable step to increase the MSW processing capacity by way of installing new plants for the same. The existing composting plant operated by MCD at Okhla is not working any more. Similarly, the other plant at Bhalswa – managed by private contractor – was also operating at less than $1/5^{th}$ of installed capacity.... MCD needs to attend to the problems faced by these compost plants urgently. The NDMC managed compost plant at Okhla was found running and there is no attempt on the part of NDMC to renovate the old plant or to install a new plant.

❑ "There is an urgent need to develop and operationalize new landfill sites, as all the three existing landfill sites (Bhalswa, Ghazipur and Okhla) have exhausted their life span since about last 5 years and are overflowing with garbage dumped without proper care. According to the MSW (Management and Handling) Rules, 2000, new landfill sites for future use need to be identified and developed by 31.12.2002. However, it was reported by MCD that new site at Jaitpur is under final stage."

February 2004. 22nd report in the series since the Supreme Court's orders. An improvement here, a deterioration there. The report is indistinguishable from its predecessors. Shutters are installed at the structures to keep out the animals. To an unexpected result: this innovation, we learn, "promotes the people throwing the garbage outside the *dhalaos*...." Additional dustbins were installed a while ago, but since then "many dustbins in the MCD area have become open sites as they are in broken state due to improper use of loaders." The major problems – landfill sites, composting plants, the "complete disorder" into which the transportation of waste has fallen – exactly as they were: "There is an urgent need to develop and operationalize new landfill sites, as all the three existing landfill sites (Bhalswa, Ghazipur and Okhla) have exhausted their life span since about last 6 [only this figure had to be changed] years and are overflowing with garbage dumped without proper care. According to the MSW (Management and Handling) Rules, 2000, new landfill sites for future use need to be identified and developed by 31.12.2002. [A gentle reminder once again, as we are already in February 2004!]...."

All the old recommendations – in bold type again.... "It is prayed before the Hon'ble Court that the municipal authorities in the NCT of Delhi be directed to make concerted efforts to achieve results in a time-bound manner.... They should also develop and implement a Master Plan for Management of Municipal Solid Wastes in a phased manner with measurable indicators to monitor the progress...." "Since the improvement in municipal solid waste management in the city has been observed to be slow-paced, it is prayed that the Hon'ble Court may direct an inspection frequency of once in six months.... It is therefore prayed that the Hon'ble Court may direct the Delhi Pollution Control Committee to monitor MSW management in the NCT of Delhi, and ensure compliance of the MSW Rules, 2000."

All the recommendations and prayers that have been repeated a score of times – the bold type and italics as ineffectual as the inspections themselves have been for eight years....

What would you bet was happening? That the Court was giving all concerned time to mend their ways? Or that, the inspection reports, having been asked for, and having been received, were just being filed? Every two to four months for eight years....

8

Converting a great problem into a greater opportunity

Each one of our cities shouts out a fact: the problem of urban waste, in particular of hazardous waste is nearing crisis-proportions. Heaps of garbage can be seen in even the most affluent colonies – ever so often, just outside the structures into which residents and municipal workers are supposed to put the waste. Newspapers routinely carry photographs of medical, infectious waste that has been thrown and is lying heaped just outside the hospitals themselves, all too often even inside the hospital compound.

The heaps grow many times faster than population for reasons that are obvious. Urban population grows faster than general population. Urban waste grows faster than urban population – what with changing consumption habits. And piles of urban waste grow faster than urban waste – what with our governmental structure becoming weaker by the week *vis a vis* its employees.

Nor is it just a matter of garbage piles getting higher. The waste – specially the hazardous waste – percolates into the aquifer, into lakes and rivers. And thus poisons us twice over. Giving a typical illustration, the report *State of the Environment, 2001,* published by the Ministry of Environment, TERI and the United Nations Environment Programme, narrates, "The Thane-Belapur industrial area, in Maharashtra, where about 1,200 industrial units are housed on a 20 km stretch close to New Mumbai, creates more than 100 tonnes of solid waste every day. About 85% of this waste is either acidic or alkaline in nature. The area also produces 5 tonnes of waste every day which is difficult to treat because of its halogen content.... The water bodies in the vicinity are polluted. The sediment in the Ulhas river has registered high levels of mercury and arsenic. Ulhas river empties into Thane Creek at its northern end. As a result, Thane Creek is one of the most polluted seawaters in the country."

And again, "The Ahmedabad-Vadodara-Surat industrial belt has over 2,000 industrial units in the organized sector and more than 63,000 small scale units manufacturing chemicals like soda ash, dyes, yarns and fertilizers. Vapi in Valsad district has around 1,800 units of which 450 fall in the category of polluting industries. Industries in all these areas usually dump their wastes in low-lying areas within a 2 kms radius. As a result, a major illegal dump yard has sprung up on the banks of the Daman Ganga. Indian Petrochemical Corporation Ltd. (IPCL) at Vadodra dumps 1,800 tonnes of hazardous wastes every month at a site near Nandesari. The IPCL dumpsite is on a hill. During the rainy season, the hazardous constituents of these wastes are washed down into the river."

And yet again, "In the Wazirpur Industrial Estate and Shahadara-Maujpur Industrial Estate as well as along the Grand Trunk Road in Delhi, small and tiny scale industries processing non-ferrous metals such as copper, brass, aluminium as well as steel rolling mills and pickling factories were dumping their heavy metal rich affluent and acids into open cess pools and drains. This had led to permeation of effluent into the water table and has contaminated groundwater, which is used by local residents as potable water supply...."

The Report goes on to recount another typical case – of two units producing acid-using dyes in Bichhri, a village in Rajasthan: "This resulted in some 8,250 cubic metres of wastewater and some 2,400-2,500 tonnes of process sludge. The toxic wastewater was let out without treatment and the process sludge was dumped in the plant premises. The wastewater flowed through Udaisagar canal across the entire region while rainwater washed the sludge across the soil into the groundwater. An official survey indicates that groundwater up to 70 feet below the ground level had been contaminated over an area of 7 sq km affecting 8,000 people in seven villages...."

The examples can be multiplied. But a few things will be evident even from these passages:

❏ While many defend public sector units on the ground that they have a greater sense of "social responsibility", these units are as guilty of disregarding official standards and notifications as private ones.

❑ The sectors that we treat as holy cows – "small scale, tiny scale" – can, and do cause as much damage as the ones it is fashionable to rail against – "large scale", "multi-national" and the rest. To take just one example, in 2000/01 the Centre for Science and the Environment focused its Green Rating Project on the auto-sector. Daewoo Motors, Hyundai, General Motors and Mercedes Benz India out-scored all the others – though the Centre also noted that these companies were introducing older engines and models into India, some of which would fail the current Green tests in their own countries. [*Down to Earth,* 30 November 2001, p.27.]

❑ The polluters are disregarding norms and notifications not in some distant, difficult to see, back-of-beyond hamlet: they are doing so in the cities themselves, indeed in the principal cities themselves, in industrial estates set up by governments themselves; in a word, our environment is getting violated right in front of the eyes of rulers.

❑ Among the entities that we have polluted are the very ones – rivers, lakes – that we worship.

Contrast such examples with the sort of facts that one comes across routinely in reports about the state of affairs in Europe, even the United States. A random sample from reports available on the Internet speaks to a contrast – each concerning an activity much more difficult to remedy than just treating hazardous waste:

❑ In 1985 Germany announced incentives for adopting catalytic converters and switching to unleaded petrol. By 1 September 1993, 97% of all newly registered cars were equipped with regulated catalytic converters.

❑ Germany slashed the production of toxic wastes by 15% in just 3 years.

❑ In Sweden, between 1982 and 1994 the number of combustion plants with nitrogen oxide reducing technologies increased ten fold. The target the country fixed was to reduce nitrogen oxide emissions – that cause acid rain – by 35% by 1995; it was exceeded in 1993 itself.

❑ Carbon dioxide emissions in Sweden decreased from 100 million tonnes in 1970 to 60 million tonnes in 1991.

❑ Between 1980 and 1991, sulfur dioxide emissions decreased by 80% in Sweden; by a quarter in Denmark between 1995 and 1997 – these reductions were achieved just by the introduction of a stiff tax on SO2 emissions.

❑ In France, between 1975 and 1983 pollutants in industrial discharges decreased by 40%. Between 1970 and 1989 total groundwater extraction decreased by 15%. Even that figure understates by far what was accomplished: the figure would have been much higher but for the fact that, for a variety of reasons that are not germane to our discussion, municipalities increased their extraction by 42%; by itself industry decreased the amounts it was extracting by 55%.

❑ Between 1975 and 1990, oxygen demanding discharges decreased by one-third in Netherlands. Net load on surface water decreased to one-third of what it had been. Between 1976 and 2000, the discharge of heavy metals – like cadmium, copper, lead, mercury, zinc – into lakes and rivers decreased by percentages ranging from 86% to 97%.

❑ Use of industrial water in several of the OECD countries in 2000 is about half of what it was 25 years ago.

❑ From 0% in 1981, wind power was generating 3% of Denmark's power by 1992.

❑ Generation of power from renewable sources quadrupled in California between 1983 and 1992.

❑ "New wind turbines developed in California are fully cost-competitive with conventional fossil fuel power plants. Significant advances in commercial generation of solar electric generation were also achieved. In just six years, one company called LUZ reduced the cost of solar thermal electricity from $ 0.25 kWh for its first plant to $ 0.08 kWh for the ninth plant...."

❑ By using taxes and public pressure, developed countries made industry phase out chloroflurocarbons – the gases that were hurting the ozone layer most.

❑ In the US, the number of times each cubic meter of water is used in manufacturing industry has increased from 1.8 in 1954 to 3.4.

❑ The way that the Danube, the Thames, the lakes in Austria have been cleaned is the sort of thing that those countries are able put on posters they publish to attract tourists.

Such examples suggest several lessons.

Some lessons

What we encountered in relation to our laws and environment is not inevitable. Technology to mitigate pollution, technology to transit to more beneficent ways of doing things is available off the shelf. The occasional success story in India itself shows that much can be done even without better technologies. The report from which those distressing examples were taken, *State of the Environment, 2001,* recalls the excellent work that was done in Surat after the plague-scare of 1994 – how the city, convulsed by fears of plague, became, in just 18 months, the cleanest city in the country. The report recounts the simple administrative devices that were adopted, the way the community was mobilized, the difference that enforcing such a simple thing as penalties for littering made, the way private sweepers and private transporters were engaged. One has only to see what the efforts of N. Chandrababu Naidu did to clean up Hyderabad, and one knows that pollution and filth are not inalienable concomitants of modernization.

But in a sense, these success stories reinforce the elementary question: Why is it that in those countries and in these instances within India laws and standards have altered conduct, but in general in India they have not? A conscientious civil servant, among whose responsibilities is that of enforcing these laws, says that the very feature that was built in to make these laws "tough" impedes convictions. Our environmental laws are criminal laws, as distinct from civil laws, he points out. The standard of evidence required for conviction under a criminal law is much more stringent than in civil laws. But it is very difficult to establish a cause and effect relationship in most environmental matters, he says. The proof is probabilistic rather than the simple – "'y' because 'x'."

Perhaps. But that can't be the sole or even the main reason – after all, the requirements of evidence being what they are, why then enact environmental laws as criminal laws in the first place? The real reasons are of a different kind:

❑ A great deal of thought has gone into the standards and laws that have been formulated in Europe and other places. A tiny –

though lethal – example will indicate what happens when this is not done. When the norm looks for concentration of pollutants per milliliter of discharge, the unit will have little difficulty in passing the test: all it has to do is to flush the effluent with a larger volume of clean water, or some other solvent. That is manifestly and doubly harmful: the pollutants get into the river and more clean water gets used up. The norm must capture both – the concentration per milliliter as well as the total volume of pollutants that are discharged.

Plain as can be – and yet one of our vital norms is still locked on to just the former. Mercury used in the caustic-chlorine industry is a cruel reminder of the consequences. The Center for Science and Environment points out that "Mercury consumption in Indian caustic-chlorine companies is at least 50 times higher than the average European consumption," but so lax are our monitoring mechanisms that "as much as 44 per cent of mercury loss goes unaccounted and even companies have no clue about this huge, alarming loss." How does this kind of a situation persist? The Center's experts observe,

"The focus of regulations for mercury pollution from mercury cell plants in India is on placing checks on mercury concentration from various point sources rather than putting a check on total mercury pollution load entering the environment. This is in contrast with regulations being implemented in Europe where, along with the concentration, regulation on total mercury being released from the plant exists.

"The existing regulatory standard of India on mercury pollution from caustic-chlorine industry measures emissions of mercury from following point sources: mercury in wastewater and mercury from hydrogen gas holder.

"The average mercury loss through wastewater in Indian mercury cells is 0.38 gm per tonne caustic soda and average mercury loss through hydrogen gas holder is 0.01 gm per tonne caustic soda. Therefore, only 0.39 gm mercury loss can be accounted as per the existing regulation.

"However, the average mercury consumption in Indian mercury cells is 146.6 gm per metric tonne of caustic soda. This means that the regulatory standards are only regulating 0.3 per cent of the total pollution. This by itself sums up the effectiveness of regulations in controlling mercury pollution.

"Even though the regulations on concentration of mercury from various point sources in India and Europe are very similar, the absence of total mercury input regulation in India has resulted in the average mercury emissions being as high as 146 grammes per metric tonne (gm/mt) caustic soda from mercury cells plants. Whereas, by implementing this standard European companies have achieved mercury emissions of 1.5 gm/mt caustic soda." [*Down to Earth*, 15 September, 2002, pp.27-28.]

❏ Having formulated the laws and standards, governments enforce them.

❏ But it isn't just fear of prosecution that impels industry to abide by the laws and standards, nor just the incentives. More important is the spirit of rule-abidingness. Much of industry in a country like Sweden has gone farther than the laws and rules required. In part this has been due to societal pressure: the pervasive effect of the Green Movement for one. But the major part has come from conviction – in these countries large sections of industry are as convinced as the rest of society that nature must not be violated.

❏ One of our habits also comes in the way: all too often we are satisfied counting problems, specially the problems of others – "They have developed, you say? But look at the mounting divorce rate. Look at the way they have polluted their rivers and lakes." That they are actually doing something about their problems, that they have already attended to several of them – such facts we do not allow to interrupt our hectoring.

In addition to these general points, the mixture of incentives and disincentives that these countries have deployed to alter the conduct of industry yields several specific lessons. We will do well to bear these in mind.

Incentives that actually spur, disincentives that actually deter

In Singapore you cannot just walk up to a car-dealer and buy a car. Since 1990, the Government has instituted a Vehicle Quota System. Vehicles have been divided into seven categories – cars of different capacities of engines, commercial vehicles and buses, motorcycles, etc. The Government specifies the number of vehicles of different kinds that may be purchased in a month. This number is determined by allowing a 3% increase in the number of vehicles per year and the number of vehicles that are liable to be taken off the roads that year. Government announces that it will release that many Certificates of Entitlement. These are put up for auction. As I write, the certificates for a car with an engine less than 1600cc cost around US $16,200 a piece. After you have bid for and won the Certificate of Entitlement, and paid for the car, you must pay a Registration Fee of about US $600, and an Additional Registration Fee that is 110% of the Open Market Value of the car.

And then you must pay an annual road tax. On a medium-sized car – with a 1600cc engine – this is about US $600.

And the dealer's charges.

The result is that while the original market value of a Toyota Corolla, the equivalent of our Maruti Baleno, is about US $10,000, by the time you can put it on the road it will cost you around US $44,100!

But each time you actually take it out on the road, you will have to pay more.

Singapore has instituted the Electronic Road Pricing system. Under it, you have to pay a stiff charge should you drive during peak hours. The rates are fixed depending on the road-space that your car occupies, and the particular road on which and the time at which you drive it – the latter set of rates has been fixed to ensure that, as far as possible, traffic flows around 45-65 km/hour on expressways and 20-30 km/hour on arterial roads.

And of course there are hefty parking charges. Even if you park your car in a residence, you have to pay a parking charge – the only exception is if you live in a condominium.

There are other levies too. The diesel tax, for instance. It is *six times* the road tax of an equivalent petrol driven car.

On the other side, hefty rebates have been decreed to induce owners of petrol-driven vehicles to switch to eco-friendly fuels. The Registration Fee and the Additional Registration Fee are reduced by 20% for hybrid or electric or CNG cars, and by 5% of the Open Market Value for CNG buses. The annual road tax is reduced by 10% for hybrid cars and 20%t for electric, bi-fuel and CNG cars and buses. Recently, to induce owners of taxis and other commercial vehicles to switch to vehicles complying with Euro IV norms, rebates of annual road tax of up to 100% of the Open Market Value of the vehicle have been announced. For certain categories, the annual road tax has been completely waived.

Several countries in Europe have adopted elements of such levies.

And of course, automobiles are just one example. These countries have levied heavy taxes on pollutants, and simultaneously given rebates to firms that install equipment which will reduce the level of that pollutant below the prescribed norm. The levies cover emissions of carbon, of heavy metals, of sulfur, an array of chemicals, choloroflurocarbons, generation of garbage, leaded gasoline, etc. Correspondingly, rebates are given for equipment that will mitigate these emissions, etc., and they are given for products that do not use as much of the targeted material.

Levies and rebates in India

In India also we have instituted a number of levies and rebates along the same lines.

Accelerated depreciation at 100% for installing pollution control equipment; reduced customs duty; excise duty of only 5% on items used for controlling pollution; exemption under a section of the Income Tax Act for those incurring expenditure to conserve natural resources; no excise duty for building materials that use 25% or more of fly ash; no customs duty on equipment required for producing building materials that use fly ash; tax concessions of various kinds for renewable energy systems like solar photovoltaic cells, wind energy generators; rebates to industries that comply with effluent quality standards; concessional rates of import duty for wood and wood articles – to save our own depleting forest cover....

The contrast is that while the taxes and rebates in, say, European countries have indeed had visible, in some cases even dramatic effects, they have not had that order of impact in India.

The contrast points to several lessons. These have been intensively studied in Europe by ecologists and economists – you will find them listed in reports such as Andre de Moor and Peter Calamai, *Subsidizing Unsustainable Development, Undermining the Earth with Public Funds,* Earth Council, 1997; *Environmental taxes: recent developments in tools for integration,* European Environment Agency, 2000. Our experience in India confirms several of the lessons. Among these are the following.

To start with, the levies must be part of a coherent approach. How can levies on cigarettes be effective if – as we do – we simultaneously in a sense underwrite a minimum price to those who grow tobacco? How can we expect farmers to desist from using soil-poisoning, cancer-causing chemical fertilizers when we give out Rs.12,000 crores every year as subsidy to use those very fertilizers? Is what we do to curtail air-pollution not diluted by the subsidies we continue to give for using diesel? CO_2 emissions from diesel are 10 per cent more than even petrol. Should we be surprised that excessive amounts of water are being pumped out of the aquifer, and that as a result the water-table is falling at an alarming rate when we subsidize the use of electricity in agriculture by Rs.35,000-40,000 crores every year? It is good to levy a stiff charge on cars that come into crowded parts of a city – but the charge will be most effective, and will be least resisted, if simultaneously a good public transport system is in place.

So, first a coherent set of policies. And one must watch out for second order effects too. The activity that is subsidised must actually wean the people away from the activity that Government had sought to penalize. We impose a diesel cess; by itself it could help nudge truckers towards alternate fuels; but when we use the proceeds primarily to build better highways – instead of, say, subsidizing alternate fuels – we clear the way for a larger number of trucks; and thereby foster even higher consumption of diesel....

Second, the entire array of instruments should be deployed – not just a levy or a rebate. As the Supreme Court's decisions in regard to buses and industrial units that were polluting the air in Delhi demonstrated, often non-market measures are the only ones that will jolt a system out of a harmful addiction. Nor is it just a question of instruments. Setting standards, fomenting peer group pressure among industrialists, mobilizing the media to focus the searchlight on violators, educating the people – all of these have to be part of the arsenal. Thus, the policies must be coherent, and they must be comprehensive.

Third, the levies have to be substantial enough, and their enforcement has to be honest enough to actually make it expensive for the harmful practices to be continued. A good benchmark is the amount that the unit or consumer would have to spend to switch to the alternative product or process – the levy must be such that the unit can see that it would gain perceptibly and in the near-enough future by switching to the alternative. Correspondingly, the rebates or incentives that are given to get people to adopt alternative products, processes or equipment have to be sufficient to make the switch actually profitable. In Sweden, a study points out, the tax on sulfur emissions is *four times* what the polluting unit would have to spend to reduce the emissions below the norm. In our case, all too often, what happens is that we hear of a good idea or someone gets one, and a sort of token step is taken. That way the objective isn't attained, and the measure – the tax or the incentive – gets discredited. Look at the tokenism that has marred – for decades – our approach to an alternative fuel like ethanol. There is another feature that several countries have built into their levies and one that we would do well to adopt. The fee on the polluting activity *rises* with every passing year: units are required to reduce their emissions to x% by year t_0; those that do not will have to pay amount "y" in t_1 – that levy itself is stiff; in t_2, they must pay "2y", and so on.

Fourth, either the alternative technology or product must be available off the shelf – as it has been for half a century in regard to ethanol – or the country must invest sufficient resources to develop it.

Fifth, the measures must be crafted for the long run. The unit availing of the incentive must not be able to retain the gain if it relapses into the harmful ways and practices that the government had set out to replace. Incentives too should be tailored to *continuing* improvement. A young Collector, S.S. Sandhu multiplied the survival rate of trees along the roads in Ludhiana by a simple device. The contractors who planted the trees used to be paid by the number of trees they planted. They would plant, collect the money, and forget the trees. Sandhu decided that they would be paid each year according to the number of trees that had survived and the height that they had attained! For the same reason, when a levy is imposed, we should not start judging it immediately. We should give it the time that is required to install the new processes and equipment, or develop the alternate technology and replace the existing capital stock.

One reason for the successes that European States have had in this sphere holds another lesson for us. We have already seen how they have coupled levies on polluting processes or activities with rebates for those who adopt the better alternative – by now the approach even has a name: "feebate". But they have gone further. They have used the amounts they have collected from environmental taxes to cut general taxes to a corresponding extent – on individuals, on corporations – as well as to reduce mandatory contributions – to social security, to pension funds etc. The point is twofold: do not look upon environmental taxes so much as a source of revenue as an instrument for redirecting economic and technological choices; and simultaneously create a constituency among the general population for the new levies.

Seventh, the fear is often expressed that should we impose such levies we would be making our units uncompetitive *vis a vis* units operating in countries – Pakistan?, Bangladesh?, Nepal? – that do *not* impose equivalent levies. Moreover, given the ease of getting items over into India from neighbours in such proximity, firms can easily choose to shift their operations to one of these countries – so that we would lose out twice over: the processes would continue to pollute our neighbourhood, and we would have lost jobs, etc. in the bargain. Europeans have therefore adopted a twofold approach. They have been in the forefront of building international opinion to induce all governments – especially those in Europe – to adopt such environmental taxation. Second, they levy compensating charges on goods that are imported from countries that do not have environmental taxes on those harmful processes, and give refunds to units that export items that require inputs on which they have had to pay an environmental tax, say fossil fuel.

Finally, of course there is the most elementary, as well the most elemental requirement – that such measures as are decreed are actually enforced. If norms for emissions are announced but monitoring facilities are not installed, or, though installed, remain "non-functional"; if the pollution gauges tell the tale but the inspectors are corrupt, everything will naturally come to naught. The courts have directed that taxis must ply in Delhi only on CNG. What is the point of such a directive if – as has happened – taxi owners convert a few registered taxis to CNG but transfer most of their business to illegal taxis – private vehicles that have not been registered as but ply as taxis and that can thereby continue to ply on petrol and diesel? And how easy it is to circumvent the directive in this way will be evident from what the *Indian Express* reported the other day: that the legal, registered taxis in Delhi are just 3,873, while the vehicles that are illegally plying as taxis number around 1,00,000. All that the latter have to do is pay Rs.200 a vehicle a month to the police and the State Transport Authority people, and to pay a thousand per vehicle when these personages come for "inspection". [*The Indian Express,* April 27-29, 2004.]

Each of these lessons has a ready, and literal application for us in India:

❏ Prepare thorough lists items and processes that harm health and the environment;
❏ Levy stiff taxes on them;
❏ Have the scale of each levy multiply with each passing year;
❏ Use the proceeds to subsidize the benign alternative;
❏ Use them to reduce taxes on the "goods";
❏ Enforce every law, rule, tax....

Over the years, "greening the budgets" has become a veritable movement in Europe. Its proponents encapsulate their goals and experience in pithy rules:

❏ "Tax waste, not work" – levy a charge on the amount of garbage that a family generates rather than on the income it earns.
❏ "Get people to pay for what they take, not for what they make."
❏ "Tax bads, not goods" – a levy on fossil fuels, not on bio-fuels; on tobacco, not on books. "Would you rather that you and your neighbour are taxed for working?," asks a key proponent, "Or for polluting each other's lungs?"
❏ "Set prices to reflect true costs to the earth" – by using levies that reflect the draft which the process or commodity imposes on non-renewable resources, the harm it inflicts on the environment and on health.
❏ "Ensure that the polluter pays."

They also urge that the proceeds from these levies be used to

❏ Subsidize those who alter their ways – for instance, those who install the effluent treatment plant;
❏ Remedy what has been damaged – for instance, the lake that has been polluted;

❑ Educate consumers to switch to alternative goods;
❑ Build peer pressure and public pressure on erring units;
❑ Finance research to develop alternative technologies.

Pollution is but one aspect

While the examples above have been about pollution, the degradation of our environment goes far beyond effluents, emissions and the like. *State of the Environment, 2001* records *inter alia* that

❑ Per capita annual availability of renewable fresh water decreased from 6008 cubic metres at the time of Independence to 2266 cubic metres in 1997.
❑ The critical level for groundwater exploitation is 80%; the rate of exploitation in Punjab is close to 89%, in Haryana it is 80%.... The crisis becomes even more evident when we go below these state-wise averages. The Central Groundwater Board pointed out in 1994 that in 6 of the 12 districts of Punjab, and in 3 districts of Haryana the utilization rate exceeded 100%; that in districts such as Mehsana in Gujarat, Coimbatore in Tamil Nadu, groundwater aquifers had got "permanently depleted" because exploitation had been exceeding recharge for long.
❑ As a result, the water table has been falling at an alarming rate: a study reported in 2002 that farmers in Mehsana were forced to lower their pumps by 10 feet every two-three years because of falling water levels; in cities like Delhi "the water table continues to fall by more than half a meter every year in certain zones"; in Punjab, the state that provides so much of our food, too it has been falling by more than half a meter every year.
❑ The consequence? "It is estimated that as much as one-fourth of India's agricultural production, about 45 million tonnes is jeopardized by groundwater over-pumping alone"....
❑ In only 4 of our 20 river basins is the water flow adequate; in 9 the flow is still at a level that the shortage is liable to be "local and rare"; but already in five basins the flow has fallen so much that "health and economic development" are now hampered by water scarcity; and in 2 it has fallen so low that "water supply is the primary constraint on life".

❑ And water is just one symptom. About 57% of our land area, for instance, has been scarred by one form of degradation or another.

❑ Per capita forest land has fallen to 0.08 hectares as against the 0.47 hectares that are needed to meet basic needs.

❑ In 1997 fuel wood consumption was about 260 million cubic metres as against a sustainable level of only 52.6 million cubic metres.

❑ Our livestock population of 467 million grazes on 11 million hectares of pasture land – that is, an average of 42 animals graze in a hectare of land against the threshold level of 5 animals. As there isn't enough pasture land left, a third of the fodder requirement is met by letting the animals graze in forests, with predictable consequences.

❑ Only 24% of the waste water gets treated in Class I cities before being dumped into rivers and lakes; the figure for Class II towns is 3.7%.

❑ India is the 6th largest and 2nd fastest growing generator of Green House Gases.

Here is a textbook case of what teachers like C.K. Prahlad have been urging us to grasp. He has stressed that our firms should learn to locate the business opportunity *in our needs* – that is the surest way even to profits.

The enormous opportunity

Remedying the environment that we have damaged – cleaning rivers and lakes, for instance; replacing harmful materials by beneficent ones – fossil fuels by renewable ones, chemical fertilizers, insecticides and pesticides by bio-ones; restoring our aquifers by rehabilitating traditional ponds, by simple water-harvesting measures – such projects offer the greatest *business opportunity* in India. Doubly so: through them we will salvage our future; and the solutions we devise for these problems will also have a ready market in other countries. Sweden's exports of environmental equipment now exceed a billion dollars. The revenue from equipment to monitor and clean the environment, from equipment that is needed to replace polluting processes and products is already close to 600 billion dollars; even at current levels of economic activity the potential market is estimated to be in the range of a trillion dollars.

Ecology restoring projects also constitute one of the largest opportunities for creating jobs for our people. Water harvesting, repairing traditional ponds, cleaning our rivers and lakes, proper segregation, collection and processing of urban wastes – activities such as these can engage millions. In many of them, the over-whelming component is to move earth. The main thing *that* needs is organization of large numbers. And for that too, we have unlimited, and grossly underutilized resources. Almost 50,000 persons retire from the armed forces every year – to take just one example. Almost all of them are in their forties and fifties. Each of them has had professional training. Each has learnt to organize and motivate others. Each has led a disciplined life. Each is imbued with the national spirit. Having worn the uniform for twenty-twenty five years, each is looked up to as he returns to his community. And yet we just let that enormous resource scatter to waste. A massive programme to harvest rain-water, to restore every traditional water storage facility, to dredge rivers and reservoirs – by constituting ex-Servicemen into companies. What opportunity could be more obvious? What could spell such certain benefit?

On the other side, as we saw briefly earlier on, the very wastes that today constitute such a burden are – literally – a resource-in-the-garb-of-a-problem.

The most researched by-product

About three-quarters of our installed power generating capacity is thermal. And about three-quarters of that is coal-based. Indian coal has high ash content – about 34% to 50%. Fly ash is the unburnt portion of coal used in these plants.

We generate about 100 million tonnes of fly ash every year. Only 10 to 15 per cent of this gets used today. 85 per cent of it is just mixed with water and dumped into "ash ponds". Precious water is wasted. Land is taken up. Air and subsoil water are polluted. A typical account reads,

> "A 1999 study by the health authorities at Santhaldih (in West Bengal's Purulia district) showed that a large number of people in the area were

suffering from lung infections and skin diseases caused by fly ash contamination of air and water. The power plant in the region, commissioned in 1973, with a 480 MW-capacity, produces 0.6 MT of fly ash every year. "The authorities had built two ash tanks at Santhaldih which had been filled up over a period of time. The fly ash, which couldn't be stored in these ash ponds, was getting scattered over 25 neighbouring villages.

"The effect of the ash was found in animals and vegetation too, so much so that the cattle feeding on the contaminated vegetation suffered from dental disorders and skin diseases. It also caused a decline in the bird and aquatic population...."

On the other side, notice that 35 to 40 per cent of our development expenditure is on construction. For this we use about 100 million tonnes of cement. But for each tonne of cement we produce we release about a tonne of carbon dioxide – and thus injure the life-protecting ozone layer. The cement industry is also one of the largest users of water, it is also a very energy-intensive industry, and, by the rock that it uses, it scars the country.

But by the techniques that were developed in Canada in the 1980s, and are in use the world over, 35 to 50 per cent of the construction material can be fly ash. The material can be used, and is being used the world over for making bricks, highways, pavements, houses, embankments, railway sleepers.... Not just that, manufacture of Pozzolona Portland Cement – that uses fly ash – requires 11 to 15 per cent less energy than that of Ordinary Portland Cement. Study after study shows that the structure is stronger, and that it lasts longer by decades.

That fly ash can be used in these ways, that doing so will yield such boons is well known. Indeed, a paper from TERI instructs me that fly ash is "the most researched by-product of the last 70 years" – it reports that there are thousands of items about it in technical literature.

Not just that, the Government launched a national Fly Ash Mission in 1994 under TIFAC – the Technology Information Forecasting and Assessment Council. Several of our premier institutions have been working on it – the Central Road Research Institute, the Central Building Research Institute, the NTPC, BHEL, the Institute for Solid Waste Research and Ecological Balance – and they have developed and tested the technologies for using it.

And it has been used too – the embankment and approach roads of the Nizamuddin bridge, the flyovers at Okhla and Sarita Vihar in New Delhi, the Raichur-Arsnagi road in Karnataka, the road built by Gujarat Ambuja at Ropar in Punjab....

Thus, a clear need, a resource piling up and poisoning us in front of our eyes, demonstrated technology, governmental notifications, visible success here and there, and yet only 15-odd percent of the material is used. Little Netherlands produces 1 million tonnes of fly ash. It uses *one hundred per cent* of it....

What accounts for this difference? What is the key that will enable us to do that which technology already in use allows, that which others have already done?

The key

The Government had by notification prescribed that manufacturers making clay bricks, tiles or blocks within a radius of 50 km of thermal plants must mix at least 25% of ash. If they do not, the notification had declared, the manufacturer's lease on the land, his right to manufacture, etc. are liable to be terminated. As the notification – its minatory provisions notwithstanding – was having little effect, Government did the predictable thing. It decreed that manufacturers not just within 50 km but those within 100 km of the thermal power plant shall be required to abide by the provisions of the notification. The new notification forbade these manufacturers from excavating topsoil within 50 km radius of coal- and lignite-based power plants, and enjoined that, should they do so, they would have to preserve, store and reapply it.

"But till date this notification remains on paper," reported *Down to Earth* [30 June, 2003]. And no one seemed either unduly perturbed or unduly enthusiastic about the stiffer provisions that were on their way. "The Government has failed to implement even the 50 km notification, how does it intend implementing the 100 km notification?," inquired a member of the Delhi Brick Kiln Owners Association. "They can go ahead and notify an area of 200 km, but what use will it be if it remains unimplemented?"

Thermal Power Plants – owned and operated by the Government itself – are no better, *Down to Earth* found out. "TPPs have budgetary allocations for fly ash disposal. Due to various reasons ['read corruption', inserted *Down to Earth*] they do not want to bring down their budget," says a Delhi-based fly ash brick manufacturer. He informs that the Badarpur Thermal Power Station in New Delhi has recently acquired 500 acres of land for fly ash disposal. It already occupies 100 acres of land as an ash pond. Elsewhere in the country fly ash seems to be pure waste: according to the Tamil Nadu Industrial Development Corporation, the state recklessly discharges almost 94% of the fly ash into the sea."

There are all sorts of schemes and regulations to promote the use of fly ash bricks. But instead of prescribing schemes and incentives for others, "Why don't government agencies such as the Delhi Development Authority (DDA), CPWD, Municipal Corporation of Delhi (MCD) promote fly ash bricks?," *Down to Earth* inquired. The answer it found? "It is easy to make money in a project if the tenders call for clay bricks as there are various qualities of clay bricks available in the market," a manufacturer explained. "And fly ash bricks have no such varieties, hence no possible cuts." "Today we want to become 'eco-friendly' by manufacturing fly ash bricks," he went on, "but are facing administrative problems [an euphemism, no doubt]. Hence our products keep lying in the godown for months together." "At present," *Down to Earth* noted, "the Rajghat power station in Delhi [owned and operated by the Government itself] has close to 80 lakh fly ash bricks stocked at its premises, with no buyers."

A mounting problem. A clear, easy way to convert it into a resource. Notifications to do so. Rules to make sure everyone abides by those notifications. Boards to enforce those notifications and rules. Incentives to induce entrepreneurs to abide by them. The product piles up in a Government owned and operated organization. Government owned and administered organizations that can use it. And yet, on the ground....

In a word, passing laws has become a substitute for enforcing them.

That is doubly destructive. What needs to be done remains not-done. Worse, the Rule of Law, indeed the very authority of State is undermined.

Thus, the key is the familiar one, and it is easily located: *implement* the good ideas we have been having for decades.

Other materials

The story is the same in regard to the 90 million tonnes of bagasse that our sugar mills produce every year; in regard to the 23 million tonnes of rice husk that comes off as we produce 90-odd million tonnes of rice; in regard to urban solid waste, to wastewater, to waste from tanneries. The bagasse can be used much more profitably to produce paper, bio-degradable plastic, films. Slag can be used in constructing embankments, pavements, highway shoulders. Rice husk can be used for feeding livestock, for fertilizing land, for producing a versatile substitute for wood, and thereby helping save our forests. The CSIR reports that the wood substitute produced from rice husk has an edge over wood and plywood – in resistance to termites, to high decay, to fire and water; that it has excellent mechanical properties, like internal bond strength, dimensional stability, elasticity, screw and nail holding capacity, abrasion resistance etc. Wastewater can be recycled many times over. Tannery wastes – both liquid and solid – can be used to produce biogas.

Indeed, aspect upon aspect of the way we produce things at present offers opportunities. Industry uses a twelfth of the water we use as a country. But 90 per cent of this is *not* consumed, it is discharged as wastewater. Were we to recycle and reuse just this discharge, we would alleviate water shortages in some of our metropolitan concentrations perceptibly. Today the power generation efficiency in our thermal power plants is 30-35 per cent. With no more than available technology this can be scaled up to 60 per cent. Technologies that have been developed in the West for chemical recovery in the paper industry are not economical unless the plant is producing significantly above 100 tonnes a day or so. To develop a version of this recovery process that would be viable for smaller plants.... Treating spent wash from distilleries.... Recovering chrome from the 80 per cent of our 2,500 tanneries that use it.... Technologies to reduce energy consumption per unit of output to international levels – in the steel industry, in producing aluminium....

And in each instance, the advantage that would accrue to the country is incalculable. To continue the last example in the list above, ".... The iron and steel sector leads in consumption [of energy] with about 10 per cent of the total.... The average energy consumed for

making one tonne of crude steel in India is in the range of 30-40 GJ –
very high compared to global standards (18-20 GJ). India currently
produces 20 million tonnes of steel. Assuming that the average energy
consumption for making one tonne of crude steel is reduced from the
current 35 GJ/tonne to 25 GJ/tonne through technology upgradation
and conservation measures, the energy saved from this sector will be
a whopping 200 million GJ (55,000 million KWH electricity) annually.
In 2000-01, the power deficit in the country stood at 39,812 million
KWH. Which means, enhancing the energy efficiency of the
integrated iron and steel sector alone can meet the current power
deficit in the country.

"Similarly, the aluminium sector, the second largest energy
consumer in the country, can meet around 7 per cent of India's
current power deficit. The energy consumed in producing one tonne
of aluminium in India is 90 GJ, compared to 70 GJ in Europe. India's
average annual aluminium production is about 0.5 million tonnes.
Bringing the Indian aluminium industry to European consumption
levels can save about 2,750 million KWH of energy...." [For these and
other examples, and telling details on them see, for instance, *Down to
Earth,* 15 June, 2003.]

Multiplying successes

Again, some plant or the other somewhere or the other in the country
is using wastes to excellent effect, some plant or the other is
improving energy input, it is switching to more benign inputs.
Both Madras Fertilizers Ltd. and Madras Refineries Ltd. have built
secondary treatment plants water from which is now used for
purposes such as cooling – an investment that has enabled them to
overcome desperate water shortage that continues to plague the rest
of Chennai. The Al Kabeer meat processing unit in Rudraram near
Hyderabad uses offal and other organic and bio-wastes to produce
biogas as well as fertilizer via biomethanation – it meets a quarter of its
power requirements in this way, and also earns substantial amounts
from the fertilizer: in just three years, the company has recouped all
the investment it made to treat its wastes.

There have been other noteworthy successes beyond recycling
waste also. In its Green Rating exercise, the Center for Science and
Environment found that even the automobile sector had affected

notable improvements: in recycling wastewater, in reducing energy consumption, in decreasing paint and primer consumption, in decreasing air emissions.... Gujarat Ambuja Cement has drastically lowered its energy consumption as well as its emissions to a level that is now the lowest in our cement industry. The firm is targeting zero waste discharge. It is modifying its procurement policy to give preference to green inputs.... Philips India has done a commendable job in reducing toxic metals and solvents, in cutting down rejections, in improving energy efficiency and lowering water consumption in its production processes.... [*Down to Earth,* 15 September, 2002; *ibid,* 15 June, 2003, pp.36, 37.]

Similarly, there have been fine improvements in what has hitherto been one of the worst polluters – the pulp and paper industry. The Green Rating exercise which the Center for Science and Environment conducted in 1999 had yielded a distressing and woeful picture of the industry. But by 2004, the Center found:

❑ The number of ISO 14,001 companies has increased significantly.
❑ Water consumption has been reduced from about 250 tonnes per tonne of paper to less than 150 tonnes per tonne of paper. Some of the units have in fact gone down almost to zero discharge. These units will soon be among global leaders in this industry, the Center notes.
❑ The consumption of chlorine, the major source of pollution in this industry, too has been reduced significantly. We now have one company which has elemental free chlorine technology.
❑ In 1999 less than 20 per cent of the wood that the industry was using was sourced from farm land. The proportion seems to have doubled.

In a sense, all we have to do is to multiply these successes across the country. And we would have converted many problems into rich resources.

The long run imperative and opportunity

Remedying our environment is one opportunity. Converting waste into wealth is another. These are opportunities we can avail of by using no more than technologies that are already available.

There is just as pressing a need for, and as vast an opportunity in organizing research to develop new technologies for these purposes. Experts have correctly emphasized that in several instances the technologies that have been developed in the West will not meet our requirements. "The small scale agro-residue based paper and pulp industry, tanneries, or molasses-driven distilleries do not exist in the West," the Center for Science and Environment points out giving typical instances. "But in India they are part of the small scale sector that accounts for 40 per cent of industrial production, 35 per cent of its direct exports and – here is the rub – 60 per cent of total pollution...." [*Down to Earth,* 15 June 2003.]

But there is an even greater opportunity for the future. And that is in bio-products. Much of the oil we import can be replaced by bio-fuels. Most of the products that are today made from the by-products of petroleum can be made from biomass – chemicals, plastics, adhesives, paints, solvents, polymers, cosmetics, acids, lubricants, building materials.... Other substitutions are possible even from existing technologies – water-based paints to replace solvent and metal-based paints in the automobile industry, for instance.

Here is a great opportunity for us. We have among the most knowledgeable farming communities in the world. We have vast areas that can be rehabilitated even as they are put to producing these items – jethropa and other hardy plants for biodiesel, for instance. We have laboratories upon laboratories that can do so much more than they are doing today.

And we have urgent needs – not just for these products but also, for instance, to reduce our dependence on imported oil. To glimpse the unlimited opportunities in this sphere as well as what even the West we deride so much is already doing in this regard, do look up Janine M. Benyus' riveting *Biomimicry, Innovation inspired by Nature,* [William Morrow, 1997; Harper Collins, 2002], or just download, *Industrial Bioproducts: Today and tomorrow* [Energetics Inc., for the US Department of Energy, Office of Energy Efficiency and Renewable Energy, Office of the Biomass Program, July 2003].

Here then is a field – developing bioproducts – that should be one of the principal points of focus for our scientists, technologists and industry in the coming decades.

That effort will be quadruply rewarded:

- ❏ We will have solved many of our problems.
- ❏ We will have provided for our needs.
- ❏ We will have set an example for the world.

We will at last have taken a step to provide what we have been talking of since Gandhiji wrote *Hind Swaraj* – an alternative to the dominant pattern of consumption and development.

A matter of life and death

9

Acting on the facts

Whatever the set of facts that we take up – infiltration from Bangladesh, the ideology that is being drilled into wards in *madrasas,* the way *madrasas* along our borders are being used for harming our country – we run into the same sequence: whenever the facts have been brought to the attention of governments, even by high officials of State themselves, governments have just looked the other way.

Annexation by inundation

"Large scale illegal migration from East Pakistan/Bangladesh over several decades has been altering the demographic complexion of this State. It poses a grave threat both to the identity of the Assamese people and to our national security. Successive Governments at the Centre and in the state have not adequately met this challenge.... I feel it is my bounden duty to the Nation and the state I have sworn to serve, to place before you this report on the dangers arising from the continuing silent demographic invasion...." Now, that is not some sundry journalist or AASU activist writing. It is the Governor of Assam – who happens to have been Deputy Chief of Staff of the Indian Army. And it is no ordinary article in which he begins in this way – it is his official report to the President of the country.

"The unabated influx of illegal migrants from Bangladesh....," General S.K. Sinha told the President "threatens to reduce the Assamese to a minority in their own state, as happened in Tripura and Sikkim."

"The long-cherished design of Greater East Pakistan/Bangladesh, making inroads into the strategic land-link of Assam with the rest of the country," he warned, "can lead to severing the entire land mass of the North East.... from the rest of the country. This will have disastrous strategic and economic consequences."

After tracing in detail the way the demographic balance has been overturned in district after district adjacent to Bangladesh, General Sinha concluded,

"This silent and invidious demographic invasion of Assam may result in the loss of geostrategically vital districts of Lower Assam. The influx of these illegal migrants is turning these districts into a Muslim majority region. It will then only be a matter of time when a demand for their merger with Bangladesh may be made. The rapid growth of Islamic fundamentalism may provide the driving force for this demand. In this context it is pertinent that Bangladesh has long discarded secularism and has chosen to become an Islamic State. Loss of Lower Assam will severe the entire land mass of the North East from the rest of India...."

[Lt. General S.K. Sinha (Retd.) *Report on Illegal Migration into Assam submitted to the President of India by the Governor of Assam,* 8 November, 1998, pp. i, 1, 18.]

Two years earlier, having failed to awaken anyone in Government, the former Governor of West Bengal, and one who had earlier been the head of the Intelligence Bureau, T.V. Rajeswar, had felt compelled to go public. In a series of articles in early 1996, he had pointed to the long-standing design to create a Greater, Islamic Bangladesh – by annexing Assam, the bordering districts of West Bengal, and parts of Bihar, and to the fact that through this illegal infiltration the design was well on the way to being realized. Indeed, he stressed, the way this influx had already converted vast, contiguous tracts into Muslim, specifically Bangladeshi Muslim dominated areas, the prospect had already arisen that a third Islamic State may be carved in the sub-continent out of India.

He recalled what the then Muslim League Premier of Bengal, Nazimuddin had told the Governor of the province, R.G. Casey – Casey had set it out for the Viceroy, Lord Wavell:

"Nazimuddin tells me that they calculated that the combined area would give them a majority of 58% of Muslims in place of 51% if only all Bengal and all Assam were to be included. He tells me that the Muslims bred faster than the Hindus and that 58% would reach 60% and more within a relatively few years. He went on to say that they believed that once this North Eastern Pakistan was established, there would be no one more keen about it than the Hindus within its borders and that he believed it possible that the Burdwan Division might come into North Eastern Pakistan in due course."

Rajeswar cited Kissinger's dire warning – should that be "wish"?

"The inevitable emergence of Bangladesh – which we postulated – presented India with fierce long-term problems. For Bangladesh was in effect East Bengal, separated only by religion from India's most fractious and most separatist state, West Bengal. They share language, tradition, culture, and, above all, a volatile national character. Whether it turned nationalist or radical, Bangladesh would over time accentuate India's centrifugal tendencies. It might set a precedent for the creation of other Moslem States, carved this time out of India. Once it was independent, its Moslem heritage might eventually lead to a rapprochement with Pakistan."

And Rajeswar drew attention to what had already come to pass:

"Muslims in India accounted for 9.9 per cent [of India's population] in 1951, 10.8 per cent in 1971 and 11.3 per cent in 1981, and presumably about 12.1 per cent in 1991. The present population ratio of Muslims is calculated to be 28 per cent in Assam and 25 per cent in West Bengal. In 1991 the Muslim population in the border districts of West Bengal accounted for 56 per cent in South and North Parganas, 48 per cent in Naida, 52 per cent in Murshidabad, 54 per cent in Malda and about 60 per cent in Islampur sub-division of West Dinajpur. A study of the border belt of West Bengal yields some telling statistics: 20-40 per cent villages in the border districts are said to be predominantly Muslim. There are indications that the concentration of the minority community, including the Bangladesh immigrants, in the villages has resulted in the majority community moving to urban centres. Several towns in the border districts are now predominantly inhabited by the majority community but surrounded by villages mostly dominated by the minority community. Lin Piao's theory of occupying the villages before overwhelming the cities comes to mind, though the context is different. However, the basic factor of security threat in both the cases is the same.

".... Figures have been given showing the concentration of Muslim population in the districts of West Bengal bordering Bangladesh starting from 24 Parganas and going up to Islampur of West Dinajpur district and their population being well over 50 per cent of the population. The Kishanganj district [of Bihar] which was part of Purnea district earlier, which is contiguous to the West Bengal area, also has a majority of Muslim population. The total population of the districts of South and North 24 Parganas, Murshidabad, Nadia, Malda and West Dinajpur adds up to

27,337,362. If we add the population of Kishanganj district of Bihar of 986,672, the total comes to 28,324,034. (All figures are based on the 1991 Census.) This mass of land with a population of nearly 2.8 crores has a Muslim majority. The total population of West Bengal in 1991 was 67.9 million and of these, 28.32 million are concentrated in the border districts, with about 16-17 million population of minority community being concentrated in this area. This crucial tract of land in West Bengal and Bihar, lying along the Ganges/Hughly and west Bangladesh with a population of over 28 million, with Muslims constituting a majority, should give cause for anxiety for any thinking Indian."

From these figures, he gave two warnings. First,

"There is a distinct danger of another Muslim country, speaking predominantly Bengali, emerging in the eastern part of India in the future, at a time when India might find itself weakened politically and militarily."

The second part of the warning is relevant even if that continuous tract does not separate into a full-fledged country:

"Let us look at the map of Eastern India – starting from the North 24 Parganas district, proceeding through Nadia, Murshidabad, Malda and West Dinajpur before entering the narrow neck of land lying through Raiganj and Dalkola of Islampur sub-division before passing through the Kishanganj district of East Bihar to enter Siliguri. Proceed further and take a look at the north Bengal districts of Darjeeling, Jalpaiguri and Cooch Behar before entering Assam, and its districts of Dhubri, Goalpara, Bonaigaon, Kokrajhar and Barpeta. A more sensitive region in Asia is difficult to locate...."

Nepal is way out of hand. In the north Bengal districts unrest has already erupted – the Gorkha National Liberation Front in the Darjeeling Hills, the Kamtapur Liberation Front in the northern districts of the state. And on the other side of that chicken's neck corridor, we have the Bodo groups, and further down ULFA.

Go over to the border districts of Assam, and you find the same phenomenon. In his report to the President, General Sinha drew attention to the differential decadal growth of population of Hindus and Muslims in Assam – 33.7% and 38.3% in 1951-61 respectively; 37.2% and 31% respectively in 1961-71; and an estimated 41.9% and 77.4% respectively in 1981-91 – and observed:

"Muslim population of Assam has shown a rise of 77.42 per cent in 1991 from what it was in 1971. The Hindu population has risen by nearly 41.89 per cent in this period.

"Muslim population [as a percentage of total population] in Assam has risen from 24.68 per cent in 1951 to 28.42 per cent in 1991. As per the 1991 Census, four districts (Dhubri, Goalpara, Barpeta and Hailakandi) have become Muslim majority districts. Two more districts (Nowgaon and Karimganj) should have become so by 1998 and one more district (Morgaon) is fast approaching this position.

"The growth of Muslim population has been emphasized in the previous paragraph to indicate the extent of illegal migration from Bangladesh to Assam because.... the illegal migrants coming into India after 1971 have been almost exclusively Muslims...."

Assam and Tripura are the states that have been most heavily infested by infiltrators. But over the last few years, infiltrators have been moving from these two states to other states, in particular the hill areas.

Response

General Sinha kept drawing attention of the high-ups in Delhi to the inundation. All that happened was that his warnings became the occasion for the "secularists" to denounce him as a "communalist" who must be removed from his post.

What was the response to your articles?, I asked T.V. Rajeswar. None, as far as the official machinery was concerned, he said. But the articles were just the most recent thing he had written on the subject, he said. He recalled that after he had been appointed Governor of West Bengal he had occasion to study the question in considerable detail, and that he had sent communications and reports about the danger to Delhi. After retirement, he wrote an account of what happened to his reports on the impact that illegal immigration was having, and of the dire consequences that were building up. The account he wrote typifies the sequence:

"After I assumed office as Governor of West Bengal in March 1989, I went into the matter [the continuing demographic invasion from Bangladesh] in great detail and I found that the problem was far more serious than I had perceived earlier. I had written to the President, the Prime Minister and the Home Minister regularly during my stay in Calcutta on this. In my very first monthly report for March, 1989 sent to the President on April 6, with copies to the Prime Minister and the Home Minister I referred to the problem of Bangladesh immigrants. In my report for the month of May 1989 I had referred to this matter in fuller detail after having visited the North Bengal districts of Cooch Behar, Jalpaiguri, Darjeeling and West Dinajpur. I also wrote a detailed letter to Chief Minister Jyoti Basu on June 5, 1989 suggesting that a census should be held in all the districts of West Bengal to assess and identify the Bangladesh immigrants, and thereafter identity cards to those residing in the border districts of West Bengal should be issued.

"After the Janata Dal Government assumed office at the Centre, I wrote in January 1990 to Shri I. K. Gujral, Minister for External Affairs, with copies to the Prime Minister and the Home Minister, suggesting that a detailed study might be carried out by a committee consisting of senior officers from the ministries of External Affairs and Home, as well as from the State Governments of West Bengal and Bihar, followed by a thorough census, along with the national census of 1991, to ascertain the dimensions of the problem of Bangladesh immigrants into India. There was no response from any of them till I left Calcutta on February 6, 1990. All these reports should be available in the Home Ministry...."

"A detailed study" was indeed completed by officials of the IB and the Home Ministry in 1992: it estimated that even by then the number of illegal migrants from Bangladesh was anywhere between *one and half to two crore.* The only action that was taken as a consequence was that Government ordered that the report be kept secret. I published the entire text. [And later included it in *A Secular Agenda,* ASA, New Delhi, 1993, pp.269-93.] All I heard was some minatory murmurs that I might be proceeded against under the Official Secrets Act!

In April 1992 Hiteshwar Saikia, then Chief Minister of Assam, said on the floor of the state Assembly that there were about 3 million illegal Bangladeshi immigrants in the state. The Muslim United Front leaders declared that he must withdraw his statement within 48 hours – or they would bring his Government down. Saikia withdrew his statement!

In August 1993, members of Parliament asked the Home Minister about the numbers who had infiltrated from Bangladesh. Three ministers got to contribute to the answer. We are "not able to sort of count them," they confessed – even as they did everything they could by convolutions to minimize the problem. And that was the end of the matter. [*ibid,* pp.251-60.]

In May 1997, Indrajit Gupta, long time General Secretary of the Communist Party of India, then the country's Home Minister was a trifle more forthcoming. He told Parliament that there were about 10 million illegal migrants in India. But as for doing something about them, his statement was the end of the matter. "At least he has acknowledged the problem," all who could make him do nothing about it said as a consolation.

The one political party at the national level that had been talking vigorously about the urgent need to stanch this invasion was the BJP. In its manifesto for the 1996 elections it stated,

"Illegal Immigration: Demographic Invasion – A Threat to Our Security

"We believe that illegal immigration from our neighbouring countries, especially Bangladesh, has a direct impact on our nation's security and has an unsettling effect on our demography. Given the sheer dimension of numbers – there are as many as 1.7 crore illegal immigrants, the bulk of them Bangladeshis, living in various parts of the country – illegal immigration is not only transforming the geography, but the sociology, the economy, indeed even the politics of this country. India is facing an explosive issue. If our demographic balance is allowed to be disturbed by inept policies and political considerations, various demographic entities are bound to come in conflict, thus adversely affecting our security environment. The invasion of illegal immigrants from Bangladesh has led to an alarming growth in a section of the population in our North East, in Assam, in West Bengal, parts of Bihar and Delhi. In certain areas, a section of the population has grown by almost 100 per cent.

"The BJP proposes to:
a. Complete barbed wire fencing along the India-Bangladesh border, beginning with the plains, to prevent infiltration;
b. Detect illegal immigrants, delete their names from voters' list and arrange for their deportation without any further delay;
c. Declare all property deals between Indians and illegal immigrants as null and void;
d. Amend immigration rules and other laws to impose stringent checks on illegal entry into India; and
e. Expedite the issuance of identity cards to all citizens of the country."

The Party reiterated its pledges in this regard in its manifesto for the 1999 elections. It declared,

"Illegal Infiltration

"The Congress and United Front Governments for their own narrow and selfish reasons have been deliberately negligent of this problem. The total number of illegal infiltrators from Bangladesh is officially ascertained at over 1.7 crore. The adverse impact of this on our economy and social and political order poses problems of grave magnitude. This cannot be allowed to continue. Our Government will:

1. Take more stringent measures to intercept illegal infiltrators and turn them back. Fencing of the border wherever possible will be urgently taken up. Border patrolling will be intensified;
2. Initiate steps to detect illegal infiltrators and delete their names from electoral rolls; and
3. Maintain a national register of citizens."

But the Party had to team up with a number of Allies. Together, they pledged to work according to a Common Minimum Programme. This document did not mention the subject at all.

An enactment, and pledges about it

An entire volume can be written about the paralysis over this vital question – a paralysis that is itself a symptom. But for the present purpose we can glimpse the state of affairs by considering just one small item – the ruinous Illegal Migrants (Determination by Tribunals) Act – henceforth, the IMDT Act as it is known in Assam. Here is the shortest possible chronology of this one matter:

23 November 1946 The Foreigners Act 1946 was enacted. This gave to the Central Government certain powers in respect of the entry of foreigners into the territory of India, their presence therein and their departure from India.

23 September 1964 The Foreigners (Tribunals) Order 1964 was put out by the Central Government. This provided that any question as to whether a particular person is or is not a foreigner was to be referred to the Tribunals that were being constituted for the purpose.

15 October 1983	Despite the existence of the Act of 1946 and despite the fact that it applied to the whole of India, the Illegal Migrants (Determination by Tribunals) Act was enacted in 1983 by Parliament to provide for the determination of illegal migrants and their deportation. This Act was made applicable only to Assam, and more specifically only to those foreigners who had entered into India after March 25, 1971 and were not in possession of valid passports or travel documents or other legal authority to enter India.
15 August 1985	A Memorandum of Settlement was entered into between the All Assam Students' Union, the State of Assam and the Union of India, commonly known as the "Assam Accord". Among other things, the Accord provided:

"The Government will give due consideration to certain difficulties expressed by AASU/AAGSP regarding the implementation of the Illegal Migrants (Determination by Tribunals) Act, 1983."

7 December 1985	In pursuance of the Accord, the Citizenship Act 1955 was amended in 1985 and a new Section 6A was inserted into the Act.
27 January 1990	A "time frame" for "clause wise implementation" of the Assam Accord was prepared, and signed by the Union Home Ministry and the Chief Secretary of Assam. It stated that a decision on the repeal of the Act of 1983 would be taken by February 28, 1991.
20 September 1990	At a meeting between the Union Home Minister, Chief Minister of Assam and representatives of the All Assam Students' Union, the Government "noted" the demand of the representatives of AASU that the Act of 1983 should be repealed, and assured the representatives of AASU that it would initiate

discussions with other political parties on the subject.

11 August 1997   At a meeting regarding the implementation of the Accord, the Central Government stated that although necessary administrative and organizational framework in the form of setting up tribunals and providing requisite staff to them had been set up, the results achieved had been extremely poor, and that there was a need to analyse carefully why the system had failed and what needed to be done to achieve the objective of detection and deportation of foreigners. On behalf of AASU, its President stated at the meeting that the former Prime Minister had visited Assam in October 1996 and had informed AASU that a decision had already been taken to repeal the IMDT Act.

6 April 1998   At a meeting between officials of the Ministry of Home Affairs, Government of India, officials of the Government of Assam and representatives of AASU, it was decided that the proposal made by the officials of the Government of Assam and the representatives of AASU seeking the repeal of the Act of 1983 would be put up to the new Government for decision.

23 September 1998 Another meeting was held between the Government of India, Government of Assam and representatives of AASU, the parties to the Assam Accord. The participants were informed that the repeal of the IMDT Act was "under the active consideration" of the Government.

22 February 1999   In his Address to Parliament, the President of India stated that the repeal of the IMDT Act was "under the active consideration" of the Government.

18 March 1999   At a meeting between representatives of the Governments of India and Assam, and the representatives of AASU, Government reiterated that the repeal of the IMDT Act was "under the active consideration" of the Government. Measures being taken to identify foreigners – e.g., issuing photo identity cards – and the steps being taken to seal the border were also discussed.

1 July 1999   At a further meeting, the representatives of AASU urged that an Ordinance be issued to repeal of the IMDT Act. They were again assured that the matter was "under the active consideration" of the Government of India.

A case in the highest court

As there seemed no hope that the suicidal IMDT Act would be repealed by Parliament, a past President of AASU, Sarbananda Sonowal at last filed a petition in the Supreme Court. He argued that the Act ought to be struck down as it so patently flew against the Constitution, and as it was patently discriminatory – laws applicable in the rest of the country made it so much easier to detect and deport foreigners than this law that had been imposed on the region of the country that was most afflicted by their invasion.

He had the greatest difficulties in finding a lawyer who would argue the case in the public interest. I had to request Mr. Ashok Desai to take up the case. He did so willingly. That was in March 2000. Since then the case has come up a score of times. Several Chief Justices have come and gone. The AGP Government in Assam which had filed an affidavit supporting the petition has been replaced by a Congress Government. This new Government has filed an "additional affidavit" – reversing the stand of the Government of Assam as stated in its original affidavit! The Government at the Centre too has changed. Successive orders of the Supreme Court tell the tale. Here they are:

17 April 2000   Let a copy of the Writ Petition be served on the learned amicus in Writ Petition (c) No.125/98. To be heard along with that Petition.

1 May 2000   Learned Additional Solicitor General prays for six weeks' further time to furnish the status report. We grant the prayer.

17 July 2000   The delay in filing the status report is condoned. Copy of the status report has been furnished to learned counsel for the parties. Responses, if any, to the status report, may also be filed within four weeks.

28 August 2000   Mr. Ashok H Desai, learned senior counsel appearing for the writ petitioner in Writ Petition (c) 131/2000 has drawn our attention to an affidavit filed on behalf of the Union of India and, in particular, to the position detailed at page 214 of the 'up-dated status position' attached to that affidavit, wherein it is stated that

> "The Government is of the view that the Illegal Migrants (Determination by Tribunals) Act, 1983 in its application to the State of Assam alone is discriminatory. The proposal to repeal this Act is under active consideration of the Government."

Mr. Desai has also drawn our attention to an affidavit filed on behalf of the State of Assam, respondent No.2, wherein it is stated on the affidavit of Shri D.J. Hazarika, Officer-on-Special Duty to the Government of Assam that,

> "The State Government has thus been insisting upon the Central Government for repeal of the IMDT Act. Now, in the Counter Affidavit filed by the Central Government it has been admitted that the Act is 'discriminatory' in nature and on such admission, the Act is liable to be struck down as unconstitutional."

Mr. R.N. Trivedi, learned Addl. Solicitor General submits that he stands by the affidavit filed on behalf of the Union of India but would like to seek further instructions in that behalf and prays for the matter to be adjourned and taken up in January, 2001. We grant his prayer.

In the meanwhile, 'up-dated status reports' may be filed by the Union of India and the concerned State Governments.

List the matter in January 2001 for directions.

8 January 2001   W.P.(C) 125/1998 & 131/2000

Heard

Rule

Learned counsel for the parties submit that they have already filed counter/rejoinder. Additional document is still to be filed, let the same be filed within six weeks.

The petitions shall be posted for final hearing before a three-Judge Bench.

List after six weeks for directions.

W.P. (C) 7/2001

Mr. R.K. Jain, learned Senior Counsel appearing for the petitioners submits that prayer (a) from the Prayer Clause may be deleted. We grant the prayer.

Issue notice

Tag with W.P. (C) 125 of 1998.

26 February 2001   Issue notice in the impleadment applications.

Let the parties complete pleadings in all these petitions within six weeks.

Learned counsel for the parties shall also, within two weeks from the date of completion of the pleadings, file brief written submissions, not exceeding five pages each. They shall be at liberty to exchange written submissions between themselves. Learned counsel for the interveners are also permitted to file their response to the writ petitions as well as written submissions.

The matter shall be listed for directions to fix time schedule for hearing after eight weeks.

9 July 2001   Learned counsel for the State of Assam prays for four weeks time to file a further affidavit. We grant his prayer. An advance copy shall be

furnished to learned counsel opposite.
Rejoinder, if any, within three weeks, thereafter.

Post for directions after seven weeks.

15 October 2001   W.P. (c) No.125 of 1998

An application has been filed on behalf of the
State of Assam seeking permission to file "a new
counter affidavit". The application is supported
by an affidavit of the Commissioner & Secretary,
Home Department, Government of Assam.

Mr. Kapil Sibal, learned senior counsel
appearing for the State submits that he does not
press prayer 'a' and that the affidavit which
has been filed along with this application, may
be treated as 'an additional affidavit'. Leaned
counsel appearing for other parties has no
objection to that course being adopted. We,
therefore, take on record the new affidavit as an
additional affidavit filed on behalf of State of
Assam and reject prayer 'a'. The application is
allowed in above terms.

Mr. Ashok Desai, learned senior counsel prays
for and is granted four weeks' time to file his
response to the additional affidavit filed by
the State. All other parties may also file their
response, if any, within the same period, to the
additional affidavit.

List the writ petitions after four weeks before a
three Judge Bench for further proceedings.

I.A. No.4 of 2001

The applicant through their learned counsel
is permitted to assist the Court at the time
of hearing of the case. The application for
impleadment is, accordingly, disposed of.

9 January 2002   Put up this matter along with W.P. (c) No.131/
2000 on January 18, 2002.

18 January 2002   All these matters deal with one and the same
question, namely, the validity of the Illegal

Migrants (Determination By Tribunals) Act 1983. In view of the controversy, rule was issued in all these matters. All the respondents have entered appearance and have filed their respective show cause.

Put up for final disposal in the third week of April 2002.

15 April 2002

On perusal of the prayers made in these petitions, it appears that in Writ Petition (c) No.131/2000 the validity of Act 39/83 is under challenge and learned counsel for the parties pray that this matter may be heard and disposed of early. Mr. Jain, learned senior counsel, also says that in Writ Petition (c) No.7/2001 the same prayer has been made. In other matters the question of implementation of the provisions of the Act and sealing of the border etc. are under consideration.

We, therefore, direct that these two petitions may be delinked from this batch of cases and posted for hearing on 22nd April, 2002. The counsel are requested to file written submissions in these two matters, if not already filed, in the meantime.

Rest of the matter may be put up in July, 2002.

22 April 2002

The petitioner has filed written submissions. Mr. Sanghi appearing for the State of Assam is requested to file his written submissions.

All other parties who want to argue must file their written submissions and serve copy of the same on the respective counsel for 10th of May, 2002.

After hearing Mr. Desai for some time and the learned Solicitor General as well as Mr. Sanghi, appearing for the State of Assam, it appears that the matter cannot be concluded today.

We, therefore, direct that these petitions be listed on 13th of August, 2002 along with WP(C)

No. 581/2001, as it is submitted that the validity
of Section 6A of the Citizenship Act, 1955 is also
under challenge. Pleadings be completed in
that matter, in the meantime.

13 August 2002   The matter is not listed.

28 October 2002   Put up on 20th November, 2002.

20 November 2002   The matter did not reach.

24 January 2003   List the matter in the month of April, 2003 for
directions.

7 April 2003   List the matter for directions in July, 2003.

7 July 2003   It is brought to our notice that a Bill has been
introduced in Parliament for repeal of the Act
which is impugned in the present petitions. In
that view of the matter, we adjourn the hearing
of these petitions. Let these petitions be listed in
January 2004.

January 2004   The matter is not listed.

16 March 2004   Call in the month of July, 2004 as requested.

By this time the country was in the midst of the campaign for General
Elections. The case was adjourned again.

Another conference

But to get back a few steps. Months continued to roll by. The BJP had
taken up the issue. The Cabinet had decided that the IMDT Act shall
be repealed. But nothing happened on the ground. Quite the
contrary. With a new Congress Government in office in Assam, a
Government dependent on the votes of the beneficiaries of the
country's inability to act on the question, ULFA had an even freer
hand. It used the hand against – not those who had usurped the land
of the Assamese – but against labour from Bihar! In Delhi the Directors
General of Police met again in a much publicized conference. The
Intelligence Bureau made a presentation on the illegal immigration
from Bangladesh, on how that country was continuing to be a haven
for terrorists striking at India, and how the two phenomena together
constituted a grave danger to our national security. The press was
formally briefed about the presentation. Papers carried elements of it.

A journalist brought me the copy of the note that had been distributed.

The note repays reading: for both reasons – it shows once again the twin facts: everyone knows what is going on, and yet nothing gets done. Here is the text of the note:

* * *

There has been an accretion to India's security threats from Bangladesh, particularly after the formation of the BNP led government there in October 2001. The points of concern include:-
  i) Shelter and training to Indian Insurgent Groups (IIGs) and use of BD soil for carrying out actions in our border States;
  ii) Acquisition of arms by IIGs in Bangladesh and their transportation for use in India;
  iii) Growth of radical Islamic groups as also private *madrasas* spewing hatred against India;
  iv) Enlargement of ISI activities with increasing use of Bangladesh soil for espionage in India as also terrorist actions by radical Islamic groups;
  v) Efforts to subvert sections in India's border States with indoctrination and training being provided to such elements;
  vi) Continuing inflow of illegal migrants resulting in demographic distortions and growing political clout of such illegal migrants in some border States.

The 4096 Kms long and porous Indo-Bangladesh border makes for easy crossing. The problem of continued unabated influx of large-scale (over 15 millions) illegal Bangladesh migrants into India has assumed serious security implications. Illegal BD migrants, driven by economic forces, have settled in various States including West Bengal (79 lakhs), Assam (50 lakhs), Bihar (4.75 lakhs in the north-eastern districts including Katihar, Sahebganj, Kishanganj and Purnia), Tripura (3.75 lakhs) and Delhi (3.7 lakhs). In Nagaland, the population of Muslims, mostly illegal migrants from Bangladesh, has more than trebled in the last decade — the figures rising from 20,000 in 1991 to over 75,000. Similarly, in Mizoram also, there has been a growth in the numbers of illegal Bangladeshi migrants though firm estimates are not yet available.

The illegal BD migrants have significantly altered the demographic complexion particularly of the border districts of West Bengal and Assam. Their ability to obtain ration cards as also enroll themselves as voters not only gives them a back-door entry to Indian citizenship but also provides them with a political clout that facilitates settlement of more Bangladeshi illegals in our country. In Assam, the illegal migrants are able to affect State politics in a major way with their having acquired a critical say in around

50 of the 126 Assembly constituencies in the State. Their presence has already led to a major movement against them in Assam and in Nagaland. Also their presence is being increasingly resented by the locals. The North East Students Organization (NESO) has also taken up the issue of illegal migration and repeal of IMDT Act with increased fervour.

Besides the demographic threat, the support to the NE based IIGs in Bangladesh, by its Army and security agencies, has become stronger. The IIGs use BD soil for shelter, training and storage and transport of arms as well as carrying out actions in India. All the major outfits in Tripura (NLFT, ATTF), Assam (ULFA, NDFB), Meghalaya (HNLC, ANVC), Nagaland (NSCN/IM), NSCN/K) and Manipur (PLA, UNLF)) have such camps primarily in the districts of Bandarban, Rangamati, Chittagong, Khagrachari, Moulvi Bazar, Habibganj, Sylhet, Mymensingh, Kurigram, Comilla and Dhaka. Cox's Bazar is the main reception point for foreign arms whereafter these are transported to India through land routes in Bangladesh.

Several top IIG leaders stay in Bangladesh, some with their families. These include Paresh Barua (C-in-C, ULFA), Ranjan Daimary (President, NDFB), Julius Dorphang (Chairman, HNLC), Dilash Marak (Chairman, ANVC), Bishwamohan Debbarma (President, NLFT) and Ranjit Debbarma (President, ATTF). These leaders are known to be in contact with Bangladesh security agencies as also the ISI. Most of the IIG leaders use Bangladesh passports, as these are easily available.

Bangladesh, particularly Dhaka, has been used as a staging point for sending members of both IIGs and jehadi groups to Pakistan and Afghanistan as also for their infiltration into India for action. Three ATTF Ugs [underground operators], who surrendered before Security Forces on October 2, 2002 revealed that ISI had arranged a 6-months training for 8 ATTF UGs at Kandhar (Afghanistan) and they were flown to Kandhar from Dhaka. Two senior leaders of NDFB (Dhiren Boro, Vice President, arrested on January 1, 2003 and Gobinda Basumatary, General Secretary, arrested on December 5, 2002) disclosed the instrumentality of ISI in training of NDFB cadres in Pakistan with the cadres being sent from and returning to Dhaka. The interrogation/debriefing reports of several ULFA leaders including Pradip Gogoi (Vice Chairman, presently in jail) and Lohit Deori revealed that several batches of ULFA cadres were flown to Pakistan from Dhaka for imparting training, which was arranged by ISI.

Asghar Ali (R/o Nalgonda, Andhra Pradesh), the person responsible for the killing of Haren Pandya, former Gujarat Home Minister, revealed during interrogation that at least 8 Muslim youths were sent to Bangladesh through Kolkata for onward journey to Pakistan for training around December 2002. Qari Salim, an ISI operative and a HuM cadre who was arrested in Guwahati in 1999, had revealed that he had come via Bangladesh and was tasked to carry out sabotage activities on the Leh-Manali Highway. The persons involved in conspiracy of the hijacking of IC-814 from Kathmandu in December 1999 had used Bangladesh for their movement to India from Pakistan.

Pak Intelligence Offices (PIOs) in Dhaka are becoming increasingly active in espionage against India. In 2002, 3 modules being run by PIOs from Dhaka, and using some BD operatives, were busted. A large number of secret documents and photographs of sensitive defence locations were recovered. Another module run by a PIO from Dhaka, also using a BD operative, was exposed in August 2003 in Sikkim while collecting defence related information pertaining to deployment/movement of Indian Army in sensitive North Bengal and Sikkim area.

Meanwhile, within Bangladesh there has been a steady growth of the Wahabi brand of Islam, which encourages 'jehadi' terrorism. The 'Qaumi' *madrasas* of Bangladesh (estimated to be 90% of total one lakh *madrasas* which are outside the ambit of government control) are the main purveyors of its doctrines with India-baiting remaining a lynchpin of their teachings. The financial aid to these *madrasas* comes through charities mainly from Pakistan and Saudi Arabia. The *madrasas* are used for indoctrination of youths from both sides of the border, as also shelter/ transit point by military/suspected Pak ISI operatives, as also as training centers by fundamentalist outfits like HUJAI, JEI, ICS, IOJ, and for infiltration into India.

Islamic organizations in Bangladesh have been distributing anti-India and fundamentalist propaganda material in North East. During October-November 2001 calendars depicting Osama Bin Laden were found in circulation in Karimganj district of Assam. Police also seized CDs and audio-cassettes at Tezpur (Nov. 2001) and at Karimganj (Nov. 2002) containing anti-India inflammatory speeches of Moulana Dilawar Hussain Syeedi, a JEI-BD MP.

The radical ambience in Bangladesh has encouraged the growth of a number of 'jehadi' groups including the Harkat-ul-Jehad-al-Islami (HUJAI-BD), Jamait-ul-Mujaheedin (JUM), Shahadat-e-Al-Hukma and Jaish-e-Mustafa. The presence of JEI-BD in the government and Islami Oikya Jote (IOJ) in the ruling alliance provides protection and encouragement to their activities as also to the indoctrination, training and shelter to radical Islamic groups from India including the SIMI, MULTA and Islamic United Reformation Protest of India (IURPI).

The growth of the clout of radical Islamic forces in Bangladesh, the increasing activities of the ISI there and the susceptibilities of the BD Government to such forces predicates greater attention to this front.

A section of Bangladeshi opinion makers have already been talking of a Bangladeshi *lebensraum* in our North East. Besides a response at the political level, there is need for greater focus on the Indo-BD border and closer coordination between the Security Agencies, Border guarding forces and State Police forces for an effective response to the growing threat from Bangladesh.

*   *   *

The presentation done, the meeting over, the press having been briefed, things continued exactly as before.

Months passed. The BJP took up the issue again. Resolutions were drafted, proposed, passed, released to the press. Public meetings were addressed in Assam. Pledges were again made that the IMDT Act would be repealed....

In the meantime, elections to the Lok Sabha were called.

And in those elections, the Government from which some hope – that should actually read, "at least *some* hope" – could have been entertained for scrapping the Act was swept from office. The Congress – the very party that had been the major beneficiary of enrolling Bangladeshis on to electoral rolls – was the dominant constituent of the new Government. And the Communists – who would never allow any advance in the matter – were the principal props of the new Government.

The person – Anwara Taimur – because of the smuggling of Bangladeshi's on to voters' lists in whose constituency the entire Assam movement had begun was sworn in as Member of the Rajya Sabha on 4 June, 2004....

Time now for the affidavits of the Central Government also to be supplemented by an "additional affidavit" reversing the stand it had taken hitherto – the way the stand of the Assam Government had been reversed.

In the meanwhile, the inundation continues.

"Killed by one word"

No elaborate deductions are needed to discern what a sequence such as this reveals about the type of State we have become: which other country, inundated with one and a half to two crore foreigners, with vast tracts of its territory – tracts of vital strategic importance – wrested from it by people just creeping in, would shut its eyes?

"One word has killed this country," one of our senior-most intelligence officials told me. "And that word is 'examination'." He recalled that he had been posted in Kashmir in the early 1980s. IB had reported that a lot of money was coming in to the local *madrasas,* that *maulvis* were arriving from UP and Bihar, that they were bringing with them an extremist sort of Islam – that all this was bound to spell trouble in the future.

"We were asked to compile detailed information about the *madrasas* that were engaged in activities of this kind," he recalled. Investigations were conducted. Information was sifted. It was sent to Delhi. At long last the Government is going to act, the officers told each other.

"But what about Articles 29 and 30?," some officers inquired. "These are minority institutions [the *madrasas*]. Under those Articles of the Constitution, minorities can run and operate institutions without let or hindrance."

"Yes, that is right. Acting against *madrasas* can have far reaching implications," everyone concluded. "We should ask the Law Ministry to examine the matter."

And then, "Because the money has been coming not just from Pakistan, but also from countries like Saudi Arabia and even Iran – countries with which we are trying to improve our relations – we should also ask the External Affairs people to examine the repercussions of moving against *madrasas*."

And the matter disappeared – another rivulet lost in the desert.

Soon, the agencies reported that some *Jamaat* men had carefully infiltrated the administration. Reporting this to Delhi, they pointed out the serious consequences that this infestation would have in the future – to take just one facet, said the intelligence official, these men would be able to mingle with officials occupying sensitive posts, and glean vital security-related information from within the administration.

The intelligence official and his colleagues were asked to immediately track down the persons. After diligent inquiries, they identified about 150 men. They again urged that at the least these persons be removed from service forthwith.

"But whether they are *Jamaat* men or not," some in Delhi reasoned, "now that they are in government, they have the protection available to every government servant under Articles 309-11. Therefore, we should 'refer the matter to the Law Ministry and the Personnel Department for examination."

And that was the end of that.

Which is the idea that we have not thought of?

Conduct a census in the border districts.

Issue photo identity cards.

Compile a National Register of Citizens.

Settle exservicemen in Kashmir.

Repeal the IMDT Act.

Fence the border....

Criminals are able to dodge enforcement agencies because we do not have an FBI-type agency that can swoop down anywhere in the country. The CBI cannot investigate even the most blatant case. The IB cannot move in to arrest a person working for an enemy country till the state government either gives permission or cooperates. There have been instances when the IB has had to shadow a man for *six* months – till he moved out of Bihar, in a case that was narrated to me – before the agency could nab him. Hence the proposal – "We must have an FBI-type agency with similar jurisdiction...." That too has been tossed around for years and years.

For 30 years at the least, we have been plagued by Naxalite violence. For more than 10/12 years everyone in the region has been aware that Maoists were establishing bases in Nepal. For all this time, conference after conference dealing with the internal security situation in India has "taken note" of the declared objective of these insurrectionists – to create a Naxalite corridor all the way from Nepal to Andhra. Conference after conference has also resolved to institute a Joint Command of the police forces of the affected states to defeat this insurrection. Yet even so elementary an instrument has not been forged.

Which is the proposal that has not been urged? Indeed, which is the one that someone or the other has not adopted?

And yet each idea has got lost in subsequent "examination".

How heartbreaking it is to be told that many of the items which were needed by the Army during the Kargil War had been on the Army's priority list for years, and had to be purchased in a sudden spurt during the operations. [Air Vice Marshal (Retd.) Kapil Kak, "India's Defence Modernization," in *India's National Security, Annual Review 2001*, Satish Kumar, ed., Vikas, New Delhi, 2002, pp.307-09.]

This manifest softness is doubly fatal: on the one hand, it leads the enemy to conclude that we *will not* fight; on the other, it leads us to conclude that we *should not* fight. It multiplies the chances of an assault on us, and simultaneously increases the chances for the assault to succeed.

The real lesson

10

Towards an enabling State

The cases we have considered above document how administration is entangled in Red Tape, how it entangles others in it, they show that administration entangles them in that tape whatever their field, and howsoever vital the function they have to discharge is for the country.

It does so in many ways, and for a variety of reasons:

1. Ministries function as silos: from another silo a question arrives, in a file; the file travels down to lower and lower forms of life; it comes to rest at the desk of the long-suffering officer somewhere near the bottom; he looks up files on this or similar questions, and prepares a draft response; the file now begins its journey up the ladder in this particular silo – at each step the preceding noting is summarized, sometimes a marginal addition of substance is made; eventually it reaches the top; the imprimatur of the appropriately high authority having been affixed, the file is sent to the silo from which the question emanated.

2. A consequence of even this first bit of the sequence should be noted: while the draft will notionally be deliberated upon as the file travels up the silo, often what has been drafted by the official low down in the silo, survives in tact; that official is one who is liable to have the narrowest perspective, he is liable to feel most constrained by precedent, he is liable to be the most "literalist".

3. Every decision has to be referred to half a dozen other silos: thus, having returned from one silo, the file now begins its journey to a third silo.... The question would have been processed for months – I can at short notice cite half a dozen examples from my own experience; various officials would have pored over it; inter-ministerial meetings would have taken place; the draft would have been circulated among different "stake-holders" – a much favoured expression these days; and yet, when the file comes up to you, the

best of officers would have recorded, "May be sent to Law Ministry for vetting."

4. As a consequence, a case gets to be "processed" for periods that are incomprehensible to those outside government:

❑ The residence of the Indian High Commissioner in Singapore is a splendid property. A tree fell on it *nine years ago*. The place remains unoccupied to this day. As it is situated right next to the building of Singapore's External Affairs Ministry, every person visiting that important office sees it – vacant, locked up, a *"bhoot-bangla"*, as a senior official of the High Commission described it. For *nine years,* officials have been exercising their minds on what repairs have to be carried out, how, and by whom. A typical debate that has ranged in the files: some rule says that the residence of a functionary of that standing should be 760 sq. metres or less; the plan made by the architect turned out to be 780 sq. metres; sorting that wiggle out took four months. Nine years. And in the meantime, Government pays Rs.6.5 lakh as rent every month for the alternative "temporary" accommodation.

❑ Everyone knows how swiftly things move in the telecom sector, how fierce competition is in it. Yet, it takes 8 to 19 months for the BSNL to process a tender. Equipment that began reaching the Northeast in May 2004 originated from a tender floated *two years* earlier. The equipment was woefully inadequate – for demand had exploded meanwhile; and also relatively obsolete – for technology had continued to advance by the day.

5. This aeonic timescale has got so ingrained that the one who cuts through the tape and does the task at normal pace, is at once denounced, questions are raised, motives attributed – in Parliament, through plants in the press. "Why this unseemly haste?," runs the insinuation:

❑ Disinvestment transactions used to take two to three years to complete, yet every time a transaction was completed, every time a debate in Parliament occurred, the cry went up, "Why this unseemly haste?"

❑ Exactly the same thing started happening as I tried to get BSNL to speed up its procurement procedures.

6. The core competence of many a civil servant, and the reason he is so indispensable is that he knows the successive turns of this maze, he knows the sign-posts along it, and the way-side inns in which one can safely put the matter to rest.

7. The system is such that it swiftly entangles in the same faded-tape every effort to reform it. The fate of the Administrative Reforms Commission, the fate of the innumerable committees that were set up to reform the industrial and import-export licensing systems, the fate of the committees that have been set up in 23 ministries to affix responsibility for time and cost over-runs in major projects.... each testifies to the quicksand-like ability of this system to swallow and digest every effort at speeding it up. Even when persons are caught red-handed, the case is quietly buried along the maze. When I was given charge of the Communications Ministry, I heard horrendous accounts of corruption in some of the PSUs under the Ministry, and about what had been happening in regard to tenders, in regard to releasing payments for work that had been completed. Officials and I held intensive meetings with the suppliers of equipment. A Procurement Manual was drawn up. It was put on the Net. But I also knew that Manuals cannot stop the resourceful. Therefore, I met the Director of the CBI, and encouraged him to put whomever he thought fit under surveillance. After that a shameful number of BSNL officials were caught – with enormous, from the perspective of a mere author like me waiting for royalties, *unthinkable* amounts in cash in their houses: cash ranging from 40 lakhs to one and a half crore was recovered from each official's house. Months passed. Formal letters were sent to CBI from the Ministry. What is the problem?, we inquired. Cash has been recovered. The man is not able to explain it. Why is the case not filed? All to no avail. Will someone engineer an "out-of-court settlement"?, I was left to wonder. Will a case be filed, and then die in court – a natural death from extreme old age?

A purpose

Of course, in the view of some the long journeys serve a purpose. Noticing that I was routinely turning down demands – for transferring officials, for relaxing tender-conditions, etc. – an experienced politician remonstrated, "That minister alone is successful who never says 'No', and never does anything. Why not just say, 'That seems a good idea, I will have it examined,' and send the damned thing on a journey? *Bhaiya, duniya aashaa par zinda rahti hai."* Indeed, by this measure, the longer the file takes to move from one obstacle to the next, the more valuable it is. Getting it to the next stop becomes an objective in itself for the fellow. And the fact that he has at last got it over one obstacle will itself rekindle the hope that his project will see the light of day, and keep him looking to you.

But its value in the light of such wisdom apart, its therapeutic value for the long-suffering apart, the endless maze has ruinous consequences:

❑ Growth is impeded.
❑ Governmental enterprises are disabled. How is BSNL to compete with private telecom players when it takes 19 months to process a tender? How is Indian Airlines to compete with private airlines when decisions on fleet etc. take a decade?
❑ Worst, this sclerotic system has given us a reputation; delays, files, long-winding corridors have come to be associated with India in the minds of others.

The reputation has consequences over and above the fact. The President of Nokia had come over for a discussion to my office one day. When will you think it worth Nokia's while to establish manufacturing facilities in India, I asked. India's telecom market was now growing at a pace that in two-three years' time establishing production here could well be a serious proposition, he said. But we have to look at many things, he added. What is by their standard a small factory produces 10 million handsets a year, he explained. Some of their factories produce 40 million handsets a year, he pointed out. A single handset has about 400 parts. Eighty of these parts are the size of specks of dust. That means that a factory producing no more than 10 million handsets will be receiving *four billion* components. You can't build up inventories of these, he said – not of those specks of dust, for instance. The components have to fly in just in time, and the handsets have to fly out just in time. The slightest delay in an office, a strike at some airport, and the whole chain will come apart.

Reminded at every turn

Observations of that sort awaken us to the contrast between the world's pace and ours. Investors come to a country or turn away, other countries will exert to cooperate with us or will look elsewhere, not so much because of internal rate of return calculations their accountants churn up on specific projects, but by the general repute of a country. And, for reasons that in view of the examples that we have encountered in this volume should not surprise us, India's reputation today is of a country in which things will get blocked one way or another. During my term in Government I would be reminded of this at every turn.

"Singapore has to fly on two wings – China *and* India," one leader of Singapore after another said. "That is why it is important for us that India grows rapidly, that relations between Indian and Singapore grow stronger. Look upon Singapore as your Hong Kong, your Shanghai."

To follow up the discussions, it was agreed that I would meet one of Singapore's key decision-makers for breakfast the next morning. "Each of your senior leaders affirmed the importance that Singapore attaches to close economic ties with India," our High Commissioner began. "I would like Mr. Shourie to hear directly from you why is it, then, that Indo-Singapore economic relations just don't take off." "Well, I will tell you," the Minister replied. "This time the main proposal from your side is to set up a 'joint study group' to explore ways of strengthening economic cooperation. But a 'joint task force' was set up *two years ago* to study the prospects for a free trade arrangement between our countries. It has had precisely one meeting."

"You see, we *want* the closest cooperation," he continued. "We have been striving to interest you in it. When you want us round, just whistle. We will come running. But till then, you will understand, we have other things to do."

That was the message – indeed, those were the very words.

In any event, a joint study group was in fact set up. After much consultation, and several months later, the Singapore members of the group arrived in India. Their High Commissioner learnt that the Indian members had not met till then, that they had been summoned to a hurried meeting earlier in the day to think up *some* ideas that could be thrown around. The incident made it to the "diary items" of a financial newspaper. That was all.

Of course, eventually the requisite studies and negotiations *will* get completed. But in the meanwhile others would have got to Singapore – the US, China, others: each, like Singapore, swift to seize the moment.

I was in Japan. One of the points of focus was to ascertain what could be done to persuade Japanese firms to invest more in India. Representatives of the latter pointed to the disputes that had arisen with some of our departments – chiefly the tax authorities. They had been mentioning these for some time, it turned out. They had taken up the question with the Finance Ministry in Delhi. They had taken it up with the Finance Secretary when the latter had visited Japan the previous year. He had announced that a single window had been set up in the Ministry to deal exclusively with the problems faced by Japanese investors. What has happened to that window, I need not tell you, a Japanese businessmen remarked – amidst knowing smiles from others.

A few months later, a delegation of Japanese businessmen came to visit me in Delhi. They were in India as part of events to mark the 50th anniversary of the establishment of diplomatic relations between Japan and India. The blessed single-window came up again. But this time there was an even more elementary hitch: the officer who had been designated to be the window had got transferred, and his replacement had not yet joined!

Devout Buddhists, the Cambodian people have high regard for India. They remember Panditji, they still think of the days of non-alignment when the leaders of our countries worked together on the great issues of the world. They have suffered to an unimaginable extent – a third of their population was wiped out during the massacres unleashed by Pol Pot, the very one who was hailed as the great revolutionary by our progressives. Along with Singapore, Cambodia is the country that has advocated our case in ASEAN most fervently. We were in Pnom Penh. We were to meet the Cambodian Government representatives. From the meeting all were to go straight to a room where the press and television crew were waiting.

A curious, but tell-tale incident occurred. From the statement that was to be issued an item had to be hurriedly deleted. It was a pledge to give $ 10 million to this stricken, and ever-so-affectionate friend, a mere $ 10 million. Why? It turned out that in fact this amount had been pledged *two years earlier* when the Cambodian Prime Minister had visited Delhi. And it had not been disbursed all this while. Why?, you will ask. Two ministries had got into a disagreement about the grant element in the loan. One said it should be kept at X%, the other felt that it should be raised to X+Y%. The file had been going to and fro for two years. The matter was settled by *diktat* literally on the eve of departure. But by then, unknown to us, Cambodia had secured aid for that particular project from elsewhere. It now wanted that those $ 10 million should not be tied to any particular project. But that required consultations with the Finance Ministry back in Delhi. And suddenly we were minutes from the moment when statement had to be released....

I ran into the same features in the Ministry of Commerce and Industry. We are not able to legislate reforms – for instance, in labour laws – for the country as a whole. One device is to create small enclaves in which the regime we need is commenced. Accordingly, in March 2000, with much fanfare Government announced the policy on Special Economic Zones. Many of the notifications translating that policy into specific laws and regulations had not been issued till mid-2003.... Similarly, every year the Export-Import policy is announced on 31 March. The policy for 2002/03 had been announced as usual on 31 March 2002. In January 2003 several of the notifications to give effect to the announcements contained in that policy released ten months earlier – for twelve months! – had yet to be issued. My first task as Minister for Commerce and Industry was to chase up those notifications!

And it can't be that general administration and policy making will be lackadaisical and winding, but in matters relating to defence and foreign affairs, the same system will deliver expeditiously – in fact, as the example of the demographic inundation from Bangladesh establishes, it is not the case. When an ailment seizes the body every follicle exhibits the same symptoms....

A multitude of such experiences has led investors, even governments to conclude that, whatever we say, whatever grand plans we announce, whatever "vision" and "policy" statements we launch, in the end things will get bogged in some swamp or the other.

More than anything, it is this impression we have to turn around. And that is one of the main considerations that we should bear in mind as we block reforms, as we bend finance ministers to roll back their announcements. It isn't just that that particular reform gets derailed, a reform that is desperately needed. It is that that reputation – of a country encoiled in a system that will, in the end, not allow it to deliver on its announcements – gets reinforced.

Reputations stick

And reputation is all. Even by itself it is enough to lead the investor to look elsewhere. We delude ourselves believing that investors will come one way or another – for they are lusting after the Indian market. Examples we are familiar with here at home will show that such presumption is nonsense.

The youth that have taken to arms, to kidnapping, to ransom and extortion in the North East have given the region a bad reputation. You and I may keep saying that Nagaland is at peace today, that ULFA is active in only a few pockets of Assam. For the busy investor, the "North East" is one composite blur: incidents anywhere in the region, reinforce the feeling in the investor's mind, "That place spells trouble." Similarly, you and I know that India is a continent – that there is trouble in Kosovo does not mean that Europe is aflame; Yes, Kashmir is still troubled but, you and I know, Punjab settled down long ago. But to the busy investor "India" is one undifferentiated whole: killings and arson in Gujarat are not killings and arson in one western part of India, they are reminders that "India" is enmeshed in internecine violence.

Still.

And a bad reputation, once acquired, sticks. Recall the militant trade unionism of West Bengal Marxists of the 1960s and '70s. Thirty-forty years have gone by. Private industry – private industry from within India – shuns the state to this day. When that is how events of thirty-forty years ago affect the perception of industrialists from within India about a region within India, how much more will they affect the foreigner, and the foreign government: his information about India is certain to be that much less detailed than of an Indian about a part of

India; and he is certain to spare much less time to learn about the country than an Indian is liable to do when it comes to assessing a region within the country.

Coherence

"You have directed the execution of a project in India," a Singapore Minister was asked, "You have also executed a project for your country in China: what is the one factor which accounts for the fact that China is growing at 9 per cent a year, and India is growing at 6 per cent?"

He replied in one word: "Focus."

His elaboration touched two levels – he pointed to one feature relating to the projects themselves, and to a feature relating to general policy and discourse. "In China I was met by two officials," he explained. "They had all the answers, they took all the decisions. And what they decided, got done. In India I was directed to the land department. There I met three officers. Each had his own version of the regulations we would have to traverse. And then for a year and a half the whole thing got stopped because a gentleman who had a small plot behind the proposed site went to court: he was rearing bees for honey, and argued that his activities would be impeded, that the land should have been acquired under one Act rather than another...."

The other point the Minister made touched focus in policy, in internalizing that policy. The Chinese have set one goal for the country – growth – he explained. They do not let anything detract them from that goal. They decide what they need to do next to attain that goal, and they ensure that those things get done. From the President down to the local authorities, they work in one direction, they speak in one voice. In India, you are deflected by something or the other every other day, on every matter you are talking at cross purposes. China was to join the WTO in December 2000. For the years preceding 2000 that deadline became the timetable for reform. You in India have been among the founder-members of WTO but to this day you are quarreling whether WTO is good for you or bad. There even are groups in your country who to this day argue that you should actually get *out* of the WTO!

That is the reputation we have to overcome. Indeed, not just the reputation. That is *the set of facts* we have to reverse. Every institution in the way of every other institution. Within every institution – for instance, the bureaucracy – anyone and everyone having enough power to throw the machine out of gear for months – raise a doubt, ask a question on file, recommend that the following alternative be examined before a final decision is taken – but no one with enough power to see a decision through. A public discourse that revels solely in problems, not solutions, that lunges for every imaginable negative in each solution....

From the point of view of the investor, thus, the fact that a policy has been announced does not end uncertainty. Even getting a specific go-ahead in Delhi does not end uncertainty. After all, he has to set up the factory in a particular locality, he has to get the power and water connections in that municipal ward. Any one of a score of meteors can crush years of effort.

A telling example

There is the other fact of life. Percy Barnevik drew attention to it some years ago at a World Economic Forum-CII conference in Delhi. You have to stop comparing yourself to India of yesterday, he said. It is no longer sufficient to be better than you were yesterday. You have to be better than rival investment destinations are today. In fact, you have to be better than potential investors think those destinations are liable to be tomorrow.

And how good are they today? A single example – the first person account by the President of one of our best companies, Sundram Fasteners – will suffice.

Like many other firms, Sundram Fasteners had seen the enormous potential of the Chinese market. They set up an office in China so as to understand at first hand the dynamics of doing business in that country. Soon enough they concluded that exporting from India was not going to work as the cost structures in the two countries were too similar. Accordingly, they decided to set up a plant in China to manufacture high tensile fasteners. They commenced a study to determine where they should locate the plant. What happened thereafter is best gleaned from the account that Mr. Sampathkumar Moorthy, President of SFL, has been kind enough to set down at my request – how I wish it could be made compulsory reading for every official and minister in India. Do read it:

* * *

The experience of Mr. Sampathkumar Moorthy

What was amazing was that every province was keen on direct investment into their province and there was a competition between various provinces. The central policy of attracting foreign investment seems to have percolated down to the provinces and even to the county level. The aggressiveness with which each county was vying for the investment was very evident. We were given to understand that the evaluation of the provincial officials was made on three main criteria:

1. how much of foreign direct investment was brought into their province;
2. What are the employment opportunities generated;
3. VAT generated by the province.

It would not be out of place to recall an incident that illustrates the aggressiveness of provinces. In the preliminary stages, when we were with one of our customers in Central China, the local provincial authorities came to know that SFL was visiting this customer and may think of setting up a factory in China. The officials requested for an appointment to meet with us and impress upon us that we should invest in their province even though all our activities were just in the initial stage. They made a total presentation on why their province was best suited and were ready to take us to show various sites. They also went out of their way to make sure that our stay in that province was comfortable and actually provided us with a car and escort so that we could travel in comfort to the next destination. This just illustrates the proactive approach taken where the officials come searching and trying to meet and attract potential investors.

Once the decision to invest in China was made, an assessment of four provinces and 12 industrial zones was carried out. Everywhere there was enthusiastic response; each zone trying to put its best foot forward. SFL finally zeroed in on the Haiyan Economic Development Zone in Zhejiang province.

The experience in dealing with the officials of the development zone and the county was memorable.

The officials were totally proactive and available all the time. The presentation and negotiations were done by the Vice Mayor of the county who was personally present and who could be reached any time even during the late hours. They tried to remove the fear of the unknown which we might have had by assuring us that everything would be taken care of by them.

First, they made it clear that it would be truly single window clearance and they would be responsible for getting all the local as well as central clearances. We just need to sign a Memorandum of Understanding with them and they would present us with the business license.

Second, everything connected with infrastructure and with requirements of the factory was promised to be made available at the doorstep. Power connection, gas, telecommunications etc. would be provided at the factory with no need to apply anywhere else or chase any officials or department.

Third, to remove all environmental constraints, provision for disposing of the sewage directly into the central sewage system was promised by the county. Effluent which would be generated in the process of our manufacture would be collected and taken to the central effluent plant to be treated and disposed so that SFL had to do nothing. The distance from the factory to the central treatment plant is 3 Kms but the entire work of laying the pipelines was agreed to be executed by the county.

Fourth, they were very flexible in the discussions and used the discretionary powers available with them. While guideline rules were given by the Center and some of them could not be changed, discretions at the county level were negotiated so that we could get the best deal. For example, the VAT refund, which was promised as 100% for the first year, 70% for the second, and 50% for the third year, could be renegotiated to 100% for the first and second year and 70% for the third year. Land is purchased by the county, its price was negotiated and finally using their discretionary powers, was offered to SFL at 50% of acquisition rates.

Fifth, all services were committed. Power was guaranteed and we were asked not to install any power generating sets. Labour would be provided by the county at standardized rates.

All in all, we were spared the anxiety of talking to various departments. We just had to fill up forms which were given by the county officials and give these back to them. On completion of this, the development zone was responsible for all processes and obtaining all clearances whether at the Central or at province level and the business license would be handed to SFL to start the activities.

Finally, the development zone and the county went out of the way to make sure that we felt comfortable in working with them. Not only the total arrangements of transporting us, arranging local sight seeing wherever required, throwing a banquet in our honor were organized. They made sure that all relevant officials were present for the final signing ceremony. During the final signing ceremony the Vice Mayor and the Mayor of the county, the Vice Mayor of Jiaxing city, the Member of the Standing Committee of all China Federation of Industry and Commerce, Division Chief of China Centre for Business Cooperation and Coordination, etc., participated. In addition, all relevant heads of department at the county level be it the Fire Chief, Police Chief, Land Chief, Environment Chief, everyone of them was present. All of them had the same assurances to offer that we should not have any problem. If there was anything to be sorted out, they asked us to get in touch with them and they would sort out the matter.

So looking back, what started out as a journey into an unknown land with fears in mind – how the environment would be, whether it would be wise to invest, whether it would be successful – we came back totally assured. The officials were behind us and all the unknowns would be taken care of by them and our job would be just to set up the factory and start production.

The entire journey was truly a memorable one, which at the end left us confident of setting up a factory in a distant land and being successful.

*   *   *

That is the treatment that an investor gets in China. Unless the investor sees that he is going to get a better treatment here than in China or Southeast Asia, he will go there. The moral is simple. Granting permissions can only be the first step. The things we keep debating endlessly – raising the cap on foreign equity, granting some tax benefits etc. – can only be a beginning. These are things the investor takes for granted – for they are available to him in every investment destination. We have to *actively woo* the investor.

Chisels initiative out

There is another feature of the present administrative system that has to be got over – one that those outside the structure do not get to see often. The maze dulls the sharpest of minds. It changes the very idea of what "work" is. Many a civil servant, when he has sent the file to the next stop, feels that he has done "work". Ever so often in Government I used to be reminded of Vinoba's quip, *"Hamaare yahan baat hi kaa kaam hai, kaam ki baat nahin."* A system conditioned in this way, seldom throws up creative solutions. We still have individuals in the civil service who are outstanding by every standard. But the system chisels every creative impulse out of them.

Consider a simple fixation that I had to contend with for four years – the fixation that, were government holdings in a company to fall below 51%, the government would lose control of that "strategic asset". Contrast this dread with what private industrial houses do as routine – they control companies with 26% equity, often with less. Reliance acquired BSES a while ago. Soon after they acquired the company, the Reliance management sought and received the shareholders' consent to amend the Articles of Association. The new Article that the shareholders approved provided that, so long as the Reliance Group of companies and/or its associates, and/or its subsidiary companies hold 26% or more of the paid-up voting equity share capital of BSES and are the single largest shareholder of the company, Reliance shall have the right to appoint the majority of the Directors on the Board, that Reliance shall have the right to appoint the Chairman and Vice Chairman of the Board, that Reliance shall have the right to "exercise control over the company" as defined in the Companies Act. Similarly, it is routine practice for our companies that issue ADRs and GDRs in international markets to vest voting rights for those shares in the Board of Directors of the Issuer Company. Studying the prospectus of the GDRs of Reliance Energy, for instance, I find that it states explicitly that those acquiring GDRs shall have no voting rights, that they shall vote as directed by the Board of Directors, or assign the proxy vote to a Director of Reliance Energy, or vote in the same manner as the shareholders the Board designates.

Three things strike one. The devices are completely within the law. They are simple as can be. And, third, the company is confident that it can retain effective control over management by these elementary changes. Surely, if the object is to retain control, the government can do so in similar ways. The point is that the system almost never throws up even such simple solutions.

Indeed, when an idea is suggested, the first reaction is what management experts refer to as IRI – the Instant Rejection Instinct. "Sir, Law Ministry may have an objection…. Sir, Company Affairs…. Sir, SEBI…."

"Sticking to principles" to dodge the untried, new course

In place of seizing the initiative, over the years the civil servant learns to duck, and look for some precedent. To say little of blazing new trails, even ordinary pragmatism gets to be shunned. Another example from China will bring out the contrast.

China is estimated to have today around 400 ballistic missiles pointed at Taiwan. These are likely to increase to 600 in the next 5 years. It is just a few years ago that China test fired several of these perilously close to Taiwan. On the other side, to arm itself against China, Taiwan is the second largest purchaser of arms from the US. In a word, on the face of things, the two countries are in a state of hostilities. Yet the two-way trade between the two is in excess of $30 billion. Officially Taiwanese investment in China is around $17 billion. In fact, because of restrictions imposed by Taiwan, much more has been invested by Taiwanese businessmen *via* Hong Kong, Caymen Islands, etc. The total Taiwanese investment that China has been able to secure from Taiwanese entrepreneurs is estimated to be not $17 billion but close to $ 70 billion. This investment has generated an estimated 3 million jobs in China. Kunshan, a city near Shanghai, is little more than an enclave of Taiwanese firms. Anywhere between 400,000 and 700,000 Taiwanese live and work in China now – they constitute 7 to 10 per cent of Taiwan's total labour force. The largest companies of the two – including companies owned in each case by the respective governments – have formed joint ventures. Taiwanese are estimated to make 3 million trips to China every year – *three million trips* when direct airlinks have *not* been established. When these are established, this figure is expected to go up to 5 million.... This migration adds directly to China's military strength too: for instance, the hardware producers enable China to develop High Performance Computers at a much faster rate – computers that are vital for testing and deployment of missiles and nuclear weapons, computers whose export to China the US has been trying to restrict. [For these facts and related information, see Report to the US Congress of the US–China Security Review Commission, *The National Security Implications of the Economic Relationship between the United States and China*, July 2002, pp.58-63, 106-07.]

Unless a breakdown liberates him, how much safer for the civil servant to "stick to principles," to "consistency" than to pursue such pragmatic policies....

When the consequences are so obvious, when they are so debilitating, why do such practices, why do such attitudes persist?

For several reasons.

Governance, and the sclerosis that has set in

Reasons

1. The governmental structure is a coral reef – it grows by spontaneous, often by accidental accretions, not by design. Two factors have reinforced this feature:

❏ Every time something untoward happens – a lapse that becomes public, some inordinate time or cost over-run – another body is set up, another layer/another stopover/another loop is added to the procedure.

❏ Fractured electorates have resulted in fractured legislatures, and that has required a larger and larger number of ministries. Responsibilities and jurisdictions have got ever more fragmented. As a result, for every decision one has necessarily to consult an ever-growing number of functionaries. Each of them thus acquires a quasi-veto over every matter.

2. The system is hierarchical. The higher the post one occupies, the more one's opinion will prevail. But the altitude of the post depends on the number of years one has put in as a civil servant – and the larger the number of years one has spent in the grind, the more thoroughly rounded-off, broken-in so to say, one is certain to be.

3. By now the norms have themselves transmogrified. As I said, many an officer thinks that he has actually done work, that he has done what is required of him when he has sent the file to the next desk. Procedural routine has drained the ability to think – I am not talking of individual officers, but of the system as a whole.

4. Equally important, events have shown officers that no harm will come to them because of delay, because some project that had been assigned to an officer did not get completed in time, etc. But that great trouble can come hurtling down on him should he try to cut through the system – motives will be pasted, inquiries may be launched. Why not just stick within the maze, and, inside the maze too, why not tread the well-worn ruts?

5. Of course, often the impulse to seek the opinion of others springs from a genuine search for the best alternative. And sometimes the initial proposal is indeed improved upon as it moves through the maze. But more often, the best is made an enemy of the good. Had the second-best been done earlier, the "interest" that would have accrued

on the matter would have far exceeded what has been gained from the improvement.

6. Often that business of "asking the Law Ministry for an opinion," of getting things decided in or endorsed by committees are appliances of protection. "Collective responsibility" in fact means that, search as you will, you will not be able to hold any one responsible.

7. When circumstances have awakened the system to the necessity of a function, a department has been created to handle it. Environment? O.K., a Ministry. One result, as we noticed, is that now one has to get the approval of yet another ministry – which means, not one granite bloc, but four or five distinct and separate layers of officers in that organization. But there is another inevitable consequence. When you set up a specialized organization – say, a Ministry for Environment – that particular value is its sole concern. As far as the Ministry of Environment is concerned, the one thing that matters is the environmental impact of a project. We thus get a number of objectives, *each of which is an over-riding one, a "matter of principle"* for some limb of government or the other. Delays, meetings to "thrash out the issue", negotiations – I almost typed, "Indo-Pak negotiations" – become the order of the day.

8. Of course, the fact that this system must be reformed too has been recognized as an important goal. And so we have the Department of Administrative Reforms. As a Department has been set up for the purpose, what should be a part of the work of every Ministry has become the exclusive responsibility of that one Department. The proposals of this Department now have to make their way through the maze like any other proposal from any other Department.

9. The system does not hear enough from those who suffer on account of it. It is said that when an organization becomes larger than a hundred or two, it stops talking to and listening to the rest of the world. Its members busy themselves talking to each other. The government is not just a hundred or two hundred strong! The BSNL alone has *three and a half lakh* employees. My friend, Jean Baneth, writes

"I once worked out an illustrative model of the self-contained government. A simple illustration is this: imagine that every civil servant spends an average of one second per month to comment on every other civil servant's work (the illustration can be reworked more realistically without changing the principles). In that case, as the workforce approaches 633600, everyone will be increasingly occupied with such comments. By the time the magic number is reached, there will be no time for any other work. Therefore, more civil servants will need to be hired, but of course, the more that are hired the more time they will spend on commenting on each other's work, and less time they will have for anything else. Similarly, just working more – which will mean, sending more comments – intensifies the difficulty."

Moreover, those who approach the governmental system come as applicants, often as supplicants. They are naturally loath to pick up cudgels against it. They just want to get their little thing done. Often, when a falsehood appears in some newspaper against someone, his reaction is to let the matter pass. For, offended, the newspaper is liable to inflict much greater trouble. So, the paper does not hear much about what it has done. The one who gets entangled in the webs of officialdom is in the same position. First, his remonstration is almost certain to be referred to the same officers for redressal. Only the exceptional man will own up to a mistake. The chair of authority, as well as anonymity, as well as the fact that the internal working of the system is going to remain invisible to the outside world – all ensure that the poor sod who has been dealt with heartlessly will just have to lump it. But should by some quirk the officer who did wrong suffer on account of what he did in that case, he can get at the complainant in myriad ways – better still he can make others in the system do so. Prudence ensures silence from the victims. The result is inevitable: as few confront the system, it hears even less than its sheer size would have led it to hear.

10. That the system has become vast as an ocean itself defeats the effort to change it. To transform this vast ocean the effort would have to be:

❑ Massive.
❑ Across the board.
❑ Simultaneous on every front.
❑ Sustained.

But circumstances militate against each of these four imperatives. Ministers are ill-equipped. Secretaries, etc. know the intricacies much better – but, as we noted, they are so thoroughly domesticated by the system that they do not have the passion which alone would sustain effort for long enough to engineer real change. Knowledge and aptitude apart, there is the simple matter of time. The effort has to be sustained, we said. But the average tenure of a minister is but a few years – if that – in a ministry. And that of a Secretary is perhaps even shorter. I remember a quick survey that N.C. Saxena had done when he was Secretary of the Planning Commission: the average tenure of Secretaries of the Central Government turned out to be just 11 months. In the states, of course, the tenure is evanescent – in UP, etc. a survey had shown the tenure of a Collector to be 8 months, that of the head of the police in the district to be 4 to 6 months. And that was the duration seven-eight years ago. With but a toothpick of jurisdiction and authority in the hands of each, and that too for such fleeting intervals, how can one ensure massive, across the board, simultaneous, sustained effort?

Things to do

The first lesson thus is for those who are outside the system: keep up the pressure. As citizens whose cases languish. As consumers who do not get the quality of service that they have been promised, that is their right to expect. As investors. When as an investor, for instance, you choose one state rather than another, broadcast why you have chosen the former and shunned the latter.

Associations of industry should, and the media should collect and publish data about the time that cases take – in different states, in different departments – as well as the successes that have been wrested by individual officers. Rank the states, rank the departments. If only each of us would devote at least a fifth of the energy that we devote to getting our own case through the maze, if we were to devote just a fifth of that energy to straightening out the maze which slows all of us down, we would materialize the change we want.

The next lesson is to look around. True, there are delays. True, the system swallows attempts to improve it.

Yet, islands have survived. ISRO, to take one instance.

Yet, the very same system is able to tackle emergencies so well – the earthquake in Gujarat, to take another instance.

Yet the same system is able to shepherd without incident three crore pilgrims as they converge at a single place during the *Kumbh*.

Yet, the Maharashtra Government was able to construct the Bombay-Pune Highway in record time.

Yet, the National Highways Authority has been executing the Quadrilateral project with exemplary dispatch.

Yet, the Delhi Metro is being built with consummate efficiency.

The thing to do, therefore, is to document the factors that have enabled the same system to perform so well in these organizations and circumstances. One of the things we will see is how so much turned on just an individual or two – Dr. Satish Dhawan in ISRO, Mr. Sreedharan in the Konkan Railway yesterday and the Delhi Metro today – and on the trust that was reposed in them by the authorities. Thereby we will learn to value competence and integrity so much more than we do.

We will also glimpse the operational rules they adopted that cut through the maze. R.C. Sinha, who steered the Bombay-Pune Highway, had crafted an entirely novel set of rules for tenders. The contractor had to sign a bond that, if any disagreement or dispute arose, he would abide by Sinha's decision. Each stage of every segment of the work had stringent deadlines. Each segment of work had targets which had to be met by the end of every week. Stiff penalty was collected for every *day* of delay. Handsome reward was given and conspicuous recognition was bestowed for every *day* saved. The Government machinery was also made to assist in ways unusual: the day that the contractor was scheduled to begin work, water, power, a structure for storage were all ready for him at the site. Payments were made every week, without fail....

Similarly, I remember Dr. A.P.J. Abdul Kalam recounting his days at ISRO, and the many operational rules he recalled. "Everything should be done in mission-mode," he counseled me, adding the impossible, "Preferably by persons under 35." A specific, clear task, he said. A small, compact team to execute it. The team completes that task, and disperses. Individuals from it and from other teams to be re-formed into a new team for the next task.... "We used to meet every Monday," he recalled. Not for a fixed agenda, but together to get over problems that had come up. Not for any pre-fixed period, but for as long as the problems required. "We had a rule: if you feel you have to write to someone about something, don't write – ring him up; if you feel you have to ring up someone for some matter, don't ring him up – go to him, and sort the matter out there and then...." Not rocket-science. Instead, the science that made rockets go up!

Having located such islands of excellence,

❑ Document the rules that have been followed in such organizations.
❑ Broadcast them.
❑ Whenever even a small island of responsibility is placed under your charge, introduce such practices.
❑ Stand by the officer who works to such rules.

Among the rules of thumb that I found to be of help are the following six:

❑ The smaller the Ministry, the better it runs. This was one of the reasons that the Disinvestment Ministry was able to execute a number of pioneering projects, and on each of them every officer was able to do innovative as well as detailed work.
❑ The Ministry should run, specially in a crisis, as an open seminar – lines of jurisdiction must have no significance, every officer should be given the confidence that his view is valued whether the particular task is his responsibility or not.
❑ The team must at all times be receptive to, indeed it must be in the habit of soliciting information from outside the governmental system – as well as ideas.
❑ It should do its best to follow ISRO-type rules in dealing with officers in other ministries.
❑ The team must have all the powers that are required for bringing that task to a conclusion – if that infernal ghost, the "Rules of Business", vests those powers in the Minister, he must devote himself to every detail of the task and in effect be a working member of the team.
❑ Those in Government who want to change things should *not* chase individual cases – no one can solve the problems of the number of individuals who are bound to be buffeted by the workings of a ministry or department. Instead, he should devote the limited energy he has, and the even more limited time he is

going to have at the post, to altering the system by which their needs are to be met – and that, as I shall just mention, by wielding the axe.

I am fortified in this last conclusion by the fate that has attended every "open *darbar*" that has been commenced in the last 10 years. Among the first things that several of our leaders who have become Prime Ministers and Chief Ministers have done upon assuming office is to announce that they will meet people in open *darbars* every week or so. Hundreds turn up – each with a harrowing tale. At first, our high dignitary gives directions "on the spot" to officials. Soon the practice has to be abandoned – for he realizes that he just can't solve the problems of a billion people by attending to them himself.

I am sure that persons with more extensive experience of working in government will be able to add many other rules to the list. But my general conviction is different. Going by the way the system swallows efforts to reform it, do not attempt to reform the operation. Wherever possible, just hack away the function. That is one of the rules of thumb that guided me in dealing with the licensing system in telecom. As we have seen, the licenses were service-specific, they were user-specific, they were technology-specific, they were area-specific, they were vintage-specific. One approach would have been to go on ironing one wrinkle out after another, to go on "rationalizing the system" as they say. I had little doubt that while we may remove some complication today, as some problem develops, the loop will be brought back again. So, I worked to, as nearly as possible, abolish the requirement altogether. The Group of Ministers fully endorsed the proposal. The Cabinet approved it. We now have one Universal Access License, and you get it for the asking – you pay the entry fee, get the authorization, and provide any service to any customer using any technology anywhere in the country. The same thing was done in altering the regime for Mergers and Acquisitions in telecom. Once the function itself is more or less abolished, and what remains is made quasi-automatic, non-discretionary, that the system remains as it was matters little – it is as if some shadow play were to continue in slow-motion in some faraway building.

This is the real route to reform – continue to transfer functions and power from the State structure to society.